365 DEVOTIONAL READINGS WITH

MARTIN LUTHER
DAY by DAY

365 DEVOTIONAL READINGS WITH

MARTIN LUTHER

DAY
by
DAY

CONCORDIA PUBLISHING HOUSE · SAINT LOUIS

Published by Concordia Publishing House
3558 S. Jefferson Avenue, St. Louis, MO 63118-3968
1-800-325-3040 · www.cph.org

Edited by Dawn M. Weinstock

Scripture quotations, unless otherwise noted, are from The Holy Bible, English
Standard Version®. Copyright © 2001 by Crossway Bibles, a publishing ministry of
Good News Publishers, Wheaton, Illinois. Used by permission. All rights reserved.

The quotations from Luther's Works, volumes 1–51 in this publication are from
Luther's Works, American Edition (56 vols.; St. Louis: Concordia Publishing House
and Philadelphia: Fortress Press, 1955–86)

The quotations from Luther's Works, volumes 58–79 in this publication are from
Luther's Works, American Edition (22 vols.; St. Louis: Concordia Publishing House,
1964–2015).

Hymn texts with the abbreviation *LSB* are from *Lutheran Service Book*, copyright
© 2006 Concordia Publishing House. All rights reserved.

The quotations from Luther's Small Catechism and Luther's Large Catechism in this
publication are from *Concordia: The Lutheran Confessions*, second edition: edited by
Paul McCain, et al., copyright © 2006 Concordia Publishing House. All rights reserved.

The quotation for August 10 in this publication is from *What Luther Says*, copyright
© 1959 Concordia Publishing House. All rights reserved.

Manufactured in China.

Library of Congress Cataloging-in-Publication Data

Luther, Martin, 1483-1546.
 [Works. Selections. English]
 Day-by-day with Luther : 365 devotions by Martin Luther / Dawn Weinstock.
    pages cm
 Includes index.
 ISBN 978-0-7586-4663-7
1. Devotional calendars. I. Weinstock, Dawn Mirly, editor. II. Title.
BR331.E6 2015
242'.2--dc23

                         2015026047

2   3   4   5   6   7   8   9   10   24   23   22   21   20   19   18   17   16

INTRODUCTION

ven after nearly 500 years, what you will read in this book sounds as though it were written yesterday. Martin Luther's writings have a poignancy and power that continue to captivate readers. A daily dose of Luther is good for the soul, because Dr. Luther points us directly to Jesus Christ and the Gospel. These daily readings, selected and edited so well by my colleague, Dawn Weinstock, are drawn from the many volumes in the American Edition of Luther's Works, including the new volumes now being released, thus providing material from Luther never before available to English-speaking readers. We pray this book is a blessing to all who use it and all who are touched by the passionate enthusiasm demonstrated by Luther for what we need the most, day by day, our dear Lord Christ!

Rev. Paul T. McCain

*And at the end of eight days, when He was
circumcised, He was called Jesus.*

LUKE 2:21

Circumcision and Name of Jesus

is name is rightly called on this day "Jesus," which is [translated] "Savior," for Savior means one who helps, redeems, saves, and cures everyone. The Hebrew language calls this one "Jesus." So the angel Gabriel spoke to Joseph in sleep: "She will bear a Son, and you shall call His name Jesus, for He will save His people from their sins" (Matthew 1:21). Here the angel himself explains why He is called Savior, "Jesus," namely, because He is help and salvation to His people. . . . What, then, is our name? Doubtless as Christ gives us all that is His, so He also gives to us His name. Therefore, all of us are called Christians from Him, God's children from Him, Jesus from Him, Savior from Him, and whatever is His name, that also is ours. As St. Paul writes: "In this hope you were saved" (Romans 8:24), for you are "Jesus" or "Savior." See, there is therefore no limit to the dignity and honor of a Christian! These are the superabundant riches of His blessings, which He pours out on us, so that our hearts may be free, joyous, peaceful, and fearless. Then we keep the Law willingly and cheerfully.

From the *Church Postil*, sermon for New Year's Day on Luke 2:21
(Luther's Works 76:47)

*For whatever was written in former days was
written for our instruction, that through endurance
and through the encouragement of the Scriptures
we might have hope.*

ROMANS 15:4

Watch, Read, Know

 his is the advice: Keep watch! Study! *Attende lectioni!*
("Attend to reading!" 1 Timothy 4:13). Truly, you
cannot read in Scripture too much, and what you do
read you cannot read too well, and what you read well you
cannot understand too well, and what you understand well
you cannot teach too well, and what you teach well you cannot live too well. . . . It is the devil, the world, and the flesh
that are ranting and raging against us. Therefore, beloved
lords and brothers, pastors and preachers, pray, read, study,
and keep busy. Truly, at this evil, shameful time, it is no time
for loafing, snoring, or sleeping. Use your gift, which has
been entrusted to you (see 1 Timothy 4:14), and reveal the
mystery of Christ (see Colossians 1:26). As St. Paul says, "If
anyone refuses to know it, let him be unknowing" (1 Corinthians 14:38). Since Baptism and the Sacrament are present,
we must not keep silent about the Word of the mystery.

From Luther's preface to Johann Spangenberg, *German Postil*
(Luther's Works 60:285)

Our Brother, Not Our Enemy

 herefore, though I feel and experience that unfortunately I cannot say "our Father" with my whole heart (as no one on earth can say it completely—otherwise we would already be in perfect bliss), yet I will experiment and begin as a little child to suck at His breasts. If I cannot sufficiently believe it, I will still not let it be false or say no to it. Although I cannot play the game as it should be done, I will not promote the opposite (as the monks and despairing hearts do, who do not regard Christ as their Brother but as an enemy and a jailer), for that would be to turn Him into the devil. Rather, I will daily learn to spell, until I learn to repeat this Our Father and this preaching of Christ as well or as poorly as I can, no matter if it is stammered and stuttered or babbled, so long as I somehow accomplish it.

From the *Church Postil*, sermon for Easter on Mark 16:1–8 (Luther's Works 77:33)

"Your will be done, on earth as it is in heaven."

MATTHEW 6:10

The Purpose of Trouble

et us learn, therefore, to submit ourselves to the counsels of God and to refrain from the cares and thoughts that God has not commanded. There is nothing safer or more acceptable to God than if we refrain from our own counsels and rely on His Word. There we shall find sufficient guidance about what we ought to do. His commands to us are faith, love, and bearing the cross. With these things, I say, we can happily occupy ourselves. Let us deal with everything else as it comes into our hands, leaving to Him the concern about its outcome. . . . But God has given men this trouble or affliction not in order to destroy them but in order to call them back from their foolish wisdom and schemes and to teach us that our wisdom amounts to nothing. . . . For it is not wisdom that accomplishes anything, not even genuine wisdom, but the will of God, so that we learn to pray (Matthew 6:10): "Thy will be done."

From *Notes on Ecclesiastes* (Luther's Works 15:25)

Elijah was a man with a nature like ours, and he prayed fervently that it might not rain, and for three years and six months it did not rain on the earth. JAMES 5:17

Cling to Christ in Prayer

These words "in My name" [John 16:23] demand faith when one prays. They show that our own worthiness should not demand that we pray or achieve fulfillment, and that our unworthiness should not prevent us from praying; they show that we are surely heard solely for the sake of Christ, our only Mediator and High Priest before God. Therefore our prayer must be centered in Him alone. All Christendom prays in this manner; it concludes and seals all its prayers and cries with the words "through Jesus Christ, our Lord." In this way it brings its offerings to God in faith. Therefore you should do likewise, in order that you may defend yourself against the terrible thoughts which detain and deter you from prayer. Be sure not to let the devil delude you when he tells you that you are unworthy; but for this very reason fall on your knees when you feel that you are not worthy and cannot become worthy. Cling to Christ, make your prayer dependent on Him. . . . By no means be in doubt or uncertain when you pray; but believe confidently that your prayer has come before God, has reached its goal, and has already been granted. For it has been offered in the name of Christ and has been concluded with the amen with which Christ Himself here confirms His Word.

From *Sermons on the Gospel of John, Chapters 14–16* (Luther's Works 24:393–94)

When they saw the star, they rejoiced exceedingly
with great joy. And going into the house they saw the
child with Mary His mother, and they fell down and
worshiped Him. MATTHEW 2:10–11

The Epiphany of Our Lord

 hese Magi here teach us the true faith. After they heard the sermon and the word of the prophet, they were not idle or slow to believe—and look at the obstacles and hindrance they faced! First, they made a mistake and came to Jerusalem, the capital, and did not find Him. The star disappeared. . . . Moreover, they were frightened . . . . They underwent a good, strong battle for their faith. . . . The light of nature and the light of grace cannot be friends. Nature wants to perceive and be certain before it believes. Grace believes before it perceives. For this reason, nature does not go further than her own light. Grace joyfully steps out into the darkness, follows the mere word of Scripture, no matter how it appears; whether nature holds it true or false, [grace] clings to the Word.

From the *Church Postil*, sermon for Epiphany on Matthew 2:1–12
(Luther's Works 76:102–3)

And behold, a voice from heaven said, "This is My
beloved Son, with whom I am well pleased."

MATTHEW 3:17

The Supreme Preacher

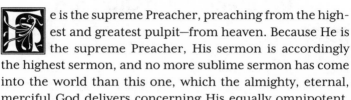 e is the supreme Preacher, preaching from the high-
est and greatest pulpit—from heaven. Because He is
the supreme Preacher, His sermon is accordingly
the highest sermon, and no more sublime sermon has come
into the world than this one, which the almighty, eternal,
merciful God delivers concerning His equally omnipotent,
beloved Son, saying, *"This is My beloved Son*, with whom I
am well pleased." . . . So, likewise, the greatest Student
and Hearer of this sermon is the Holy Spirit Himself, the
Third Person of the divine Majesty. These are all sublime
indeed—Preacher, Sermon, and Hearer—and there can be
none greater. This is why the dear angels keep silence and
do not make themselves heard. Rather, they are listening to
the supreme Preacher: God, the almighty Father, and what
He is preaching concerning His beloved Son, with whom
He is well pleased. . . . But now you may say: "What good
does it do me? Christ is God's Son, begotten of the Father in
eternity, conceived by the Holy Spirit without sin and born
true man of the Virgin Mary. . . . But I am a poor sinner,
conceived and born in sin. Therefore, because of my sin,
surely my Baptism will not be such a glorious occasion?" You

should by no means speak or think like this . . . . Rather, you should not separate your Baptism from Christ's Baptism. You must come with your Baptism into Christ's Baptism so that Christ's Baptism is your Baptism and your Baptism Christ's Baptism, in every respect one Baptism.

From *Two Beautiful and Comforting Sermons of Dr. Martin Luther*
(Luther's Works 58:361–62)

And the tempter came and said to Him, "If You are the Son of God, command these stones to become loaves of bread." But He answered, "It is written, 'Man shall not live by bread alone, but by every word that comes from the mouth of God.' " MATTHEW 4:3–4

The God of Life

ere Christ gains the victory and teaches [us] how to gain the victory—because God is to be preferred to food, for He is not a God of the belly, but the God of life, just as He proves on the basis of Moses that "man does not live by bread alone, but by every word," etc. (Deuteronomy 8:3). Therefore, man possesses not only this life of the body by means of bread, but also the present life and the life to come in the Word or in God. This temptation is one of greed and of caring for this life so that you neglect the Word of God.

From *Annotations on Matthew* (Luther's Works 67:25–26)

"If you knew Me, you would know My Father also."

JOHN 8:19

To Know the Father

 o not begin backwards, or from above, attempting to know the Father beforehand. You will fail. But do this. Close your eyes, and say: "I know nothing of God or of the Father unless I come here and listen to Christ." For anything preached or invented outside this Man's Word, no matter what it may be or how sublime it may sound, is not the Father, but remains blindness, error, yes, the devil himself. "If you knew Me, you would know My Father also. But if you do not know Me, you also know nothing about the Father; for He has declared that He wants to be recognized through the Son." The Father takes us away from all universities, from the laws of all wise people, from the lives of all the saints, from all religions, faiths, and doctrines, from all monastic cowls and tonsures, and says: "He who would know Me, the Father, must give ear to Christ, the Son."

From *Sermons on the Gospel of John, Chapters 6–8* (Luther's Works 23:351)

*"For the gate is narrow and the way is hard
that leads to life."*

MATTHEW 7:14

The Christian's Narrow Path

he life of a Christian is as hard as if he were walking on a narrow path, in fact, on nothing but razors. Beneath us in the world is the devil, who is continually snapping at us with his jaws in order to bring on impatience, despair, and murmuring against God. In addition, the world is advancing on us, and it refuses either to yield to us or to let us pass. And around our neck lies our own flesh. Thus we are hemmed in on every side. The way itself is so narrow that it would be difficult enough even if there were no dangers or obstacles in the way. Nevertheless we have to go through or become the property of the world and the devil. Think about this, and guide yourself accordingly. If you want to be a Christian, then be one. It will never be any different. You will never make the way any wider . . . . But let this be your comfort: first, that God is standing next you; and second, that after you have gone through, you will enter a beautiful and wide room.

From *The Sermon on the Mount* (Luther's Works 21:245–46)

*I have suffered the loss of all things and count them as
rubbish, in order that I may gain Christ.*

PHILIPPIANS 3:8

Where Our Treasure Lies

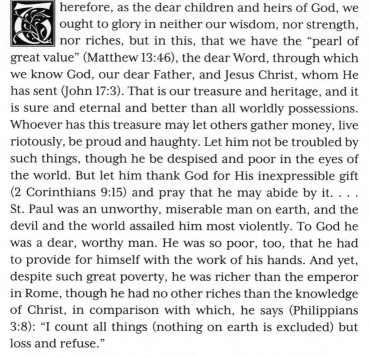

herefore, as the dear children and heirs of God, we
ought to glory in neither our wisdom, nor strength,
nor riches, but in this, that we have the "pearl of
great value" (Matthew 13:46), the dear Word, through which
we know God, our dear Father, and Jesus Christ, whom He
has sent (John 17:3). That is our treasure and heritage, and it
is sure and eternal and better than all worldly possessions.
Whoever has this treasure may let others gather money, live
riotously, be proud and haughty. Let him not be troubled by
such things, though he be despised and poor in the eyes of
the world. But let him thank God for His inexpressible gift
(2 Corinthians 9:15) and pray that he may abide by it. . . .
St. Paul was an unworthy, miserable man on earth, and the
devil and the world assailed him most violently. To God he
was a dear, worthy man. He was so poor, too, that he had
to provide for himself with the work of his hands. And yet,
despite such great poverty, he was richer than the emperor
in Rome, though he had no other riches than the knowledge
of Christ, in comparison with which, he says (Philippians
3:8): "I count all things (nothing on earth is excluded) but
loss and refuse."

From *Commentary on Psalm 23* (Luther's Works 12:161–62)

Christ is the end of the law for righteousness
to everyone who believes.

ROMANS 10:4

Justified through Faith

utside of Christ there is no blessing or justification, not only because of the Law but also because there is no other faith. God wants to keep His promise made to Abraham, to whom He promised blessing for all the world in his Seed and in no one else's seed (see Genesis 22:18). Therefore, He will not sanction a new or different faith for anyone, or let His promise be a lie or recall it. Therefore, faith in Christ justifies, as Paul says, "Christ is the end of the Law; whoever believes in Him is righteous" (Romans 10:4). What does that mean? Nothing else than that all who believe in Christ are justified through faith and receive His Spirit and grace. With that there is an end of the Law, so that he is never under the Law.

From the *Church Postil*, sermon for New Year's Day on Galatians 3:23–29 (Luther's Works 76:13–14)

God is love, and whoever abides in love abides in God,
and God abides in him.

1 JOHN 4:16

The Picture of Love

 f we were to talk for a long time about how love is a high, noble quality in the soul, the most precious and perfect virtue of all—as the philosophers and teachers of works do—that is all nothing compared to what he loudly pours forth, saying, "God Himself is love, and His essence is nothing but pure love." If someone wanted to paint God accurately, then he would have to find a picture that is nothing but love, since the divine nature is nothing other than the fiery furnace and ardor of love, which fills heaven and earth. In turn, if someone could paint and picture love, then he would have to make a picture which is not artistic or human, not angelic or heavenly, but God Himself. So the apostle can paint things here in such a way that he makes out of God and love just one thing. He does this to coax and draw us through this noble, precious, and delightful picture all the more to strive also to have love for one another and to be on our guard against envy, hatred, and dissension.

From *Several Beautiful Sermons from 1 John* (Luther's Works 78:371)

Little children, let us not love in word or talk
but in deed and in truth.

1 JOHN 3:18

The Pretense of Sanctity

he sectarians today . . . have abandoned Christ, chopped down the tree, and subverted the foundation. Therefore they build on the sand (Matthew 7:26) and cannot build anything except wood, hay, and stubble (1 Corinthians 3:12). They make a magnificent show of love, humility, and the like. But in fact, as John says (1 John 3:18), they do not love in deed and in truth but in word and speech. They also make a pretense of great sanctity, and by this pretense of sanctity they impress people into supposing that their works are wonderful and are pleasing to God. But if you shine the light of the Word on them, you will discover that they are mere trifles having to do with silly and meaningless matters. . . . Therefore it is as necessary that faithful preachers urge good works as that they urge the doctrine of faith. For Satan is enraged by both and bitterly resists them. Nevertheless, faith must be implanted first; for without it one cannot understand what a good work is and what is pleasing to God.

From *Lectures on Galatians* (1535) (Luther's Works 27:52–53)

So also faith by itself, if it does not have works,
is dead. . . . I will show you my faith by my works.

JAMES 2:17–18

Praise for Noah's Faith

 oah is praised as an example for us because he did not have a dead faith, which is actually no faith at all, but a living and active faith. He is obedient when God gives him a command; and because he believes God both when He gives a promise and when He utters a threat, he painstakingly carries out God's direction in regard to the ark, the gathering of the animals, and the food. The particular praise of Noah's faith is that he stays on the royal road; he adds nothing, changes nothing, and takes nothing away from God's directive but abides completely by the command he hears.

From *Lectures on Genesis* (Luther's Works 2:77)

Christ Jesus . . . became to us wisdom from God,
righteousness and sanctification and redemption.

1 CORINTHIANS 1:30

To Know Christ

ou may ask, "What does it mean to know Christ? Or, what does He bring us?" Answer: You learn to know Christ when you comprehend the words of the apostle recorded in 1 Corinthians 1:30, "Christ was given to us by God to be our wisdom, righteousness, sanctification, and redemption." You comprehend this fully when you realize that all your wisdom is damnable stupidity, your righteousness damnable unrighteousness, your purity damnable impurity, your redemption miserable damnation; and when you thus discover that before God and all creatures you are actually a fool, a sinner, an unclean and condemned man, and when you show not only with words but also with all your heart and your deeds that you are left with no other comfort and salvation than the fact that Christ is given you by God and that you believe in Him and partake of Him, whose righteousness alone can preserve you, as you appeal to it and rely on it.

From *Exposition of the Lord's Prayer for Simple Laymen* (Luther's Works 42:58)

*"I have not come to bring peace, but a sword.
For I have come to set a man against his father, and a
daughter against her mother, and a daughter-in-law
against her mother-in-law. And a person's
enemies will be those of his own household."*

MATTHEW 10:34–36

The True God

hrist with these words makes Himself equal to God. For He says that parents are to be hated on account of Him. But the glory of holding preeminence over parents belongs to God alone. For only the One who commanded obedience to parents can relax this obedience. Therefore, Christ is here showing Himself to be God . . . For the prophets did not speak like this, nor did they dare to accord themselves preeminence over parents or magistrates. Rather, they preached that God was to have preeminence over everything, while they boasted of themselves as His ministers; the apostles did likewise, especially Paul, who says that He preaches Jesus Christ and not himself (2 Corinthians 4:5). All of these words show that this crucified man is the true God. This is the scandal of scandals for the Jews and for all nations. This is still the case, and so it must remain forever, because on account of Him as on account of the true God we must treat everything else as inferior, and He Himself is to be exalted over all things as the true God. Thus, under lowly words, His infinite majesty makes itself known to believers. The godless pass these things by with a deaf ear.

From *Annotations on Matthew* (Luther's Works 67:116)

January 17

*[Jesus] said to them, "But who do you say that I
am?" Simon Peter replied, "You are the Christ,
the Son of the living God."*

MATTHEW 16:15–16

True Man, True God

 t is of no avail for salvation if you think of Christ
according to human opinion—that He is a righteous,
holy, good man or prophet, even the greatest one.
Rather, the Father's revelation from heaven must be added:
that He is the Christ, the Son of God—that is, that He is true
man and true God, and then that He is the promised King
and Priest. And in these few words is encompassed the entire
doctrine of the Christian faith. For the fact that He is the Son
of the living God means that He is true God, which Scripture
elsewhere demonstrates at greater length. However, the fact
that He is a man is evident in and of itself since, having con-
versed with human beings [Baruch 3:38], He was found as a
man, (Philippians 2:7), and as He Himself says here: "Who do
they say that the Son of Man is?"

From *Annotations on Matthew* (Luther's Works 67:272)

January 18

Let our people learn to devote themselves to
good works, so as to help cases of urgent need,
and not be unfruitful.

TITUS 3:14

Surrendering the Self

 hus it is not your good work that you give some alms or that you pray, but that you surrender yourself completely to your neighbor and serve him, wherever he needs and wherever you can, be it with alms, prayer, work, fasting, counsel, comfort, instruction, admonition, rebuke, pardon, clothing, food, and finally even with suffering and dying for him. Tell me, where now are such works to be found in Christendom? [I wish to God I had a voice like a thunderbolt so that I could preach to all the world and tear the little words "good works" out of all people's hearts, mouths, ears, and books—or at least give them the right understanding of those words.]

From the *Church Postil*, sermon for Advent 1 on Matthew 21:1–9 (Luther's Works 75:42, bracketed text from footnote 44)

Yet we know that a person is not justified by works
of the law but through faith in Jesus Christ, so we
also have believed in Christ Jesus, in order to be
justified by faith in Christ and not by works of the law,
because by works of the law no one will be justified.

GALATIANS 2:16

The Purpose of Good Works

We must do good works, but our confidence must not be built on them, but on Christ's work. We should not attack sin, death, and hell with our works, but send them away from us to the righteous Savior, to the King of Zion, who rides on the donkey. He knows how to treat sin, death, and hell: He kills sin, chokes death, and devours hell. Let that man take care of such matters, and apply your works to your neighbor, so that you have a sure testimony of faith in the Savior who kills death.

From the *Church Postil*, sermon for Advent 1 on Matthew 21:1–9 (Luther's Works 75:48)

If we say we have no sin, we deceive ourselves,
and the truth is not in us.

1 JOHN 1:8

The Helper Who Comforts

 herefore, a Christian must somewhere in his heart feel his sin and be frightened of death, because everything that afflicts other sinners oppresses him. The unbelievers are so stuck in their sins that they pay no attention to this, but these, the believers, certainly feel it. But then they have a Helper, the Holy Spirit, who comforts and strengthens them until He has completely carried it out and put an end to it; then they will no longer perceive any of those things. . . . It does not matter if we feel evil desires, as long as we struggle against them. For that reason, such a person must not judge according to his feelings as if all were lost, but work at the remaining sins he feels all his life, let the Holy Spirit work on him, and sigh without ceasing that he might be free of those sins. This sighing never ceases in the believers, and it goes deeper than can be expressed, as St. Paul says in Romans 8:26. But they have a precious Listener, namely, the Holy Spirit Himself, who certainly perceives this longing and gives such consciences divine comfort.

From the *Church Postil*, sermon for Pentecost on Acts 2:1–13
(Luther's Works 77:329)

[Jesus] saw a man called Matthew sitting at the
tax booth, and He said to him, "Follow Me."
And he rose and followed Him.

MATTHEW 9:9

Comrades in Sin

nd it is a wondrous comfort that He chooses such unworthy sinners as apostles, so that they might not become prideful about having such a lofty office or, rather, so that no sinner might lose heart or despair of Christ. For who are the ones who sit in the highest choir and innermost senate of the saints? They are none other than splendid sinners and tax collectors who, according to their own righteousness, would deserve to sit in the midst of hell. Therefore, Peter has no reason to look down on me or boast against me, no matter how great a sinner I am. For Peter has good reason to recall that he was my good comrade in the gravest of sins.

From *Annotations on Matthew* (Luther's Works 67:65)

*We who are strong have an obligation to bear with
the failings of the weak, and not to please ourselves.*

ROMANS 15:1

Expecting Perfection

 o one will be patient with the faults of the other, but each demands that the other be perfect. They think only of each other's [faults], and try this or that way to have more peace and rest than the other, on top of dislike [for each other]. Whoever can dismisses his neighbor and pushes him away, and then covers himself [with the excuse] that he did it because of love for righteousness, that he did not want to have wicked persons around him, but only the godly and good people like himself. This evil holds sway chiefly in those who are something special in comparison to others, who lead respectable lives and are more favored than others. These puff themselves up and put on airs. Whatever is not like them must stink; they condemn it, despise it, for they alone are the pretty kitten in the house.

From the *Church Postil*, sermon for Advent 2 on Romans 15:4–13 (Luther's Works 75:68–69)

Fathers, . . . bring [your children] up in the discipline
and instruction of the Lord.

Ephesians 6:4

A Father's Duty

t is the duty of every father of a family to question and examine his children and servants at least once a week and see what they know or are learning from the catechism. And if they do not know the catechism, he should keep them learning it faithfully. . . . Our children should be used to reciting [the Commandments, the Creed, and the Lord's Prayer] daily when they rise in the morning, when they sit down to their meals, and when they go to bed at night. . . . For the holy fathers or apostles (whoever first taught these things) have summarized the doctrine, life, wisdom, and art of Christians this way. These parts speak, teach, and are focused on them.

From *Short Preface to the Large Catechism* (*Concordia*, pp. 356–58)

And falling to the ground he heard a voice saying to him, "Saul, Saul, why are you persecuting Me?" And he said, "Who are You, Lord?" And He said, "I am Jesus, whom you are persecuting. But rise and enter the city, and you will be told what you are to do."

ACTS 9:4–6

The Conversion of Saul

he Master here is great, and He produces a great student, Paul, the only one who heard this [sermon] and thereafter became our teacher, who still teaches us today. For Christ here is saying: "Did you hear that, Paul? The whole world is wavering in darkness and error and does not know Me. But you are to call them and lead them from darkness into light, from the devil's kingdom into the kingdom of God, from death to life." "Yes, [but] how?" [Paul asks.] "By what means am I to accomplish this?" "Through the Word, which you, Paul, have now heard from Me in this sermon, namely, that you should preach repentance and the forgiveness of sins in My name. And whoever believes in Me (that I am the true Son of God) is righteous before God and will receive eternal life."

From *Sermon on the Conversion of St. Paul* (Luther's Works 58:381)

[Abram] built there an altar to the LORD, who had appeared to him. GENESIS 12:7

An Altar to the Lord

ere for the first time you see that though the holy patriarch is an exile and a sojourner, nevertheless, on account of the promise made to his seed, he gives consideration to a definite habitation. Now for the first time he builds an altar to the Lord, who had appeared to him. That is, he appoints a definite place where the church should come together to hear the Word of God, offer prayers, praise God, and bring sacrifices to God; for this is what it means to build an altar. . . . Abraham did not arbitrarily select this place for his altar. The Lord Himself, who appeared to Abraham there, selected it; for the Lord is its first founder. He shows Himself there because He wants to be worshiped there and to have His promise proclaimed. Likewise later, when Jacob had seen the angels ascending and descending on a ladder, he said (Genesis 28:17): "This is none other than the house of God, and this is the gate of heaven." Therefore because the Lord is the first to tarry there and sow His Word, He truly dedicates or consecrates the place, so that it is not secular but sacred and serves sacred purposes; for it is the Word by which all things are consecrated (1 Timothy 4:5). At this place, however, the Word is proclaimed, not by a human being but by God Himself.

From *Lectures on Genesis* (Luther's Works 2:284–85)

[Abraham] believed the L<small>ORD</small>, *and He counted it to him as righteousness.* G<small>ENESIS</small> 15:6

Abraham's Extraordinary Faith

f you should ask whether Abraham was righteous before this time, my answer is: He was righteous because he believed God. . . . Abraham's faith was extraordinary, since he left his country when commanded to do so and became an exile; but we are not all commanded to do the same thing. Therefore in that connection Moses does not add: "Abraham believed God, and this was reckoned to him as righteousness." But in the passage before us he makes this addition when he is speaking about the heavenly Seed. He does so in order to comfort the church of all times. He is saying that those who, with Abraham, believe this promise are truly righteous. Here, in the most appropriate place, the Holy Spirit wanted to set forth expressly and clearly the statement that righteousness is nothing else than believing God when He makes a promise.

From *Lectures on Genesis* (Luther's Works 3:20)

But I, through the abundance of Your steadfast love,
will enter Your house. I will bow down
toward Your holy temple in the fear of You.

PSALM 5:7

Fear and Reverence

nly the saints revere God, because they alone acknowledge the greatness of His majesty and the limitless sea of His wisdom and the abyss of His goodness shown to us. He who acknowledges it more and more will also revere God more and more. But those who have little or no regard for it will have little reverence and will not be awe-struck but act and strut about and walk up to Him. But the saints are filled with fear and reverence, so that they are afraid to look at Him and call on Him. . . . The more the saints come to know the goodness, wisdom, and majesty of God, the more they conduct themselves with fear and reverence toward Him, so that they truly rejoice in Him with fear. Consequently, if you are not yet filled with awe and reverence, fear and trembling, do not think you know God. "Serve the Lord with fear" (Psalm 2:11), and "Let all the ends of the earth fear Him" (Psalm 67:7). Psalm 47:2 "For the Lord is high, terrible." "How terrible is this place" (Genesis 28:17). This fear is the highest form of worship of God, and it is not worship unless it is one of perfect love and faith and hope.

From *First Lectures on the Psalms* (Luther's Works 10:346)

January 28

[Cast] all your anxieties on Him,
because He cares for you.

1 PETER 5:7

Do Not Worry

 o not at all worry. If something should happen to make you worry—as it must, since you have many offenses on earth—then act this way: Do not at all attempt to deal with your worry, whatever it may be, but leave the worry behind, turn with prayer and supplication to God, and ask Him to accomplish all you wanted to accomplish with your worries. Do that with gratitude that you have a God who cares for you and to whom you may boldly refer all your concerns. But whoever does not act that way when something happens, but first wants to estimate it with his reason and manage it with his own ideas, and thus handle his own worries, meddles with much misery, loses his joy and peace in God, accomplishes nothing at all, but only digs in the sand and sinks in further and cannot get out.

From the *Church Postil*, sermon for Advent 4 on Philippians 4:4–7 (Luther's Works 75:166)

I can do all things through Him who strengthens me.

PHILIPPIANS 4:13

Joy in Trials

he godless are unaware of this feeling of joy in trials. Nor is it a power of human strength, but of the Holy Spirit, which so transforms human beings in such a way that they think nothing of what terrifies others and laugh at what others lament. Now, this is a great power: to be able to turn an unbearable yoke into one that is not only bearable but even pleasant and light, not by changing the load itself but by changing the person carrying it. For the person himself is clothed with new strength, which "can do all things through Him who strengthens him," as Paul [says] (Philippians 4:13). For if I were commanded to bear heaven and earth, I would surely be utterly terrified. But if someone else were to supply a power that is enough to bear it very easily, as if I were tossing a ball, now I would not only be able to bear it, but I also would even play and be delighted in carrying it! And this is the strength of Christ, who therefore says clearly "My burden." It is as if He were saying: "My burden is unlike other burdens. My burden does not weigh down but lifts up, and it bears rather than being borne."

From *Annotations on Matthew* (Luther's Works 67:148)

Let anyone who thinks that he stands take heed
lest he fall.

1 Corinthians 10:12

Our Marvelous Christ

 now that Christ is marvelous in His saints (see Psalm 68:35), and beware of judging or condemning anyone, unless you see and hear publicly that he speaks and believes against the Gospel. Whoever speaks or acts against [the Gospel], you may freely judge that he is apart from Christ, under the devil; pray for him and admonish him so that you convert him. Otherwise, if you find that he praises and honors the Gospel, then act according to the doctrine of St. Paul: "Who are you to pass judgment on the servant of another? If he falls or stands, it is to his own lord that he stands or falls. And he may indeed be upheld, for God is able to make him stand" (Romans 14:4). Likewise: "Let whoever stands take heed, lest he fall" (1 Corinthians 10:12). Christ wants to be at the same time secret and open, at the same time found and not found. For that reason, among the fruits of the Spirit in which we can know Him and improve in Him, He lets there be some weaknesses with which He conceals Himself and at which the wanton judges are offended.

From the *Church Postil,* sermon for Epiphany 5 on Colossians 3:12–17 (Luther's Works 76:296)

Nothing Apart from God

hrist the Lord says of Himself: "No man has ascended into heaven but He who descended from heaven, the Son of Man who is in heaven." We must learn this article of faith well and retain it, for very much depends on our knowing the Savior aright and clinging to Him in steadfast faith. Whoever passes that article of faith by, passes God by; but whoever discovers it, discovers God. Everything is concentrated in the Son, and outside the Son all is vain. Therefore this proclamation about the Son of God is no unimportant matter. It is ordained that we should seek nothing apart from the Son and that we shall find nothing apart from Him either in heaven or on earth. Without Him all is lost. As long as we live, therefore, we should admonish pious and God-fearing hearts to learn and to practice this article of faith diligently.

From *Sermons on the Gospel of John,* Chapters 1–4 (Luther's Works 22:331–32)

"This child is appointed for the fall and rising
of many in Israel."

LUKE 2:34

The Purification of Mary and the Presentation of Our Lord

hrist came to be a light and Savior of all the world, as Simeon said, and everyone is justified and saved through faith in Him. For that to happen, all other righteousness which is sought in ourselves with works apart from Christ must be rejected. . . . [The works-righteous] depend on their works, they stumble against faith, they fall on Christ, so that they burn, condemn, and persecute all who reject their works or consider them useless . . . . As now the falling and breaking is nothing other than unbelief and sinking into works, so the rising and being built upon this rock is nothing other than believing and withdrawing from works. These are the believers. Christ has been appointed for the rising of them and no one else. And as at Christ's time many in Israel rose in Him, so it will be until the end of the world, for nobody can rise through his works, or through the doctrines of men, but only through Christ. This is brought about by faith, as has often been said, without any works or merit. The works must first follow after the rising.

From the *Church Postil*, sermon for the Sunday after Christmas on Luke 2:33–40 (Luther's Works 75:406–7)

February 2

[God] made Him to be sin who knew no sin, so that
in Him we might become the righteousness of God.

2 CORINTHIANS 5:21

The Lamb's Mission

 t is laudable and good to comply with these Commandments. By doing so we abstain from outward sin in the world. But it is futile to try to expunge sin before God through the Law. The one thing that is effective in this respect is spoken of here: "Behold, the Lamb of God, who takes away the sin of the world!" And in Isaiah 53:6 we read: "The Lord has laid on Him the iniquity of us all." And again (Isaiah 53:8): "The Lord will strike Him for the transgression of my people." Everything centers in Christ. Therefore a Christian must adhere to this verse with simplicity of heart and not let anyone rob him of it. Then he will be aware of the blindness of all heathen, of the papists, and of the godless, who themselves want to render satisfaction with pilgrimages and with good works. They make much of these and console themselves with purgatory. But they are blind. For Holy Scripture declares that the sin of the world does not lie on the world, or St. John's sin on St. John, or St. Peter's on Peter; for they are unable to bear it. The sin of the world lies on Christ, the Lamb of God. He steps forth and becomes a vile sinner, yea, sin itself (2 Corinthians 5:21), just as if He Himself had committed all the sin of the world from its beginning to its end. This is to be the Lamb's office, mission, and function.

From *Sermons on the Gospel of John,* Chapters 1–4 (Luther's Works 22:167–68)

Of His own will He brought us forth by the word
of truth, that we should be a kind of firstfruits
of His creatures.

JAMES 1:18

The New Man

hus the whole man must crawl into the Gospel, become new, and take off the old skin, as the snake does when its skin becomes old. It seeks out a narrow hole in the rock, crawls into it, sheds its old skin, and leaves it in the hole. Thus man must also rely on the Gospel and God's Word and confidently follow its promises, which never lie. In this way he takes off his old skin—leaves behind his light, his opinion, his will, his love, his delight, his speech, his deeds—and becomes an entirely new man, who sees everything differently than before, judges differently, forms an opinion differently, thinks differently, wills differently, speaks differently, loves differently, desires differently, acts and conducts himself differently than before.

From the *Church Postil*, sermon for the Third Day of Christmas on John 1:1–14 (Luther's Works 75:308–9)

I believed, even when I spoke: "I am greatly afflicted."

PSALM 116:10

Believe and Be Joyful

 ut if you believe, then it is impossible that your heart will not laugh for joy in God, and become free, sure, and courageous. . . . Therefore, your love breaks forth and does for everyone whatever it can, preaches and proclaims the truth wherever it can, and rejects everything which is not preached or lived according to this doctrine. Then the devil and the world cannot hear or see such things, and do not want what they do to be rejected by you. They will hang around your neck everything great, learned, rich, and powerful, and make you into a heretic and a madman. Then, just like your Lord Christ, you will come to the cross for the sake of the truth; you must be reviled in the worst way possible, and put in danger your body, life, property, honor, friends, and everything, until they drive you away from them out of this life into eternal life. Still you must rejoice in all of this, gladly endure everything and regard it as good, and once again be good to them, always remembering that you were before as they are now in the sight of God. Such faith and love certainly does this. That is a truly Christian life, which does for others as God has done for him.

From the *Church Postil*, sermon for the Second Day of Christmas on Titus 3:4–8 (Luther's Works 75:233–34)

[Jesus said,] "How often would I have gathered
your children together as a hen gathers her brood
under her wings."

MATTHEW 23:37

Under Christ's Wings

ee how the natural mother hen acts. Hardly any other animal takes such great interest in her young. She changes her natural voice and adopts a miserable and plaintive voice. She looks, she scratches [the ground], and calls her chicks. When she finds something, she does not eat it, but leaves it for the chicks. With all earnestness she battles and cries against the hawk, and willingly spreads out her wings and lets her chicks crawl under and on her, no matter what she suffers. This is indeed a delightful picture. So also Christ has adopted a plaintive voice, has preached repentance to us, and from His whole heart pointed out to everyone their sin and misery. He scratches in the Scriptures and calls us to them and lets us eat them. He spreads His wings over us with all His righteousness, merit, and grace, and takes us lovingly under Him, warms us with His own natural heat—that is, with His Holy Spirit, who comes through Him alone—and fights for us against the devil in the air (see Ephesians 2:2).

From the *Church Postil*, sermon for St. Stephen's Day on Matthew 23:34–39 (Luther's Works 75:337–38)

[Abraham believed that] God . . . gives life to the dead
and calls into existence the things that do not exist.

ROMANS 4:17

How Suffering Improves Faith

 od says]: "I can call into existence the things that do not exist (Romans 4:17) and change sadness and all heartache into sheer happiness. I can say: 'Death and grave, be life! Hell, become heaven and bliss! Poison, be precious medicine and refreshment! Devil and world, be of even greater service to My beloved Christians than the blessed angels and the pious saints!' For I can and will cultivate My vineyard in this way. All kinds of suffering and adversity will only improve it." Therefore even if all the devils, the world, our neighbors, and our own people are hostile to us, revile and slander us, hurt and torment us, we should regard this as no different from applying a shovelful of manure to the vine to fertilize it well, cutting away the useless wild branches, or removing a little of the excessive and hampering foliage. When our enemies think that they have inflicted great harm on us and avenged themselves well, all they actually achieved is to teach us all the greater patience and humility, and to make us believe all the more firmly in Christ.

From *Sermons on the Gospel of John,* Chapters 14–16 (Luther's Works 24:198)

*"The words that I have spoken to you are spirit
and life."*

JOHN 6:63

A Book Such As This

 ad to say, there are few, even among those who should do better, who honestly say even once in their lifetime to Scripture or to one of the psalms: "You are my beloved book; you must be my very own psalm." The neglect of Scripture, even by spiritual leaders, is one of the greatest evils in the world. Everything else, arts or literature, is pursued and practiced day and night, and there is no end of labor and effort; but Holy Scripture is neglected as though there were no need of it. Those who condescend to read it want to absorb everything at once. There has never been an art or a book on earth that everyone has so quickly mastered as the Holy Scriptures. But its words are not, as some think, mere literature; they are words of life, intended not for speculation and fantasy but for life and action.

From Luther's preface to *Commentary on Psalm 118* (Luther's Works 14:46)

As for me, I said in my prosperity, "I shall never
be moved." By Your favor, O LORD, *You made my*
mountain stand strong; You hid Your face;
I was dismayed. PSALM 30:6–7

The Devil's Deceit

hen God has given us an excellent faith, so that we live in the strong confidence that we have a gracious God through Christ, then we are in paradise. But before we expect it, things can change so that God causes our hearts to fall down and we think that He wants to tear the Lord Christ out of our hearts. He can be so concealed from us that we can have no comfort in Him. Rather, the devil inserts terrible thoughts about Him into our hearts, so that our conscience feels that it has lost Him. Then [our conscience] wavers and trembles as if we had merited only wrath and hostility from Him by our sins. . . . Why does God let His loved ones experience this? To be sure, it does not happen without reason, nor from wrath or hostility, but from great grace and kindness. He wants to show us how He deals with us in a friendly and fatherly way in all things, and how faithfully He cares for His own people and guides them so that their faith is always trained more and more and becomes stronger and stronger.

From the *Church Postil*, sermon for Epiphany 1 on Luke 2:41–52
(Luther's Works 76:195–96, 197–98)

As many of you as were baptized into Christ

have put on Christ.

GALATIANS 3:27

Christ Is Our Clothing

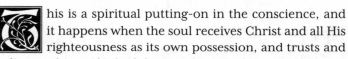 his is a spiritual putting-on in the conscience, and it happens when the soul receives Christ and all His righteousness as its own possession, and trusts and relies on this as if it had done and merited this itself, just as a person is accustomed to receive his clothes. . . . We gladly hear that He is our clothing and mediates for us as for His clothing; but we are unwilling to tolerate it when He wants to cleanse His clothing. If we want to be His clothing, then we truly must tolerate it when He wants to cleanse it; He cannot and will not go about in dirty clothing. . . . Therefore, it is a good sign when He brings much suffering and does not stop cleansing His clothing with all kinds of suffering; where He does not do this, His clothing is not there.

From the *Church Postil*, sermon for New Year's Day on Galatians 3:23–29 (Luther's Works 76:20, 22)

The saying is trustworthy, for: If we have died with Him, we will also live with Him; if we endure, we will also reign with Him. 2 TIMOTHY 2:11–12

Where the Cross Is Found

hen faith begins, God does not forsake it; He lays the holy cross on our backs to strengthen us and to make faith powerful in us. The holy Gospel is a powerful Word. Therefore it cannot do its work without trials, and only he who tastes it is aware that it has such power. Where suffering and the cross are found, there the Gospel can show and exercise its power. It is a Word of life. Therefore it must exercise all its power in death. In the absence of dying and death it can do nothing, and no one can become aware that it has such power and is stronger than sin and death. . . . God lays a cross on all believers in order that they may taste and prove the power of God—the power which they have taken hold of through faith. *But rejoice insofar as you share Christ's sufferings* (1 Peter 4:13). St. Peter does not say that we should feel Christ's sufferings in order to share them through faith. No, he wants to say: Christ suffered. Therefore bear in mind that you, too, suffer and are tried. When you suffer in this way, you have communion with the Lord Christ. For if we want to live with Him, we must also die with Him. If I want to sit with Him in His kingdom, I must also suffer with Him, as St. Paul often says (Romans 6:5; 2 Timothy 2:11).

From *Sermons on 1 Peter* (Luther's Works 30:126–27)

I am sure that neither death nor life, nor angels nor rulers, nor things present nor things to come, nor powers, nor height nor depth, nor anything else in all creation, will be able to separate us from the love of God in Christ Jesus our Lord. ROMANS 8:38–39

Why God Gives Us Faith

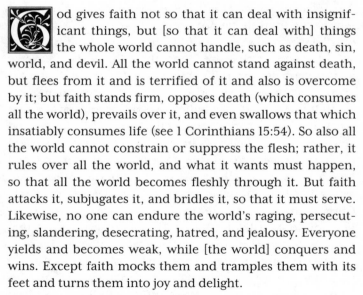

od gives faith not so that it can deal with insignificant things, but [so that it can deal with] things the whole world cannot handle, such as death, sin, world, and devil. All the world cannot stand against death, but flees from it and is terrified of it and also is overcome by it; but faith stands firm, opposes death (which consumes all the world), prevails over it, and even swallows that which insatiably consumes life (see 1 Corinthians 15:54). So also all the world cannot constrain or suppress the flesh; rather, it rules over all the world, and what it wants must happen, so that all the world becomes fleshly through it. But faith attacks it, subjugates it, and bridles it, so that it must serve. Likewise, no one can endure the world's raging, persecuting, slandering, desecrating, hatred, and jealousy. Everyone yields and becomes weak, while [the world] conquers and wins. Except faith mocks them and tramples them with its feet and turns them into joy and delight.

From the *Church Postil*, sermon for Epiphany 4 on Matthew 8:23–27   (Luther's Works 76:284)

If anyone does sin, we have an advocate with the
Father, Jesus Christ the righteous.

1 JOHN 2:1

The Devil's Nature

And this is the devil's nature and true color by which he should be recognized. He is such a wicked spirit that he can make great sins so small that they will not be seen; and, on the other hand, he can make small sins great, so that someone gnaws at, torments, and kills himself over them. Therefore, a Christian ought to learn not to let his conscience be easily troubled. But if he believes in Christ and desires to be righteous, if he contends against sin as much as he can, yet in the expectation that at times he will trip and stumble, then he does not allow such stumbling to destroy his good conscience. Instead, he says, "May this wrongdoing and stumbling depart from me along with the other infirmities and sins that I must include in the article of the Creed, 'I believe in the forgiveness of sins,' and the Fifth Petition of the Our Father, 'Forgive us our trespasses.' "

From *Sermons on the Gospel of John,* Chapters 17–20 (Luther's Works 69:203)

"So the last will be first, and the first last."

Our Hope Is in Him

o here is the summary of this Gospel: no one is so high, or will get so high, that he does not have to be afraid that he may become the very lowest (see 1 Corinthians 10:12). On the other hand, no one has fallen so deeply, or can fall so deeply, that he cannot hope to become the highest, because all merit is abolished and only God's goodness is praised. It has been determined most surely: "The first shall be the last, and the last shall be the first." When He says, "The first shall be the last," He takes away all your arrogance and forbids you to exalt yourself above any prostitute, even if you were Abraham, David, Peter, or Paul. But when He says, "The last shall be the first," He prevents all your despair and forbids you to cast yourself below any saint, even if you were Pilate, Herod, Sodom, and Gomorrah.

From the *Church Postil*, sermon for Septuagesima on Matthew 20:1–16 (Luther's Works 76:319)

Welcome one another as Christ has welcomed you, for the glory of God.

Romans 15:7

A Wondrous Thing!

 hat is, to the glory of God, or that God may hereby be glorified. The glory of God is a wondrous thing! For He is glorified when sinners and the weak are received. For His glory lies in the fact that He is our benefactor. Therefore it is for His glory, that is, an occasion for His kindness, when those are brought to Him who will receive His blessing. Thus we are not to bring the strong, the holy, the wise. For in them God cannot be glorified, since He cannot be a blessing to them, for they do not need Him.

From *Lectures on Romans* (Luther's Works 25:516)

"The light is among you for a little while longer. Walk while you have the light, lest darkness overtake you."

JOHN 12:35

The Pure Gospel

 he preaching of the Gospel is not an eternal, lasting, and continuing teaching, but rather is like a traveling rain shower, which moves on. What it hits, it hits, and what it misses, it misses. It does not return, it does not stand still, but the sun and the heat follow and lick it up. Experience shows that in no place in the world has the Gospel remained clear and pure beyond one man's memory. Rather, as long as those who introduced it remained, it continued and increased. When they were gone, the light was also gone, and soon schismatic spirits and false teachers followed. . . . So also now, we have the pure Gospel and it is the time of grace and salvation and favorable days (2 Corinthians 6:2), but this will soon be over, if the world stands longer. . . . Be careful to receive the Gospel with thanks and fear.

From the *Church Postil*, sermon for Lent 1 on 2 Corinthians 6:1–10 (Luther's Works 76:356–57)

Be sober-minded; be watchful. Your adversary
the devil prowls around like a roaring lion, seeking
someone to devour. 1 PETER 5:8

We Must Be Alert

 hether someone acts arbitrarily against Christ, without Christ, or under the guise of His name, it is immaterial; it is all against Christ. Therefore we must be on the alert against the devil, who assails us either with doctrine that runs counter to Christ, as the tyrants do, or with doctrine that is devoid of Christ, as the canon laws do. And others will come with the Scriptures and give themselves the semblance of the Lord Christ; this, of course, is also against Christ. Christ alone must remain the Bridegroom; He alone is vested with authority and must be heard, as the voice from heaven declared (Matthew 17:5). And now all those who are not Christ's own, that is, all those who are not His spokesmen, really ought to keep silence. We should be satisfied with Him. We should not wait for Moses, much less for others; for God has put His Word into His mouth. He alone is to have a voice in the chamber, for the Father entrusted this to Him; and we are to hearken to no other, be it Moses or an angel from heaven, as St. Paul says (Galatians 1:8).

From *Sermons on the Gospel of John,* Chapters 1–4 (Luther's Works 22:445)

I worked harder than any of them, though it was not I,
but the grace of God that is with me.

1 CORINTHIANS 15:10

All That We Are and Have

 have done it [the translation of the Bible] as a service to the dear Christians and to the honor of One who sitteth above, who blesses me so much every hour of my life that if I had translated a thousand times as much or as diligently, I should not for a single hour have deserved to live or to have a sound eye. All that I am and have is of His grace and mercy, indeed, of His precious blood and bitter sweat. Therefore, God willing, all of it shall also serve to His honor, joyfully and sincerely. . . . And I am more than plentifully repaid, if even a single Christian acknowledges me as an honest workman.

From *On Translating* (Luther's Works 35:193)

"This is My beloved Son, with whom I am well pleased;
listen to Him."
MATTHEW 17:5

Dying for Christ

ithout an appearance of angels, and strengthened by the Word alone, the martyrs met death for the sake of the name of Christ. Why should we, too, not be satisfied with the same thing? Baptism is a sufficiently manifest and clear appearance. So are the Eucharist, the Keys, the ministry of the Word. They are equal to—yes, they even surpass—all the appearances of all angels, in comparison with which Abraham had only droplets and crumbs. Hence I am not concerned about angels . . . . In spiritual matters we should not regard the angels as necessary, because God's promise has been amply displayed and made manifest in Christ. He has left me His Word, with which I instruct and strengthen myself. Nor is it the case that I fear that He is so fickle and changeable that sometimes He proclaims one doctrine and sometimes another. . . . We have the Word of God, the Eucharist, Baptism, the Ten Commandments, matrimony, ordinances of the state, and the administration of the household. Let us be satisfied with these and occupy ourselves with them until the end of the world.

From *Lectures on Genesis* (Luther's Works 4:126–27)

February 19

Simon Peter answered Him, "Lord, to whom shall we
go? You have the words of eternal life."

JOHN 6:68

Cling to Christ

he Christian Church emulates the example set here by St. Peter and says: "To whom shall we go? Lord, I know none but Thee. I know of no other message; Thou hast words of life. Thy sermon has the proper ring; it is impressive and vigorous; its bones are full of marrow; it delivers from eternal death, from sin, and from all misery." . . . Where eternal life and salvation are concerned, St. Peter and all godly men dismiss all other doctrines and know of none but that of this one Man Christ . . . . Those words will satisfy me. This is beautifully spoken. He will not attach himself to the physical form of Christ but will cling to His words. And to them we, too, will adhere; for these words impart eternal life.

From *Sermons on the Gospel of John,* Chapters 6–8 (Luther's Works 23:194)

*[Jesus] also went up [to the Feast of Booths], not
publicly but in private. The Jews were looking for Him
at the feast, and saying, "Where is He?"*

JOHN 7:10–11

Weak But Strong

ere Christ appears weak. He sneaks up to Jerusalem as though He feared the Jews. But fear does not move Him to disregard the command and Word of God because of their defiant attitude. No, He complies with God's command to preach the Gospel; He goes up to Jerusalem and preaches there. . . . Thus the Lord Christ also consoles us. He will have us know that our experiences will be like His. At times we will be weak, while our enemies and adversaries will appear as strong and boasting blusterers. But Christ will still see us through. . . . God takes pleasure in strengthening the weak and in weakening the strong. For His name is Creator, who makes all out of nothing and then again makes nothing out of all.

From *Sermons on the Gospel of John*, Chapters 6–8 (Luther's Works 23:215–16)

[In Christ] we have redemption, the forgiveness

of sins.

COLOSSIANS 1:14

Our True Treasure

ow what is the treasure with which we have been redeemed? It is not perishable gold or silver; it is the precious blood of Christ, the Son of God. This treasure is so costly and noble that the mind and reason of no man can comprehend it. Just one drop of this innocent blood would have been more than enough for the sin of the whole world. Yet the Father wanted to pour out His grace on us so abundantly and to spend so much that He let His Son Christ shed all His blood and gave us the entire treasure. Therefore He does not want us to make light of and think little of such great grace; but He wants us to be moved to conduct ourselves with fear, lest this treasure be taken away from us.

From *Sermons on 1 Peter* (Luther's Works 30:36)

Do not use your freedom as an opportunity
for the flesh, but through love serve one another.

GALATIANS 5:13

Throw Out the Old

 or that reason we must again rebuke and not give way to the shameless spirits who assert that we should not frighten people with the Law nor immediately hand them over to the devil. Rather, we must teach them and tell them that the old yeast must be swept out and that they are not Christians nor do they have faith if they let their flesh have its wantonness and purposely remain and persist in sins against conscience. This is so much the worse and damnable when it is done under the name and cover of the Gospel and Christian freedom, for in that way the name of Christ and of the Gospel is slandered and despised. For that reason, this must simply be thrown away and driven out, since faith and a good conscience cannot exist with it.

From the *Church Postil*, sermon for Easter on 1 Corinthians 5:6–8 (Luther's Works 77:15)

I thank You that You have answered me and have
become my salvation. Psalm 118:21

Singing for Joy

his is a happy verse, singing out of pure joy: "Art Thou not a wonderful and delightful God, to govern us so amazingly and so kindly? Thou exaltest us when Thou humblest us. Thou makest us righteous when Thou makest us sinners. Thou leadest us to heaven when Thou castest us into hell. Thou grantest us the victory when Thou causest us to be defeated. Thou givest us life when Thou permittest us to be killed. Thou comfortest us when Thou causest us to mourn. Thou makest us to rejoice when Thou permittest us to weep. Thou makest us to sing when Thou causest us to cry. Thou makest us strong when we suffer. Thou makest us wise when Thou makest fools of us. Thou makest us rich when Thou sendest us poverty. Thou makest us masters when Thou permittest us to serve." Innumerable are the wonders included in this verse; and all Christendom together praises God for them in these few short words: "I thank Thee that Thou hast humbled me, and hast helped me again."

From *Commentary on Psalm 118* (Luther's Works 14:95)

He is not ashamed to call them brothers, saying,
"I will tell of Your name to My brothers; in the midst
of the congregation I will sing Your praise."

HEBREWS 2:11–12

Unwavering Belief

herefore, even though your own unworthiness hits you in the head when you should pray, and you think: "My sins are too great! I worry that I cannot be Christ's brother," strike out and defend yourself as best you can from giving way to these thoughts. Here you are in great danger of the sin against the Holy Spirit. Confidently and boldly you should answer the devil's suggestions: "I know very well what I am, and you do not need to tell or teach me that, for it is not your business to judge about that. Therefore, go away, you lying spirit, for I should not and will not listen to you. But here is my Lord Christ, God's only Son, who died for me and rose from the dead. He tells me that all my sins are forgotten and that He now wants to be my Brother and that I in turn should be His brother. He wants me to believe this from my heart without any wavering."

From the *Church Postil*, sermon for Easter on Mark 16:1–8
(Luther's Works 77:31)

February 25

Who is it that overcomes the world except the one who
believes that Jesus is the Son of God?

1 JOHN 5:5

Victorious Faith

 he real, victorious faith is the one that believes that Jesus Christ is God's Son. It is an invincible power worked in the hearts of Christians through the Holy Spirit. It understands with certainty and does not flutter back and forth or gape at its own thoughts, but takes hold of God in Christ as His Son sent from heaven, through whom He reveals His will and heart and delivers us from sin and death to grace and new, eternal life. This confidence and trust, which does not rely on its own merit or worthiness but on Christ, the Son of God, and on His might and power, contends against the world and the devil. Therefore, this faith is not a cold, worthless, empty, and idle thought . . . but a living, active power, so that wherever it is, its fruit, victory, and conquest must follow—or, if they do not follow, then faith and the new birth are not there.

From the *Church Postil,* sermon for the Sunday after Easter on 1 John 5:4–12 (Luther's Works 77:119–20)

Therefore, since we have been justified by faith, we have peace with God through our Lord Jesus Christ.

ROMANS 5:1

Christian Peace

 his is Christian faith, which gives peace to the heart, [not] when affliction is absent but when it is most severe. And this is the difference between earthly and heavenly peace: [in the former case,] if someone is suffering, he does not have peace, etc. [But] Christian peace embraces external discord. Poverty, death, [and] persecution are present, but [Christian peace] does not feel those things within, and the heart abounds with more joy when they are present than when they are not. This peace surpasses reason and understanding; this peace comforts a person and sets the troubled heart at rest. Amid these things, the [Christian] has peace where others have discord. Where does this come from? From faith in Christ. For if I believe that by His resurrection He has conquered sin [and] death and that He abides with me, so that I shall lack nothing, then I cannot become timid. If death assails me, I say, "Christ is risen and has conquered death." If I am poor, I look at the wealth of Christ. And whatever other danger might confront [the Christian], he turns his eyes to Christ.

From *Sermons on the Gospel of John*, Chapters 17–20 (Luther's Works 69:335–36)

The kingdom of God does not consist
in talk but in power.
1 CORINTHIANS 4:20

The Fruits of Faith

 aith in the resurrection and fruits of faith] should not remain only in words. Christ's aim is not that we would hear and speak of them, but that we would feel them in our lives. How does it help if we preach much about life to a dead man, if he does not become alive from it? Or about righteousness to a sinner, if he still remains in sin? Or about truth to an erring sectarian, if he does not desist from his error and darkness? So also it is not only useless but also harmful and damnable to hear about the glorious and blessed comfort of the resurrection if the heart never experiences it, but all that remains is the sound in the ears or the foam on the tongue, and nothing more follows from it than does among those who have never heard about it.

From the *Church Postil*, sermon for Easter Wednesday on Colossians 3:1–7 (Luther's Works 77:103)

If we confess our sins, He is faithful and just to forgive
us our sins and to cleanse us from all unrighteousness.

1 John 1:9

None Are Righteous

n this alone we are saved, therefore, that having sin and living in sin we grieve because we have it and cry to God for deliverance, in accord with John's saying (1 John 1:8–9): "If we say we have no sin, we deceive ourselves, and the truth is not in us. If we confess our sins, He is faithful and just and will forgive our sins and cleanse us from all unrighteousness." In this way, yes, in this way, "The sacrifice acceptable to God is a broken spirit; a broken and a contrite heart, O God, Thou wilt not despise" (Psalm 51:17). "For there is no man who does not sin," says Solomon in his prayer (1 Kings 8:46). And Moses in Exodus 34:7 says: "Before whom no man of himself is innocent." And again, Ecclesiastes 7:20 says: "There is not a righteous man on the earth who does good and never sins." And again, "Who can say, 'I have made my heart clean?'" (Proverbs 20:9). Therefore: "There is none righteous. All have turned aside" (Psalm 14:3; Romans 3:10, 12). Thus we pray: "Forgive us our debts" (Matthew 6:12).

From *Lectures on Romans* (Luther's Works 25:247)

[Christ] died for all, that those who live might no
longer live for themselves but for Him who for their
sake died and was raised. 2 CORINTHIANS 5:15

Put Off the Old

his delightful, sweet preaching will not help you, when you say, "Christ died and rose for sinners; therefore, I hope, even for me." Yes, right, but if you always insist on remaining in your old skin, and use this preaching only as a cover for your shameful greed, then it is written: "Do not apply this comfort to yourself, for even though He died and rose for all, He has not yet risen for you, for you have not yet laid hold of that resurrection by faith. You have seen the smoke but have not felt the fire. You have heard the words but have not received their power." But if you want to boast and take comfort in this preaching rightly, that by His dying and rising Christ has helped you, then you must not remain in your old sinful life but put on a new skin. His dying and resurrection occurred so that you also finally would die with Him to the world and become like His resurrection, that is, begin to become a new man, as He is in heaven, one who does not have the desire or love for greed and deception of his neighbor but is satisfied with what God gives him through his work and is generous, kind, and charitable to those who need him.

From the *Church Postil*, sermon for Easter Wednesday on Colossians 3:1–7 (Luther's Works 77:110)

March 1

After making purification for sins, He sat down at the
right hand of the Majesty on high.

HEBREWS 1:3

Listen With Joy

ere he comes to the Gospel proper. Everything
which can be said about Christ is of no help to us
until we hear that all of it is said for our good and
benefit. Why would it be necessary to preach to us, if it happened for His sake alone? But now this applies completely
to us and our salvation. Therefore, let us listen with joy,
for these are exceedingly precious words. Christ, who is so
great, the heir of all things, a radiance of divine honor, the
imprint of the divine essence, who upholds the universe not
through someone else's power or assistance but by His own
activity and power—in short, who is all in all—He has served
us, poured out His love, and made purification for our sins.
He says "our," "our sins" [Hebrews 1:3], not His sins, not
the sins of unbelievers. The purification is in vain and does
nothing for those who do not believe this.

From the *Church Postil*, sermon for the Third Day of Christmas on
Hebrews 1:1–12 (Luther's Works 75:266)

"Why are you troubled, and why do doubts arise in your hearts?"

LUKE 24:38

The Fault in Our Nature

his text cannot be purchased with money or goods because a distressed heart can learn and conclude from it: even if the devil were to cite all the passages in the Bible in order to frighten the heart, if he does that too much and does not give comfort afterward, then it is surely the devil, even if you should seem to see the form of Christ hanging on the cross or sitting at the right hand of the Father. It may well be that Christ comes and frightens you at first, but that is surely not His fault, but the fault of your nature, because you do not correctly recognize Him. However, it is the devil himself who attacks you with fright and does not cease until he brings you into despair. Therefore, you must here separate very far from each other the frightening of Christ and of the devil. Although Christ may begin with frightening, yet He surely brings along comfort and does not want you to remain in fright.

From the *Church Postil*, sermon for Easter Tuesday on Luke 24:36–47 (Luther's Works 77:83)

"I am the good shepherd. The good shepherd lays
down his life for the sheep."

John 10:11

The Sheep Know the Shepherd

 f you know this Shepherd, you can defend yourself against the devil and death, saying: "Sadly, I have not kept God's Commandments, but I crawl under the wings of this dear hen (my dear Lord Christ [Matthew 23:37; Luke 13:34]) and believe that He is my dear Shepherd, Bishop, and Mediator before God, who covers and defends me with His innocence and gives me His righteousness. Whatever I have not kept, He has kept; what is more, whatever I have sinned, He has paid for with His blood," etc. He died and rose again not for Himself but for me, since He says here that He gives His life not for Himself but for His sheep (John 10:11), that is, as St. Peter says, "The righteous died for the unrighteous" (1 Peter 3:18), etc. So, then, you are secure, and the devil along with his hell must leave you alone, for he certainly cannot get anything from Christ, who has already overcome him. He defends and keeps you, if you believe in Him as His lamb.

From the *Church Postil*, sermon for Easter 2 on John 10:11–16
(Luther's Works 77:185)

*"My peace I give to you. Not as the world gives
do I give to you. Let not your hearts be troubled,
neither let them be afraid."*

John 14:27

Christt Preserves His Church

hrist has preserved and protected His Church so
that it is called "peace," even though this peace
is stuck in the midst of thorns and briars, that is,
affliction and trial, in which both the devil and the world
scratch and sting, torment and afflict you for the sake of the
Word and confession of Christ. Just as the Word is a message
of grace, love, and peace from God and Christ toward us, so
the Word is here in the world a message of wrath and hostility. That is why this peace must always stand in faith. When
through the devil's suggestions the heart feels oppressed,
anxious, and even frightened enough to run away from God,
let it enclose itself in this Word of Christ and guard itself,
saying: "Nevertheless, I know that I have God's promise
and the Holy Spirit's testimony that He wants to be my dear
Father and is not angry with me, but grants me peace and all
good through His Son, Christ."

From the *Church Postil*, sermon for Pentecost on John 14:23–31
(Luther's Works 77:358)

Our citizenship is in heaven, and from it we await a
Savior, the Lord Jesus Christ.

PHILIPPIANS 3:20

Two Kingdoms

hristians participate in two kinds of life or government. Here on earth, where the world dwells and has its homeland and heaven, we are not citizens. "But our citizenship," St. Paul says, "is with Christ in heaven" (Philippians 3:20), that is, in the life to come, for which we wait. We hope to be released, as did those in Babylon, and to come where we will remain citizens and lords forever. However, because we must remain in the misery of our Babylon as long as God wants, we are to do as they were commanded to do: to live here with people, eat and drink, keep house, cultivate fields, govern and conduct ourselves peacefully with them, even pray for them, until the hour comes for us to journey home.

From the *Church Postil*, sermon for Easter 3 on 1 Peter 2:11–20 (Luther's Works 77:199)

[You have come] to the sprinkled blood that speaks a better word than the blood of Abel.

HEBREWS 12:24

Sure Comfort

e have the forgiveness of sins only for the sake of the Mediator and the mercy seat, Christ, through the redemption in His blood, and are pronounced righteous before God (Romans 3:24–25). He clearly and plainly uses the word *gratis* (Romans 3:24)—without our merit and not for the sake of our works—so that we can have sure comfort and need not doubt grace and salvation, even though we are very unworthy and still have sins remaining.

From the *Church Postil*, sermon for Ascension on Mark 16:14–20 (Luther's Works 77:279)

Those who belong to Christ Jesus have crucified the
flesh with its passions and desires.

GALATIANS 5:24

Do Not Deceive Yourself

 o one should deceive himself. Whoever belongs to Christ, says Paul, crucifies the flesh with all its diseases and faults. . . . This takes place when they not only repress the wantonness of the flesh by fasting or other kinds of discipline, but when, as Paul said earlier (Galatians 5:16), they walk by the Spirit; that is, when the threat that God will punish sin severely warns them and frightens them away from sinning; and when, instructed by the Word, by faith, and by prayer, they refuse to yield to the desires of the flesh. . . . Dressed in the armor of God, with faith, hope, and the sword of the Spirit (Ephesians 6:11–17), they fight back at the flesh; and with these nails they fasten it to the cross, so that against its will it is forced to be subject to the Spirit. Eventually, when they die, they will put it off completely; and in the resurrection they will have a flesh that is pure, without any passions or evil desires.

From *Lectures on Galatians* (1535) (Luther's Works 27:96–97)

March 8

"I am going away . . . . Where I am going,
you cannot come."

JOHN 8:21

All This Is Vain

herefore be on your guard against flesh and blood, against unbelief and schismatic spirits. Let everyone diligently learn to know Christ, hear the preaching of the Gospel, and accept Christ. But Christ sees few doing this, and therefore He must have these thunderclaps to crush the hearts, yes, the world and all men. All this [works and self-appointed worship] is vain, and we are doomed unless at the end God comes to our rescue and we die in faith in Christ.

From *Sermons on the Gospel of John*, Chapters 6–8 (Luther's Works 23:360)

*The saying is trustworthy and deserving of full accep-
tance, that Christ Jesus came into the world to save
sinners.* 1 TIMOTHY 1:15

The Temptation of False Doctrine

o those who are afraid and have already been terrified by the burden of their sins Christ the Savior
and the gift should be announced, not Christ the
example and the lawgiver. . . . Therefore let every Christian
learn to be able to shake off the false idea of Christ that
Satan urges upon him in his terror and affliction, and to say:
"Satan, why are you debating with me now about deeds? I
am already frightened and troubled enough because of my
deeds and my sins. Indeed, since I am already troubled and
burdened, let me hear, not you with your accusation and
condemnation but Christ, the Savior of the human race,
who says that He came into the world to save sinners (1 Timothy 1:15), to comfort the despairing, and to proclaim release
to the captives (Luke 4:18). This is the real Christ in the most
precise sense of the word . . . . I shall listen to Christ, of whom
the Father has said (Matthew 17:5): 'This is My beloved Son,
with whom I am well pleased; listen to Him.' " Let us learn
to encourage ourselves with faith this way amid the temptation and persuasion of false doctrine; otherwise the devil
will either lead us astray through his agents or kill us with his
flaming darts (Ephesians 6:16).

From *Lectures on Galatians* (1535) (Luther's Works 27:35)

Peter and John answered them, "Whether it is right in the sight of God to listen to you rather than to God, you must judge, for we cannot but speak of what we have seen and heard." ACTS 4:19–20

Our Certain Faith

W e can stand the loss of our possessions, our name, our life, and everything else; but we will not let ourselves be deprived of the Gospel, our faith, and Jesus Christ. And that is that. Accursed be any humility that yields or submits at this point! Rather let everyone be proud and unremitting here, unless he wants to deny Christ. With the help of God, therefore, I will be more hardheaded than anyone else. I want to be stubborn and to be known as someone who is stubborn. Here I bear the inscription "I yield to no one." And I am overjoyed if here I am called rebellious and unyielding. Here I admit openly that I am and will be unmovable and that I will not yield a hairbreadth to anyone. Love "bears all things, believes all things, hopes all things, endures all things" (1 Corinthians 13:7); therefore it yields. But not faith; it will not stand for anything. . . . So far as his faith is concerned, therefore, a Christian is as proud and firm as he can be; and he must not relax or yield the least bit.

From *Lectures on Galatians* (1535) (Luther's Works 26:99–100)

March 11

He was pierced for our transgressions;
He was crushed for our iniquities.

ISAIAH 53:5

Set Your Conscience Free

his fright comes when we see the strict wrath and unwavering seriousness of God toward sin and sinners, since He even did not want to give His own dearest Son to free sinners unless He did full penance for them, as He said, "For the sin of My people I have struck Him" (Isaiah 53:8). What will happen to the sinner, when His dearest Son was struck in that way? An unspeakable and unbearable seriousness must be there when such an immeasurably great person goes to meet it, and suffers and dies for it. If you profoundly reflect on the fact that God's Son, the eternal Wisdom of the Father, Himself suffers, then you will indeed be frightened; the more [you reflect], the more profoundly [you will be frightened]. . . . When one has become aware of his sins in this way and is completely frightened in himself, he must be careful that his sins do not remain in his conscience, or sheer despair will certainly result from it. Rather, just as [the sins] proceeded and were recognized from Christ['s suffering], so we should throw them back on Him and set our conscience free.

From *Meditation on the Holy Suffering of Christ* (Luther's Works 76:426, 429–30)

March 12

"Away with this man, and release to us Barabbas." LUKE 23:18

The Precious Treasure

hat is the way things must go; that is how things have always gone and how they will always go. And this is the course and custom of the world: that the more precious is the treasure and blessing that God gives, the more hostile the world and devil are to it. Gold is the least of blessings; nevertheless, the devil cannot tolerate that it be used properly. Well-ordered authority and external peace are fine, beautiful gems; but the devil cannot tolerate them and so stirs up continual murder and bloodshed in the world, so that there is nothing in the world but murder upon murder. He cannot bear that human beings have a naturally beautiful body, and so the world is a den of robbery and thievery [of health and beauty]. But when it comes to the sublime gifts of God, such as the Holy Scriptures, the Gospel, the divine truth, Christ, and so forth—when this treasure, bringing righteousness and life, comes into the world, it will happen just as our text says: Barabbas will be set free; Christ will be crucified. Rather than leaving the truth uncondemned, they must sooner tolerate all devils.

From *Sermons on the Gospel of John, Chapters 17–20* (Luther's Works 69:218)

It is written, "I will destroy the wisdom of the wise,
and the discernment of the discerning
I will thwart." 1 CORINTHIANS 1:19

The Judgment of Reason

hen God proposes the doctrines of faith, He always proposes things that are simply impossible and absurd—if, that is, you want to follow the judgment of reason. It does indeed seem ridiculous and absurd to reason that in the Lord's Supper the body and the blood of Christ are presented, that Baptism is "the washing of regeneration and renewal in the Holy Spirit" (Titus 3:5), that Christ the Son of God was conceived and carried in the womb of the Virgin, that He was born, that He suffered the most ignominious of deaths on the cross, that He was raised again, that He is now sitting at the right hand of the Father, and that He now has "authority in heaven and on earth" (Matthew 28:18). Paul calls the Gospel of Christ the crucified "the Word of the cross" (1 Corinthians 1:18) and "the folly of preaching" (1 Corinthians 1:21), which the Jews regarded as offensive and the Greeks as a foolish doctrine. Reason judges this way about all the doctrines of the faith; for it does not understand that the supreme form of worship is to hear the voice of God and to believe . . . . *But faith slaughters reason and kills the beast that the whole world and all the creatures cannot kill.*

From *Lectures on Galatians* 1535) (Luther's Works 26:227–28)

March 14

In the days of His flesh, Jesus offered up prayers and supplications, with loud cries and tears, to Him who was able to save Him from death, and He was heard because of His reverence.

HEBREWS 5:7

Dutiful Love and Godly Fear

he Greek word . . . means "godly fear" ["reverence"] as well as "dutiful love." Therefore they take it to mean dutiful love, namely, the love the Father naturally has for the Son . . . so that the meaning is that even though we were completely deserving of wrath, yet it was proper for the Father's love to hear the Son for us, so that the love He could not deny the Son is set against our iniquity, because of which He could have denied everything to every one of us. Therefore with this word the apostle calls forth for us confidence in God because God considered His love, not our iniquities. . . . The word can be taken in an active sense, namely, the godly fear with which Christ revered the Father . . . . Therefore the meaning will be that Christ was heard, not because we were worthy—indeed, we were completely unworthy on account of our irreverence—but because His godly fear was worthy and was so great that He was heard for the sake even of those who were altogether unworthy and irreverent.

From *Lectures on Hebrews* (Luther's Works 29:177–78)

March 15

We know that the law is spiritual.

ROMANS 7:14

The Law of the Spirit

 od's commandment demands not only external conduct and appearances, but it also lays hold of the heart and demands its perfect obedience. Therefore, it also judges a person not only according to his external life and behavior but also according to his innermost heart. However, the world does not understand and pay attention to that, for it knows nothing more than public, external sins, such as murder, adultery, theft, and whatever the lawyers label as "sin" and rebuke. But it does not know and does not see the true problem and its root, such as despising God; the innate, inward impurity of the heart; disobedience toward God's will; etc. These things are and remain in all people who are not sanctified through Christ.

From the *Church Postil*, sermon for Easter 4 on John 16:5–15 (Luther's Works 77:229)

"Truly, truly, I say to you, whatever you ask of the Father in My name, He will give it to you." JOHN 16:23

When to Pray

 f you refuse to pray until you know or feel yourself worthy and fit, you need never pray any more. For as was said before, our prayer must not be based upon or depend upon our worthiness or that of our prayer, but on the unwavering truth of the divine promise. Whenever our prayer is founded on itself or something else, it is false and deceptive, even though it wrings your heart with its intense devotion or weeps sheer drops of blood (Luke 22:44). We pray after all because we are unworthy to pray. The very fact that we are unworthy and that we dare to pray confidently, trusting only in the faithfulness of God, makes us worthy to pray and to have our prayer answered. Be as unworthy as you may, but know most seriously that it is a thousand times more important, yes, that everything depends on your honoring God's truthfulness and your never giving His promise the lie by your doubts. Your worthiness does not help you; and your unworthiness does not hinder you. . . . All your life you must, therefore, guard against deeming yourself worthy or fit to pray or to receive, unless it be that you proceed with bold courage, trusting in the truthful and certain promises of your gracious God, who thereby wants to reveal His mercy to you.

From *On Rogationtide Prayer and Procession* (Luther's Works 42:88–89)

God has done what the law, weakened by the flesh,
could not do. By sending His own Son in the likeness
of sinful flesh and for sin, He condemned sin
in the flesh.

ROMANS 8:3

The Contrary Death

henever I feel remorse in my conscience on account of sin, therefore, I look at the bronze serpent, Christ on the cross (John 3:14–15). Against my sin, which accuses and devours me, I find there another sin. But this other sin, namely, that which is in the flesh of Christ, takes away the sin of the world. It is omnipotent, and it damns and devours my sin. Lest my sin accuse and damn me, it is itself damned by sin, that is, by Christ the crucified, "who for our sake was made to be sin, so that in Him we might become the righteousness of God" (2 Corinthians 5:21). Thus in my flesh I find a death that afflicts and kills me; but I also have a contrary death, which is the death of my death and which crucifies and devours my death.

From *Lectures on Galatians* (1535) (Luther's Works 26:159–60)

If anyone is in Christ, he is a new creation.

2 Corinthians 5:17

The Good Man

 have often said, in order to speak and judge correctly about these matters, that we must carefully distinguish between a good man (what the philosophers call *bonus vir)* and a Christian. We also praise being a good man, and there is nothing more laudable on earth. It is God's gift just as much as sun and moon, grain and wine, and all creation. However, we do not mix and brew those things into each other, but let a good man have his praise before the world, and say: "A good man is certainly an excellent, precious man on earth, but he is not for that reason a Christian." He could even be a Turk or a heathen (as formerly some were highly renowned). It cannot be otherwise than that among so many wicked people a good man must at times be found. However, no matter how good he is, despite that goodness he still is and remains Adam's child, that is, an earthly man under sin and death.

From the *Church Postil*, sermon for Easter 4 on John 16:5–15
(Luther's Works 77:236)

Through the law I died to the law,
so that I might live to God.

GALATIANS 2:19

Law to the Law

hus with the sweetest names Christ is called my Law, my sin, and my death, in opposition to the Law, sin, and death, even though in fact He is nothing but sheer liberty, righteousness, life, and eternal salvation. Therefore He became Law to the Law, sin to sin, and death to death, in order that He might redeem me from the curse of the Law, justify me, and make me alive. And so Christ is both: While He is the Law, He is liberty; while He is sin, He is righteousness; and while He is death, He is life. For by the very fact that He permitted the Law to accuse Him, sin to damn Him, and death to devour Him He abrogated the Law, damned sin, destroyed death, and justified and saved me. Thus Christ is a poison against the Law, sin, and death, and simultaneously a remedy to regain liberty, righteousness, and eternal life.

From *Lectures on Galatians* (1535) (Luther's Works 26:163)

We are members of His body.

EPHESIANS 5:30

Joined by Faith

ut faith must be taught correctly, namely, that by it you are so cemented to Christ that He and you are as one person, which cannot be separated but remains attached to Him forever and declares: "I am as Christ." And Christ, in turn, says: "I am as that sinner who is attached to Me, and I to him. For by faith we are joined together into one flesh and one bone." Thus Ephesians 5:30 says: "We are members of the body of Christ, of His flesh and of His bones," in such a way that this faith couples Christ and me more intimately than a husband is coupled to his wife. Therefore this faith is no idle quality.

From *Lectures on Galatians* (1535) (Luther's Works 26:168)

The law of the Spirit of life has set you free in Christ
Jesus from the law of sin and death.

ROMANS 8:2

What Binds the Law?

nd this statement of Paul's, "I through the Law died to the Law," is full of comfort. . . . Then, when the Law accuses and manifests his sin, his conscience immediately says: "You have sinned." If now you hold to what Paul, the apostle of Christ, teaches here, you will reply: "It is true. I have sinned." "Then God will punish and damn you." "No." "But that is what the Law of God says." "I have nothing to do with this Law." "Why is that?" "Because I have another Law, one that strikes this Law dumb. I am referring to liberty." "What liberty?" "That of Christ, for through Christ I am liberated from the Law." Therefore the Law which is and remains a Law for the wicked is liberty for me, and it binds the Law that damns me. Thus the Law that once bound me and held me captive is now bound and held captive by grace or liberty, which is now my Law. The accusing Law now hears this Law say: "You shall not bind this man, hold him captive, or make him guilty. But I will hold you captive and tie your hands, lest you hurt him who now lives to Christ and is dead to you."

From *Lectures on Galatians* (1535) (Luther's Works 26:161)

[God has] called you out of darkness into His
marvelous light.

1 PETER 2:9

Reason Is Darkness

ere you see that Peter states clearly that there is only one light and concludes that all our reason, no matter how clever, is utter darkness. For although reason can count one, two, three, can also see what is black or white, large and small, and can judge about outward things, yet it cannot see what faith is. Here it is stone-blind. And even if all men were to put all their wisdom together, they could not understand one letter of the divine wisdom. Therefore St. Peter is speaking here of another light, a light that is marvelous; and he tells us bluntly that we are all in darkness and in blindness if God does not call us into His true light.

From *Sermons on 1 Peter* (Luther's Works 30:65)

Truly no man can ransom another, or give to God the price of his life, for the ransom of their life is costly and can never suffice.

PSALM 49:7–8

Ransomed

 hose who trust in their own strength and in riches are such that even a brother who is still extremely kind to his brother cannot ransom him before God. . . . But if, somehow, he does redeem, it is a man who redeems (that is, as a man he can redeem in a temporal sense with regard to this life). But our redemption is from God. . . . If man redeems, and not God, then it follows that *he shall not give to God his ransom*, to whom it should be given most of all, if we are to be redeemed; but he gives it to a man as the price of the redemption of his body, but not of the soul. . . . Even as one redeemed in this way, he will still be in captivity and labor forever. And he will continue to live perpetually the worst kind of life, for he has not died with Christ, that he might live with Him.

From *First Lectures on the Psalms* (Luther's Works 10:226–27)

Mary said, "Behold, I am the servant of the Lord;
let it be to me according to Your word."

LUKE 1:38

The Annunciation of Our Lord

 ernard says concerning the faith of the Virgin Mary when it had been announced to her by the angel that she would be the mother of Christ that the strength of faith of the Virgin who could believe the words of the angel was no less a miracle than the incarnation of the Word itself. Therefore the greatest things in the histories of the saints are the words which God speaks with the saints. Although their virtues and deeds should be praised . . . yet they, like the feet, should be put in the lowest place. But the head in the life of the saints is the speaking of God itself.

From *Lectures on Genesis* (Luther's Works 5:234)

March 25

Abstain from the passions of the flesh.

1 PETER 2:11

To Tame the Flesh

ven though man has become righteous, he is not yet completely rid of evil lusts. To be sure, faith has begun to subdue the flesh; but the flesh continues to bestir itself and rages nevertheless in all sorts of lusts that would like to assert themselves again and do what they want. Therefore the spirit must busy itself daily to tame the flesh and to bring it into subjection, must wrestle with it incessantly, and must take care that it does not repel faith. Therefore those who say that they have faith, think that this is enough, and, in addition, live as they please, are deceiving themselves. Where faith is genuine, it must attack the body and hold it in check, lest the body do what it pleases. For this reason, St. Peter says that we must be sober. But he does not want the body to be destroyed or to be weakened too much. . . . It is good to fast. But one fasts in the right way by not giving the body more food than is needed to keep it healthy, and by letting it work and wake, in order that the old ass may not become too reckless, go dancing on the ice, and break a leg but may be bridled and follow the spirit.

From *Sermons on 1 Peter* (Luther's Works 30:27–28)

March 26

Good news came to us just as to them, but the message
they heard did not benefit them, because they were not
united by faith with those who listened.

HEBREWS 4:2

The Gospel Truth

 hen I hear that Jesus Christ died, took away my sin, gained heaven for me, and gave me all that He has, I am hearing the Gospel. The Word is soon gone when it is preached; but when it falls into the heart and is grasped by faith, it can never slip away. No creature can invalidate this truth. The depths of hell can do nothing against it; and even if I am already in the jaws of the devil, I must come out and remain where the Word remains, if I can take hold of it.

From *Sermons on 1 Peter* (Luther's Works 30:45)

In Your majesty ride out victoriously for the
cause of truth and meekness and righteousness;
let Your right hand teach You awesome deeds!

PSALM 45:4

The Spiritual King

hen you hear the king mentioned [in this psalm], do not think of a king of the world or a king in purple and gold, but a King in the spirit, who reigns in truth, not in wealth and tyranny. For he says "proceed prosperously and reign" (v. 4). And do this because of truth and meekness and justice. And "Your right hand shall lead You wonderfully," that is to say, not according to men, who do not discern such a reign. Therefore those three, truth, meekness, righteousness, are most fittingly mentioned, especially so that His rule may not be thought of as physical. Also the words "shall lead You wonderfully" are along the same line. For when he said "proceed prosperously and reign," he adds "because of truth," et cetera, as if to say: "So that through those and in these Your rule shall consist, You shall prosper toward it."

From *First Lectures on the Psalms* (Luther's Works 10:221)

Be gracious to me, O Lord, for I am languishing;
heal me, O Lord, for my bones are troubled. My soul
also is greatly troubled. Psalm 6:2–3

The Anxious Heart

We also see many godly hearts that are always sad and dejected, being anxious and troubled at their own thoughts, despairing in their temptations from the devil. "Where," say the world and our own flesh, "is the Holy Spirit about whom you Christians boast?" Therefore, a Christian should be wise here so that he does not pass sentence and judge according to his own thoughts and feelings, but know that against just this temptation and weakness he must cling to the Word and the comforting sermon which the Holy Spirit preaches to all poor, distressed hearts and consciences. Christ says about the office which He is to carry out through the Holy Spirit: "The Spirit of the Lord is with Me. Because the Lord has anointed Me, He has sent Me to preach to the wretched, to bind up the broken hearts, likewise to comfort all the sorrowful" (Isaiah 61:1–2). From this you should learn (as you hear at this place and everywhere in the Gospel) that God does not want to have you sad and frightened, but cheerful and confident of the sure, truthful promise of His grace, which the Holy Spirit Himself preaches to you.

From the *Church Postil*, sermon for Pentecost on John 14:23–31
(Luther's Works 77:334–35)

Therefore be imitators of God, as beloved children.
And walk in love, as Christ loved us and gave Himself
up for us, a fragrant offering and sacrifice to God.

EPHESIANS 5:1–2

Giving Ourselves

his fruit is that, just as we have eaten and drunk the Lord Christ's body and blood, we in turn let ourselves be eaten and drunk, and also speak to our neighbor the words: "Take, eat and drink." This is not a mockery, but entirely serious: that you give yourself with all your life, just as Christ has done for you in these words, with all that He is. It is as if He would say: "I Myself am here given for you. I present you with this treasure. What I have, you also shall have. When you are in want, I also will be in want. Here you have My righteousness, life, and salvation, so that neither sin nor death, neither hell nor any distress will overcome you. As long as I am righteous and alive, you also will remain godly and alive." He speaks these words to us. We must also lay hold of them and speak them to our neighbors, not only with our mouths but also with our deeds, in this way: "Look, my dear brother, I have received my Lord. He is mine, and I now have enough of all fullness and to spare. So take what I have, and everything will be yours; I put it at your disposal. If it is necessary that I die for you, I will also do it." This goal is placed before us in this Sacrament, so that this proof [of love] toward our neighbor may appear in us.

From *Sermon on Confession and the Sacrament* (Luther's Works 76:444–45)

The desires of the flesh are against the Spirit,
and the desires of the Spirit are against the flesh.

GALATIANS 5:17

The Battle of the Flesh

hen someone becomes aware of this battle of the flesh, he should not lose heart on this account; but by the Spirit he should fight back and say: "I am a sinner, and I am aware of my sin; for I have not yet put off my flesh, to which sin will cling as long as it lives. But I will obey the Spirit rather than the flesh. That is, by faith and hope I will take hold of Christ. I will fortify myself with His Word, and thus fortified I will refuse to gratify the desires of the flesh." . . . Thus there is great comfort for the faithful in this teaching of Paul's, because they know that they have partly flesh and partly Spirit, but in such a way that the Spirit rules and the flesh is subordinate, that righteousness is supreme and sin is a servant.

From *Lectures on Galatians* (1535) (Luther's Works 27:72–74)

*I decided to know nothing among you except Jesus
Christ and Him crucified.*

1 CORINTHIANS 2:2

God's Ordered Power

 ou should direct your attention to the ordered power of God and the ministrations of God; for we do not want to deal with the uncovered God, whose ways are inscrutable and whose judgments are unsearchable (Romans 11:33). We must reflect on God's ordered power, that is, on the incarnate Son, in whom are hidden all the treasures of the Godhead (Colossians 2:3). Let us go to the child lying in the lap of His mother Mary and to the sacrificial victim suspended on the cross; there we shall really behold God, and there we shall look into His very heart. We shall see that He is compassionate and does not desire the death of the sinner, but that the sinner should "turn from his way and live" (Ezekiel 33:11). From such speculation or contemplation spring true peace and true joy of heart. Therefore Paul says (1 Corinthians 2:2): "I determine to know nothing except Christ." We have leisure to speculate on this with profit.

From *Lectures on Genesis* (Luther's Works 3:276–77)

Jesus said to him, "Go; your son will live."
The man believed the word that Jesus spoke to him
and went on his way.

JOHN 4:50

The Omnipotent Prayer

he prayer of faith is omnipotent, as Christ says, "All things are possible for one who believes!" (Mark 9:23). We may not always perceive that those things for which we ask in faith are present, but they have assuredly been obtained, and they will appear in their proper time.

From *Annotations on Matthew* (Luther's Works 67:60)

Jesus turned, and seeing her He said, "Take
heart, daughter; your faith has made you well."
And instantly the woman was made well.
MATTHEW 9:22

A Beautiful Faith

ehold, that is a beautiful faith, which realizes its unworthiness and yet does not permit itself to be hindered on this account to place its confidence in Christ, nor to doubt His grace and help, but breaks through the Law and everything that frightens it away from Him; yes, if the whole world would attempt to hinder and thwart, yet it does not think of leaving this man until it has laid hold on Him. Therefore it presses through all barriers and attains what it seeks in Christ, and immediately experiences the power and work of Christ, even before He begins to speak. For it cannot apply to Christ in vain, even as Christ Himself testifies, when He says: "Thy faith hath made thee whole." Besides, faith like this is so pleasing to Christ that He does not wish it to remain concealed in her and that the power and work made effective by it should remain a secret, but what is in her heart must be published to everybody so that her faith may be praised before the whole world and be strengthened in her.

From the *Church Postil*, sermon for Trinity 24 on Matthew 9:18–26 (Luther's Works (Lenker) 5:352–53)

"But take heart; I have overcome the world."

John 16:33

Confidence That Sustains

e are sustained by this confidence; and we have no doubt that Christ is powerful enough not only to sustain us but to conquer all the power of the oppressors and the wiles of the heretics. He gave ample evidence of this in the case of the Jews and the Romans, whose fierceness and persecution He once bore. He had to bear the wiles of the heretics also; but in time all of them were overthrown and destroyed, and He remained the King and the Victor. Regardless of how much the Papists rage today or of how the sectarians distort and corrupt the Gospel of Christ, Christ will remain King forever, and the Word of the Lord will stand forever (1 Peter 1:25); and all His enemies will be annihilated.

From *Lectures on Galatians* (1535) (Luther's Works 26:456–57)

Christ redeemed us from the curse of the law
by becoming a curse for us.

Our Sure Confidence

ith gratitude and with a sure confidence, therefore, let us accept this doctrine, so sweet and so filled with comfort, which teaches that Christ became a curse for us, that is, a sinner worthy of the wrath of God; that He clothed Himself in our person, laid our sins upon His own shoulders, and said: "I have committed the sins that all men have committed." Therefore He truly became accursed according to the Law, not for Himself but, as Paul says, ["for us"]. . . . But because He took upon Himself our sins, not by compulsion but of His own free will, it was right for Him to bear the punishment and the wrath of God—not for His own Person, which was righteous and invincible and therefore could not become guilty, but for our person. By this fortunate exchange with us He took upon Himself our sinful person and granted us His innocent and victorious Person.

From *Lectures on Galatians* (1535) (Luther's Works 26:283–84)

Give ear, O My people, to My teaching;
incline your ears to the words of My mouth. PSALM 78:1

Listen, Learn, Live

he apostles have proclaimed these words and the Law throughout the world. And the psalmist opened his mouth in parables which are now known everywhere. "And hidden mysteries from the beginning" (Psalm 78:2) have been uttered everywhere, so that what follows might be true, "How great things we have heard and known, and our fathers (that is, the apostles and their successors) have told us" (v. 3) in writings and words. "And they have not been hidden from their children in another generation" (v. 4). No one can say that he does not know what Christ said and did for us. "Declaring the praises of the Lord and His powers (namely, as recorded in the Gospel) and His wonders, which He has done" in casting down the devil and in the victory over death through His suffering. "And He established a testimony in Jacob" (that is, the Gospel among His people) "and appointed a law in Israel, which He commanded our fathers to teach to their children (v. 5), that the next generation might know them, the children yet unborn, and rise up and tell them to their children" (v. 6). This the Lord did when He so urgently commanded the Gospel to be preached and that the talent be put out for interest, so that no one would have an excuse in His presence.

From *First Lectures on the Psalms* (Luther's Works 11:44–45)

April 6

[May God grant you the] strength to comprehend
with all the saints what is the breadth and length and
height and depth, and to know the love of Christ that
surpasses knowledge.

EPHESIANS 3:18–19

The Excellent Thing

hen a Christian hears this—that God's Son has come to us from heaven, preached to us, and given Himself to us—should he not (if he rightly and fully believes it) be amazed and overwhelmed with joy? For who can sufficiently express or comprehend what a great and excellent thing it is that God's Son has become our flesh and blood and is our own? Indeed, the angels in heaven cannot be filled with enough amazement that God has so dearly loved us poor, lost human beings and shown us such inexpressible kindness that He Himself becomes a man, speaks with us, lives among us, dies for us on the cross, etc.

From *Four Sermons Preached in Eisleben*, sermon on Matthew 13:24–30 (Luther's Works 58:448)

How long will you love vain words and seek after
lies? But know the LORD *has set apart the godly*
for Himself; the LORD *hears when I call to Him.*

PSALM 4:2–3

Acknowledge and Know Him

With [the Lord] is plenteous sweetness. The Law only killed, but it did not make alive [that is, it showed how a person should be put to death, but it did not make alive, that is, it did not show how a person was to be made alive], and man only hurts but does not soothe, whereas God "pours in wine and oil" (Luke 10:34). Therefore if anyone will hear this voice of the Spirit, "Why do you seek vanity and lies?" and submit to this rebuke and smiting, and say to him: "But what shall we do, O prophet? How may we escape a heavy heart? Who will set us free from this vanity and lying?" then the prophet will show them the true Savior and the "redemption which the Lord sent to His people" (Psalm 111:9), saying: " 'Know,' O sons of men, and understand what I say to you, for it will be for your good. Behold, 'the Lord has made His Holy One wonderful,' " as if to say: "Acknowledge and know Him as the Holy One of the Lord (namely, that He is Himself holy and makes you holy) whom you shall see doing wonderful things, as Isaiah 35:6 prophesied: 'Then shall the lame man leap like a hart.' Then know that 'the Lord has visited His people' (Luke 7:16) and 'has made His Holy One wonderful' for you. 'If you believe in Him, you will be saved' (Mark 16:16). If you will cry to Him, the Lord will hear you, for He is the beginning of salvation, and without Him 'there is salvation in no one else' (Acts 4:12). Therefore you must know and acknowledge Him above all, if you want to avoid vanity and lying. But you acknowledge and know Him, if you observe His miracles, since 'these very works bear witness' (John 5:36) concerning Him and the Lord has made Him wonderful so that you may know Him and cry to Him . . . ."

From *First Lectures on the Psalms* (Luther's Works 10:63)

[Forgive] one another, as God in Christ forgave you.

EPHESIANS 4:32

Forgive and Forget

[Christian faith ready to rest completely on God's Christ] requires a person cheerfully to forgive and forget injury that he has suffered. That is what God has done with us and continues to do when He forgives sin: He expunges it from the record and no longer remembers it. Still it is neither necessary nor possible for a man to forget it in the sense that he never thinks of it again, but in the sense that your heart is just as friendly toward your neighbor as it used to be before he injured you. If the stump remains in your heart and you are not as friendly and kind toward him as you used to be, that is not forgetting or even cordially forgiving. You are still the scoundrel who comes before the altar with his sacrifice and tries to serve God even while his heart is crammed full of anger, envy, and hate. But very few people pay any attention to this at all. They all walk around in their beautiful mask; they fail to see the relation of their heart to this commandment, which summarily rejects any anger or ill will against the neighbor.

From *The Sermon on the Mount* (Luther's Works 21:82–83)

For I delivered to you as of first importance
what I also received: that Christ died for our sins
in accordance with the Scriptures, that He was buried,
that He was raised on the third day in accordance
with the Scriptures.

1 CORINTHIANS 15:3–4

Proof Is in the Scriptures

 ere you notice how Paul adduces Scripture as his strongest proof, for there is no other enduring way of preserving our doctrine and our faith than the physical or written Word, poured into letters and preached orally by him or others; for here we find it stated clearly: "Scripture! Scripture!" But Scripture is not all spirit, about which they drivel, saying that the Spirit alone must do it and that Scripture is a dead letter which cannot impart life. But the fact of the matter is that, although the letter by itself does not impart life, yet it must be present, and it must be heard or received. And the Holy Spirit must work through this in the heart, and the heart must be preserved in the faith through and in the Word against the devil and every trial. Otherwise, where this is surrendered, Christ and the Spirit will soon be lost. Therefore do not boast so much of the Spirit if you do not have the revealed external Word; for this is surely not a good spirit but the vile devil from hell. The Holy Spirit, as you know, has deposited His wisdom and counsel

April 10

and all mysteries into the Word and revealed these in Scripture, so that no one can excuse himself. Nor must anyone seek or search for something else or learn or acquire something better or more sublime than what Scripture teaches of Jesus Christ, God's Son, our Savior, who died and rose for us.

From *Commentary on 1 Corinthians 15* (Luther's Works 28:76–77)

"If you abide in Me, and My words abide in you, ask whatever you wish, and it will be done for you."

JOHN 15:7

The Lord Will Answer

 herefore, no one has the right to make his own way to God through his own devotion or works. . . . You must come to Him through the Seed of Abraham and be blessed through Him, according to the wording of the testament of God. . . . Since the divine nature is so high and intangible for us, He has for our good taken on Himself the nature most familiar to us: our own. That is how He wants to care for us; that is where He wants to be found, and nowhere else. Whoever calls on Him here is immediately heard. Here is the throne of grace, where no one who comes is excluded. The others, who let Him dwell here in vain and would otherwise serve and call on the God who created heaven and earth, already have their answer when [the psalmist] says, "They call, but there is no helper; to the Lord, but He does not answer them" (Psalm 18:41).

From the *Church Postil*, sermon for the Sunday after Christmas on Galatians 4:1–7 (Luther's Works 75:383)

April 11

*Do not be conformed to this world, but be transformed
by the renewal of your mind.*

ROMANS 12:2

Our Broken Will

t is necessary for us to be careful not to follow the ways of the world or our own reason and good opinions, but rather always to break our mind and will, and do and suffer otherwise than our reason and will assert, so that we are not conformed to the world but do the opposite. So we will daily be transformed and renewed in our minds; that is, we daily, more and more, cling to what the world and reason hate. For example, we daily prefer to be poor, sick, and despised fools and sinners, and finally regard death as better than life, foolishness as more precious than wisdom, shame as more noble than honor, poverty as more blessed than wealth, and sin as more glorious than piety. The world does not have that mind-set, but is minded differently in all things; it remains in that old mind-set unchanged and unrenewed, stubborn and decrepit.

From the *Church Postil*, sermon for Epiphany 1 on Romans 12:1–6 (Luther's Works 76:188–89)

*[God] raised [Christ] from the dead and seated Him
at His right hand in the heavenly places . . . . And He
put all things under His feet.*

EPHESIANS 1:20, 22

Under Christ's Feet

hrist is a much greater and higher lord than Adam was before the fall. For nothing was subjected to Adam or put under his feet, but everything is put under Christ's feet, so that the whole world and all His enemies will have to be His footstool (Psalm 110:1). Therefore this text cannot be neglected, since it strongly proves the doctrine that Christ is true God and man. If He were not man, He could not be called . . . Son of Man. If He were not God, He could not be Lord over all the works of God nor have all things under His feet. For no one has a right to be Lord over heaven, earth, angels, man, life—yes, over sin and death—except one who is true God by nature.

From *Commentary on Psalm 8* (Luther's Works 12:134)

Pray without ceasing.

1 THESSALONIANS 5:17

Continuous Prayer

herefore wherever there is a Christian, there is none other than the Holy Spirit, who does nothing but pray without ceasing. Even though one does not move one's lips and form words continuously, one's heart nonetheless does beat incessantly; and, like the pulse and the heart in the body, it beats with sighs such as these: "Oh, dear Father, please let Thy name be hallowed, Thy kingdom come, Thy will be done among us and everyone!" And when blows fall, when temptations thicken, and adversity presses harder, then such sighing prayers become more fervent and also find words. A Christian without prayer is just as impossible as a living person without a pulse. The pulse is never motionless; it moves and beats constantly, whether one is asleep or something else keeps one from being aware of it.

From *Sermons on the Gospel of John*, Chapters 14–16 (Luther's Works 24:89)

By faith Abraham obeyed when he was called to go
out to a place that he was to receive as an inheritance.
And he went out, not knowing where he was going.

HEBREWS 11:8

An Active Faith

 hristian faith is ready to rest completely on God's Word with all confidence and courage, and then to go joyfully on its way. Therefore Peter says: Then the loins of your mind are girded, and your faith is genuine, if you have such courage, no matter whether property, honor, body, or life are involved. With these words he has surely given an excellent description of a genuine and true faith. It must not be an indolent and sleepy faith and only a dream. No, it must be a living and active thing, so that one devotes oneself to it with all confidence and clings to the Word, no matter what happens, in order that we may press forward through fortune and misfortune. Thus when I must die, I must rely boldly on Christ, readily put forth my neck, and trust in the Word of God, which cannot lie to me. Then faith must go straight ahead, let nothing lead it astray, and ignore everything it sees, hears, and feels. This is the kind of faith St. Peter demands—a faith that consists in such power, not in thoughts or words.

From *Sermons on 1 Peter* (Luther's Works 30:28)

For by grace you have been saved through faith.
And this is not your own doing; it is the gift of God,
not a result of works, so that no one may boast.

EPHESIANS 2:8–9

How to Go to God

 herefore it is necessary to mark the words well. For with the words "No one can come to Me" Christ intends to say that faith is God's gift. And He is willing to give it, if only we request it of Him. To come to Him means to believe in Christ. But he who does not believe is far from Him. You assume that faith is your doing, your power, your work; and thereby you interfere with God's work. It is the gift of God, so that He alone may be accorded the honor and no man may boast of his strength. It is the Father who draws us and gives us the Word, and the Holy Spirit and faith by the Word. It is His gift, not our work or power. St. Paul also tells us that in Ephesians 2:8–9: "For by grace you have been saved; and this is not your own doing; it is the gift of God, lest any man should boast." This is the essence of true Christianity, against which the world has always contended madly and foolishly and against which it still rages. Here there is no boasting of any work but only of the Father's drawing.

From *Sermons on the Gospel of John, Chapters 6–8* (Luther's Works 23:181)

The poor man died and was carried by the angels

to Abraham's side.

LUKE 16:22

Scripture Testifies

 ust as in the church we are said to be gathered to our people through Baptism, through the Gospel and the sacraments, and we know that we are among our people, so when we die in the promise of Christ made to Abraham, we are transferred by the angels into the bosom of Abraham, or to our people. And we have often stated that the promises of the fathers pertain to the resurrection and the future life, not only to physical life but to the other, spiritual and eternal life, when the works of natural life, of nourishing, of generation, and similar works will cease. But where that people is, we do not know. . . . It suffices for us that Scripture testifies that from the beginning of the world those who believed in the Seed of the woman did not perish and were not consigned to oblivion but were gathered to their people.

From *Lectures on Genesis* (Luther's Works 8:315–16)

Take counsel together, but it will come to nothing;
speak a word, but it will not stand, for God is with us.

ISAIAH 8:10

When God Does Not Enter

here sits the king or prince, wise and clever by himself, having the matter well in hand from every possible angle. . . . Not a single one of these people would direct a sigh up to heaven to seek advice and a plan of action from God. They are either such godless people that their conscience will not permit prayer or invocation; or they are so certain and smug in their wisdom and affairs that they scornfully forget to do it, as though they had no need of it; or they are usually accustomed to lay their plans this way, calloused in their unbelief. In the meantime our Lord God has to sit idly above. He does not dare to enter into the plans of such clever people, and He chats meanwhile with His angel Gabriel and says: "My dear fellow, what are these wise people doing in their council chamber, that they do not draw us into their deliberations? They must be wanting to build the Tower of Babel again. Dear Gabriel, go down there and take Isaiah with you, and read them a secret lesson through the window and say: 'With seeing eyes you shall see nothing, with hearing ears you shall hear nothing, with understanding hearts you shall understand nothing' (Isa. 6:10). 'Take counsel together, and let it come to naught. Speak the word, and let it not stand. For Mine is both proposing and disposing' (Isa. 8:10). So shall it be."

From *Commentary on Psalm 101* (Luther's Works 13:149–50)

April 18

None But Christ

he holy Christian people are externally recognized by the holy possession of the sacred cross. They must endure every misfortune and persecution, all kinds of trials and evil from the devil, the world, and the flesh (as the Lord's Prayer indicates) by inward sadness, timidity, fear, outward poverty, contempt, illness, and weakness, in order to become like their Head, Christ. And the only reason they must suffer is that they steadfastly adhere to Christ and God's Word, enduring this for the sake of Christ, Matthew 5:11, "Blessed are you when men persecute you on My account." They must be pious, quiet, obedient, and prepared to serve the government and everybody with life and goods, doing no one any harm. No people on earth have to endure such bitter hate . . . to the point where those who hang, drown, murder, torture, banish, and plague them to death are rendering God a service. No one has compassion on them; they are given myrrh and gall to drink when they thirst. And all of this is done not because they are adulterers, murderers, thieves, or rogues, but because they want to have none but Christ, and no other God. Wherever you see or hear this, you may know that the holy Christian church is there.

From *On the Councils and the Church* (Luther's Works 41:164–65)

With the heart one believes and is justified,
and with the mouth one confesses and is saved.

ROMANS 10:10

Faith Takes Hold

aith takes hold of Christ and has Him present, enclosing Him as the ring encloses the gem. And whoever is found having this faith in the Christ who is grasped in the heart, him God accounts as righteous. This is the means and the merit by which we obtain the forgiveness of sins and righteousness. "Because you believe in Me," God says, "and your faith takes hold of Christ, whom I have freely given to you as your Justifier and Savior, therefore be righteous." Thus God accepts you or accounts you righteous only on account of Christ, in whom you believe. . . . When we have taught faith in Christ this way, then we also teach about good works. Because you have taken hold of Christ by faith, through whom you are righteous, you should now go and love God and your neighbor. Call upon God, give thanks to Him, preach Him, praise Him, confess Him. Do good to your neighbor, and serve him; do your duty. These are truly good works, which flow from this faith and joy conceived in the heart because we have the forgiveness of sins freely through Christ.

From *Lectures on Galatians* (1535) (Luther's Works 26:132–33)

As the Lord has forgiven you,
so you also must forgive.

Colossians 3:13

With Malice Toward None

ll kinds of flaws and unpleasant things must crop up among us. We must not give vent to our anger even if we bite our tongue with our teeth, our fist strikes our eye, our foot trips, or our head runs up against a wall; but we must reason thus: "Well, he is your fellow member, your brother or neighbor. What do you propose to do about it? He erred; there was no malice involved, and he means no ill. Perhaps it was done in weakness and ignorance. You did receive a blow from him. It hurts, but are you willing to cast your fellow member away for this reason? It is a little spark. Spit on it, and it will go out. Otherwise the devil will come with his venomous breath or through evil tongues and fan it into an inextinguishable fire, and it will develop into discord and hatred that cannot be allayed but will harm the whole body. For the devil is a spirit who does not desist and cease if he is not restrained."

From *Sermons on the Gospel of John*, Chapters 14–16 (Luther's Works 24:248)

But to the wicked God says: "What right have you to recite My statutes or take My covenant on your lips? For you hate discipline, and you cast My words behind you." PSALM 50:16–17

Same, but Different

 hey call themselves Christians, believers, the church, and boast of having God and His Word, etc. We do the same thing. Both of us use the same words. Here we are in agreement. But when it comes to substance and understanding, we are as far apart as possible. . . . One must look to see where the doctrine of the Gospel concerning faith in Christ, without additions and supplements, is taught in the right manner and is accompanied by its fruits and true good works in accordance with this Word. On the other hand, one must look to see where the opposite takes place, where the Gospel and faith are mentioned only with the mouth, and other things, with which faith and Christ are denied, are put forth in opposition; where, because of a false trust, self-devised works are valued more highly than true good works, as is also shown by the fruits, since there is a determination to defend this against the true doctrine and faith with excommunication, murder, etc.

From *Sermons on the Gospel of John*, Chapters 14–16 (Luther's Works 24:330–31)

*"I give them eternal life, and they will never perish,
and no one will snatch them out of My hand."*

JOHN 10:28

Grace to Hear It

ou claim that Christ is a judge who punishes sinners severely, and that therefore I must pay and atone for my sins lest Christ slay me with His sword. Thus you teach me work-righteousness and the intercession of the saints. But I know that I am baptized, that I hear God's Word, and that I believe this article of faith, that is, believe in Jesus Christ. God has granted me grace to hear and to believe, and, thus equipped, I came to Him by the will of the Heavenly Father. This is sufficient for me. Why should I fear? And whom should I fear? For He says here: "Him who comes to Me I will not cast out." This I will accept, love, and cherish. Therefore I will surely remain secure with Him. For here I am dearly and unmistakably assured that I will not be rejected and cast out. And in another passage it is written that no one will snatch me out of His hand (John 10:28). Christ is determined to protect and defend me, so that no one will take me from Him, even though all the devils and the gates of hell (Matthew 16:18) were against me.

From *Sermons on the Gospel of John*, Chapters 6–8 (Luther's Works 23:60)

*Though I walk in the midst of trouble, You preserve
my life; You stretch out Your hand against the wrath
of my enemies, and Your right hand delivers me.*

<small>PSALM 138:7</small>

Help in the Midst of Trouble

hen they think they are already done for, when
everywhere there is despair and no hope of escaping, then the Lord is present and helps them. In this
way the Lord is present in the middle of the years, that is, He
is the Helper in the middle of troubles and at the right times,
as we have it in the psalm (Psalm 138:7). Job also speaks this
way: "When you think you are done for, etc." He is teaching
us in an eminent way all those things about the exodus of
the children of Israel from Egypt through the sea, how they
passed through the sea safely, although Pharaoh was pressing on and pursuing them with his entire army and they
already thought they were done for. He gave them water out
of a rock in the desert; food fell from heaven, etc.

From *Lectures on Habakkuk* (Latin text) (Luther's Works 19:136)

"Straighten up and raise your heads, because your redemption is drawing near." LUKE 21:38

The Greatest Love

or that love of God is so great that we are able to have confidence on the Day of Judgment, on which the whole world will tremble. Isaiah 28:16: "Behold, I am laying in Zion for a foundation a Stone, a tested Stone, a precious Cornerstone, of a sure foundation." Therefore through the knowledge of this love we also have faith, so that we can pass muster at the judgment. Thus Christ also warns by means of the parable of the fig tree in Luke 21:28: "Look up, and raise your heads, because your redemption is drawing near." This is what the blood of love which was shed for us does—the blood which is more precious than all the merits and deaths of all the saints. But the fact that we do not consider this fittingly and do not treat of this blood in a manner that is sufficiently fitting, this is due to our very education, by which we have been brought up in various ways ever since our childhood to observe human traditions and inventions. The devil knows this weakness of the flesh, namely, that we do not fittingly value the blood of Christ. Therefore if consciousness of a great sin weighs you down, comfort yourself with this blood of love. Surely the whole world does not grasp the tiniest syllable of the statement that God is love. No human religion can hold its own in the face of the judgment, but it is solely in the blood of Christ that we have confidence on the Day of Judgment.

From *Lectures on 1 John* (Luther's Works 30:301–2)

April 25

*"How awesome is this place! This is none other than
the house of God, and this is the gate of heaven."*

GENESIS 28:17

God Reveals His Glory

 herefore we should acknowledge and make much of the boundless glory of God by which He has revealed Himself to us in His church. For it is not the kind of house in which He creates as He created all things in the beginning out of nothing. No, it is a house in which He speaks with us, deals with us, feeds us, and cares for us when we are asleep and when we are awake. But how few there are who believe this! This is true, and it is a very great Word, in which the angels in heaven take delight. When they hear it, they are filled with joy and gladness because of this knowledge of the church. Yet they cannot look at, consider, and admire it enough. For the church includes God, who dwells with us in such a way that He quickens, guards, and heals us; and by this dwelling together He brings it about that in this life there is the house of God and the gate of heaven.

From *Lectures on Genesis* (Luther's Works 5:249)

You stand fast through faith. So do not become proud,
but fear.

ROMANS 11:20

The Humility of Peter

 his [Peter's temptation to deny Christ] was also necessary for Peter in his own person, so that he might be humbled. For Peter was eventually to be filled with the gifts of the Holy Spirit. Then it would have been impossible for him not to have become arrogant and presumptuous and finally to have departed with the devil into the pit of hell. This is why God permits him to fall, so that he might remain humble and have to take off his hat not only before the Virgin Mary but also before you and me. Thus, no matter how great a sinner you may be, look at Peter. You will not find any sin to equal his, except for obduracy and presumption, which is a sin unto death (1 John 5:16). . . . Thus Peter's example should be taken to heart, for it is helpful and salutary to sinners and to saints alike: to sinners, that they may not despair; to saints, that they may not become presumptuous and proud.

From *Sermons on the Gospel of John*, Chapters 17–20 (Luther's Works 69:187–88)

April 27

[Christ] loves us and has freed us from our sins
by His blood and made us a kingdom, priests to His
God and Father.

REVELATION 1:5–6

We Are All Kings

he same thing is true with regard to the fact that we are all kings. "Priests" and "kings" are all spiritual names just as "Christians," "saints," and "church" are. And just as you are not called a Christian because you have a great deal of money and property but because you have been built on the Stone and believe in Christ, so you are not called a priest because you are tonsured or wear a long coat but because you may approach God. In like manner, you are not a king because you wear a golden crown and have many lands and people under you, but because you are a lord over all things, death, sin, and hell. If you believe in Christ you are a king just as He is a King. Now He is not a King after the manner of earthly monarchs. He does not wear a golden crown. Nor does He ride along with great pomp and many horses. No, He is a King over all kings—a King who has power over all things and at whose feet everything must lie. Just as He is a Lord, so I, too, am a lord. For what He has, that I, too, have.

From *Sermons on 1 Peter* (Luther's Works 30:63–64)

April 28

Now if I do what I do not want, it is no longer I who do
it, but sin that dwells within me.

ROMANS 7:20

The Chief Sin

 his is original sin or the sin of the nature or the sin of the person, the truly chief sin. If this did not exist, there would be no actual sin. This sin is not done, like all other sins, but it exists, lives, and does all sins and is the essential sin. It sins not for an hour or a while; but wherever and as long as the person exists, sin is also there. God looks only at this natural sin. This [sin] can be driven away by no law, by no punishment, even if there were a thousand hells; only the grace of God, which makes the nature pure and new, can sweep it away. . . . As little as being born or receiving natural life depends on each person's power, so little does being without sin or being free from it depend on his ability. He alone who has created us must take it away. Therefore, He first gives us the Law, by which man recognizes this sin and thirsts for grace; then afterward He gives the Gospel and helps him.

From the *Church Postil*, sermon for New Year's Day on Luke 2:21 (Luther's Works 76:41–42)

But thanks be to God, who in Christ always leads us
in triumphal procession.

2 CORINTHIANS 2:14

Waging War

ere above all we must know that God is among us and fights for us, and in this knowledge we wage the wars of the Lord with safety and good cheer. Our powers, however, which are wisdom, knowledge, understanding, as well as our weapons, namely, the sword of the Spirit and Scripture, are nothing but the outward work under which God Himself is powerful among us and fights and conquers. Thus Paul says (2 Corinthians 10:4): "Our weapons are not flesh, but the power of God," lest we boast as though we were the conquerors; but God alone, who works all in all for us, makes us triumph in every place (2 Corinthians 2:14).

From *Lectures on Deuteronomy* (Luther's Works 9:205)

God created man in His own image, in the image
of God He created him.

GENESIS 1:27

God's Delight

 see no other reason for the repetition [of the word "image"] unless we should understand it for the sake of emphasis as an indication of the Creator's rejoicing and exulting over the most beautiful work He had made, so that Moses intends to indicate that God was not so delighted at the other creatures as at man, whom He had created according to His own similitude. . . . But without a doubt, just as at that time God rejoiced in the counsel and work by which man was created, so today, too, He takes pleasure in restoring this work of His through His Son and our Deliverer, Christ. It is useful to ponder these facts, namely, that God is most kindly inclined toward us and takes delight in His thought and plan of restoring all who have believed in Christ to spiritual life through the resurrection of the dead.

From *Lectures on Genesis* (Luther's Works 1:68)

May 1

I will instruct you and teach you in the way you should
go; I will counsel you with My eye upon you.

PSALM 32:8

Above Our Understanding

ou ask that I deliver you. Then do not be uneasy about it; do not teach Me, and do not teach yourself; surrender yourself to Me. I am competent to be your Master. I will lead you in a way that is pleasing to Me. You think it wrong if things do not go as you feel they should. But your thinking harms you and hinders Me. Things must go, not according to your understanding but above your understanding. Submerge yourself in a lack of understanding, and I will give you My understanding. Lack of understanding is real understanding; not knowing where you are going is really knowing where you are going. . . . Behold, that is the way of the cross. You cannot find it, but I must lead you like a blind man. Therefore not you, not a man, not a creature, but I, through My Spirit and the Word, will teach you the way you must go. You must not follow the work which you choose, not the suffering which you devise, but that which comes to you against your choice, thoughts, and desires. . . . In brief, God wants us to have a true, simple faith and firm trust, confidence, and hope.

From *Seven Penitential Psalms* (Luther's Works 14:152)

By faith we understand that the universe was created
by the word of God, so that what is seen was not made
out of things that are visible.

HEBREWS 11:3

Something Out of Nothing

 t is God's nature to make something out of nothing; hence one who is not yet nothing, out of him
God cannot make anything. Man, however, makes
something else out of that which exists; but this has no value
whatever. Therefore God accepts only the forsaken, cures
only the sick, gives sight only to the blind, restores life only
to the dead, sanctifies only the sinners, gives wisdom only
to the unwise. In short, He has mercy only on those who
are wretched, and gives grace only to those who are not in
grace. Therefore no proud saint, no wise or righteous person, can become God's material, and God's purpose cannot
be fulfilled in him. He remains in his own work and makes a
fictitious, pretended, false, painted saint of himself, that is,
a hypocrite.

From *Seven Penitential Psalms* (Luther's Works 14:163)

I wait for the LORD, *my soul waits,*
and in His word I hope.

PSALM 130:5

Those Who Wait

 ow there are some who want to set the goal, appoint the hour and measure, and prescribe to God how they are to be helped. And if they do not experience this, they despair; or, if possible, they seek help elsewhere. These do not tarry and wait for the Lord. God is supposed to wait for them, be ready at once, and help exactly as they themselves have designed. Those who wait for the Lord, however, ask for mercy; but they leave it to God's gracious will when, how, where, and by what means He helps them. They have no doubt about His aid, but they do not give it a name. They let God christen and name it, even if it is delayed immeasurably long. But he who designates the help, does not receive it; for he does not wait and submit to God's council, will, and delay.

From *Seven Penitential Psalms* (Luther's Works 14:192)

[God] leads out the prisoners to prosperity,
but the rebellious dwell in a parched land.

PSALM 68:6

The Captive Conscience

 e who feels no sin will not be impelled to seek grace; he will pay no attention either to the Gospel or to faith. Therefore the Law is conscience's jailer, chains, fetters, and prison. The Law points to sin and exposes it, and thus it takes conscience captive (Romans 4:15; 7:7, 8). God does not deliver us from these bonds whenever we deem it necessary, but He permits us to be humbled and tormented in them until we thirst for grace. Now He comes and gives us His Word, to which we cling, and leads us out of captivity. Thus we escape a terrified and despondent conscience, and we get a good and sure conscience. That is the twofold work and performance of Christ in us: He kills us, and He resurrects us; He humbles us, and He exalts us, each in His good season. . . .

From *Commentary on Psalm 68* (Luther's Works 13:7–8)

I go to the Father, and you will see Me no longer."

Where Is Righteousness?

 ut in this verse I hear Christ say that my righteousness consists in His going to the Father and in His ascension into heaven. There my righteousness has been deposited, and there the devil will surely have to let it remain; for he will not make Christ a sinner or reprove or find fault with His righteousness. If I am a sinner and my life does not pass muster before God, and if I find no righteousness in myself, I have another treasure, which is the righteousness of which I boast and on which I rely. This is Christ's going to the Father, which He has presented to me as a gift." . . . Here you learn that the righteousness of which Christ is speaking is not our work or doing, but that it is His going to the Father or His ascension.

From *Sermons on the Gospel of John*, Chapters 14–16 (Luther's Works 24:347–48)

[God] only is my rock and my salvation, my fortress;
I shall not be shaken.

PSALM 62:6

My Refuge

s long as you believe this, you are really safe, even though it were to rain and snow nothing but Turkish and Tartar sultans and angry kings and princes, with all their power, for nine years without interruption, and all the devils besides! I have used the word "Refuge" for the Hebrew . . . which means "a rock." For we call "refuge" that on which we depend and with which we are comforted. Thus he wants to say now: I know that my salvation comes from Him. Why? Because I have not selected any man, no matter how great, mighty, or rich he might be, as my boast, my refuge, my comfort, and my salvation; nor have I set my heart or my hope on any man. But for this I have chosen God, from whom alone all my happiness and salvation is to come and will come. He calls God his "Rock" or his "Refuge" because he sets the sure and certain confidence of his heart on Him.

From *Four Psalms of Comfort* (Luther's Works 14:233–34)

[Jesus] answered, "It is not right to take the children's bread and throw it to the dogs." She said, "Yes, Lord, yet even the dogs eat the crumbs that fall from their masters' table." MATTHEW 15:26–27

When God Is Just

hen we do not endure God's judgment and cannot say yes when He considers and judges us to be sinners, then all hostility comes down on us. If the condemned could do it, they would be saved in a moment. We certainly say with our mouths that we are sinners, but when God Himself says this in our hearts, then we no longer stand, and we desperately desire to be godly and regarded as the godly, as long as we would be free from His judgment. But it must be so; if God is to be just in His words [Psalm 51:4] that you are a sinner, then you can make use of the right which God has given to every sinner, namely, the forgiveness of sins. Then you not only eat the crumbs under the table like the dogs, but you also are a child [of God] and have God as your own, just as you want.

From the *Church Postil*, sermon for Lent 2 on Matthew 15:21–28 (Luther's Works 76:381–82)

Trust in Him at all times, O people; pour out your heart before Him; God is a refuge for us.

PSALM 62:8

Open Your Heart

 f you are lacking something, well, here is good advice: "Pour out your heart before Him." Voice your complaint freely, and do not conceal anything from Him. Regardless of what it is, just throw it in a pile before Him, as you open your heart completely to a good friend. He wants to hear it, and He wants to give you His aid and counsel. Do not be bashful before Him, and do not think that what you ask is too big or too much. Come right out with it, even if all you have is bags full of need. Out with everything; God is greater and more able and more willing than all our transgressions. Do not dribble your requests before Him; God is not a man whom you can overburden with your begging and asking. The more you ask, the happier He is to hear you. Only pour it all out, do not dribble or drip it. For He will not drip or dribble either, but He will flood you with a veritable deluge.

From *Four Psalms of Comfort* (Luther's Works 14:237–38)

Those of low estate are but a breath; those of high estate are a delusion; in the balances they go up; they are together lighter than a breath.

PSALM 62:9

The Worth of Humanity

ere you may ask: "What? Is humanity worth nothing, even though it is a creature of God?" I answer: David is not speaking about the creature as such but about the use of the creature. That is, humanity is certainly a good thing; but it is not put to good use. . . . In what way? Because people try to put their trust in them and to build on them. For such use they are worth nothing. Why? Because they are uncertain in their hearts and in their lives. Sand and water are a good thing too; but if I wanted to build a house on them, they would be worth nothing and less than nothing. When I drink water, however, or wash with it, then it is not worthless but a precious and useful thing; for this is what it was made for, this is its proper use. . . . How is it possible that men are lighter or smaller than nothing? What can be smaller than nothing? I answer: That which is obviously nothing does not deceive anyone. But anyone who trusts in that which is nothing suffers a twofold loss: first, because he finds nothing; secondly, because he loses what he has expended on it. Anyone who has a mere nothing has a simple nothing and does not expend anything on it. But anyone who trusts in men not only finds nothing but loses what he has expended on them. Thus his hope and his expense come to naught on the nothing in which he hoped.

From *Four Psalms of Comfort* (Luther's Works 14:239)

Unless the LORD builds the house, those who build it labor in vain.

PSALM 127:1

God's Purpose for Parents

lthough God would be able to rear children without parents, as He proved in the case of Adam and Eve and still proves daily in the case of orphans, He does not wish to do it this way but has ordained that He will do it through the parents and with the parents. He could also rule the house without householders, and He often does that. Yet He does not wish to do it this way but wishes to do it with the householders and through the householders, as Psalm 127:1 says, "Unless the Lord builds the house, those who build it labor in vain." And so He could also maintain peace, punish the evil, protect the good without sword and princes. Yet He does not wish to do it this way but has ordained that the princes should help Him; that is, He wishes to work with them and through them. Therefore all rules are His and are true, divine rules; nor does He need angels or men to prove His wonderful might, wisdom, and goodness.

From *Lectures on Zechariah* (German text) (Luther's Works 20:171–72)

In return for My love they accuse Me,
but I give Myself to prayer.
PSALM 109:4

What the World Is Asking For

 hey refuse to tolerate good deeds. Very well, one must commit it to God and continue praying. Oh, how pious the world is! It does not want evil, and it cannot tolerate good. What, then, does it want? Hell-fire and the devil! That's what it is asking for, and that's what it will get! . . . Even if such people had no other trouble, don't you think it is trouble enough to have such a stubborn, blind, and obdurate heart that it neither sees nor hears and will not listen, but goes right ahead in the opinion that it is being blessed rather than cursed and rejects true blessing as though it were a curse? O Lord God, if we are to sin, let us commit some other sin than this!

From *Four Psalms of Comfort* (Luther's Works 14:260, 268)

He who touches you touches the apple of His eye.

ZECHARIAH 2:8

When One Suffers, All Suffer

henever the lowliest member of Christendom suffers, immediately the whole body feels it and is roused, so that all the members at once come running, crying out, and shouting. For our Head, Christ, hears it and feels it in the same way. And though He holds back for a time, nevertheless, when He begins to glare and His nose flares, He will not be coming in jest. . . . See what a precious promise this is, for the great comfort and assurance of Christians against their persecutors, to know that He is so deeply and personally affected by our sufferings that He calls it "touching the apple of His eye" and will tolerate it just as little as anyone could endure much poking in the apple of his own eye. And so when the devil assaults a Christian, he lays hold of something that will make him bite his own tongue and burn his finger.

From *Sermons on the Gospel of John*, Chapters 17–20 (Luther's Works 69:78–79)

Since therefore Christ suffered in the flesh,
arm yourselves with the same way of thinking.

1 PETER 4:1

Crucified with Christ

n the fourth chapter of the third book of his *On the Trinity* St. Augustine teaches that the suffering of Christ is both a sacrament and an example—a sacrament because it signifies the death of sin in us and grants it to those who believe, an example because it also behooves us to imitate Him in bodily suffering and dying. The sacrament is what is stated in Romans 4:25: "Who was put to death for our trespasses and raised for our justification." The example is what is stated in 1 Peter 2:21: "Christ suffered for us, leaving you an example, that you should follow in His steps." Paul treats of the sacrament very extensively in Romans 6 and 8, in Colossians 3, and in many other passages. Thus he says . . . that he is crucified with Christ according to the sacrament, because he has put sin and lusts to death. What the apostle is saying is this: Those who seek to be justified through the works of the Law not only fail to crucify their flesh but even increase its lusts—so far are they from being able to be justified. For the Law is the strength of sin (1 Corinthians 15:56) in that it stimulates lust and its contrary inclination even while forbidding it. But since faith in Christ loves the Law, which forbids lust, it now does the very thing the Law commands; it attacks and crucifies lust.

From *Lectures on Galatians* (1519) (Luther's Works 27:238)

May 14

Bondservants, obey your earthly masters with fear and
trembling, with a sincere heart, as you would Christ,
not by the way of eye-service, as people-pleasers, but
as bondservants of Christ.

EPHESIANS 6:5–6

The Servant's Wage

servant, for example, who works and neither sees nor thinks any farther than this: My master gives me my wages and that's why I serve him; otherwise I have no regard for him. He does not have a pure heart or intention, for he works only to obtain a bit of bread. When this ceases his service also ceases. But if he were good and a Christian, this is what he would say: I'm not going to work because my master pays me or does not pay me, or because he is good or bad; but rather because the Word of God is there and it tells me: Servants, be obedient to your masters, as to Christ [Ephesians 6:5]. Then it issues of itself from the heart, which has laid hold on the Word and esteems it, and he says: All right, I will serve my master and take my wages, but the chief reason why I do so will be that in this way I shall be serving my dear God and Lord Christ, who has commanded me to do this and I know that this is well pleasing to Him. There you see a true work performed out of a pure heart.

From *Sermon on the Sum of the Christian Life* (Luther's Works 51:270–71)

The eyes of the Lord are on the righteous,
and His ears are open to their prayer.

1 PETER 3:12

The Eyes of the Lord

rite this verse into your heart with firm faith and see if it does not produce peace and benefits for you. Can you believe that God sits above and does not sleep or look elsewhere and forget you, but with open, wide-awake eyes always looks at the righteous who suffer from force and injustice? Why, then, would you complain and become displeased by the harm and wrong that happens to you, when He turns His gracious eyes to you and as the true Judge and God intends to help you? I would pay all the world's possessions for this eye and for this faith, if I could have it. There certainly is no lack of His looking at us, but only of our faith. In addition, he says, "His ears are also open to the prayers of the righteous" [1 Peter 3:12]. Just as He looks at you with gracious, kind eyes, so also He listens with sharp, open ears to your lamenting, sighing, and praying. He listens willingly and with pleasure, so that as soon as you just open your mouth, He grants is and says, "Yes."

From the *Church Postil*, sermon for Trinity 5 on 1 Peter 3:8–15
(Luther's Works 78:199)

And if children, then heirs—heirs of God and fellow heirs with Christ, provided we suffer with Him in order that we may also be glorified with Him.

ROMANS 8:17

Our Inheritance

Having heard that Christ, in His own person, had to enter into His glory through suffering and death (Luke 24:26), we are to know that so it must also be for His kingdom on earth, that is, for His Christendom. His person serves as a model, and all those who are Christians must conform to His image. For this reason His kingdom has had to endure the cross and suffering since the beginning of time; and we must follow the path to glory and life through misery, persecution, shame, and death. If He, our Lord and Head, had to do this, why should we expect something better? To sum it up: Whoever will be under this Lord, must accustom himself to drink and suffer with Him on the way in order that he may be raised to glory with Him, as St. Paul says (Romans 8:17).

From *Commentary on Psalm 110* (Luther's Works 13:347)

Do we then overthrow the law by this faith? By no
means! On the contrary, we uphold the law.

ROMANS 3:31

Fulfilling the Law

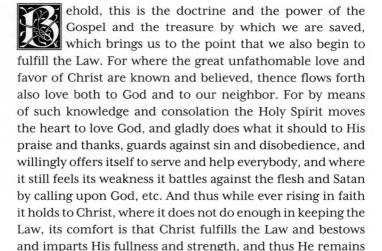

ehold, this is the doctrine and the power of the
Gospel and the treasure by which we are saved,
which brings us to the point that we also begin to
fulfill the Law. For where the great unfathomable love and
favor of Christ are known and believed, thence flows forth
also love both to God and to our neighbor. For by means
of such knowledge and consolation the Holy Spirit moves
the heart to love God, and gladly does what it should to His
praise and thanks, guards against sin and disobedience, and
willingly offers itself to serve and help everybody, and where
it still feels its weakness it battles against the flesh and Satan
by calling upon God, etc. And thus while ever rising in faith
it holds to Christ, where it does not do enough in keeping the
Law, its comfort is that Christ fulfills the Law and bestows
and imparts His fullness and strength, and thus He remains
always our righteousness, salvation, sanctification, etc.

From the *Church Postil*, sermon for Trinity 13 on Luke 10:23–37
(Luther's Works 79 (Lenker) 5:54)

May 18

"Come to Me, all who labor and are heavy laden,
and I will give you rest." MATTHEW 11:28

Christr, Our Comforter

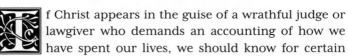

I f Christ appears in the guise of a wrathful judge or lawgiver who demands an accounting of how we have spent our lives, we should know for certain that this is not really Christ but the devil. For Scripture portrays Christ as our Propitiator, Mediator, and Comforter. This is what He always is and remains; He cannot be untrue to His very nature. Therefore when the devil assumes the guise of Christ and argues with us this way: "At the urging of My Word you were obliged to do this, and you failed to do so; and you were obliged to avoid that, and you failed to do so. Therefore you should know that I shall exact punishment from you," this should not bother us at all; but we should immediately think: "Christ does not speak this way to despairing consciences. He does not add affliction to those who are afflicted. 'A bruised reed He will not break, and a dimly burning wick He will not quench' (Isaiah 42:3). To those who are rough He speaks roughly, but those who are in terror He invites most sweetly: 'Come to Me, all who labor and are heavy laden' (Matthew 11:28); 'I came not to call the righteous, but sinners' (Matthew 9:13); 'Take heart, My son; your sins are forgiven' (Matthew 9:2); 'Be of good cheer, I have overcome the world' (John 16:33); 'The Son of Man came to seek and to save the lost' (Luke 19:10)."

From *Lectures on Galatians* (1535) (Luther's Works 27:11–12)

[Jesus] said to them, "It is written, 'My house shall be called a house of prayer.'" MATTHEW 21:13

Gifts of the Sacraments

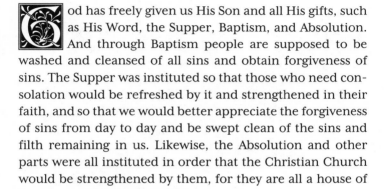od has freely given us His Son and all His gifts, such as His Word, the Supper, Baptism, and Absolution. And through Baptism people are supposed to be washed and cleansed of all sins and obtain forgiveness of sins. The Supper was instituted so that those who need consolation would be refreshed by it and strengthened in their faith, and so that we would better appreciate the forgiveness of sins from day to day and be swept clean of the sins and filth remaining in us. Likewise, the Absolution and other parts were all instituted in order that the Christian Church would be strengthened by them, for they are all a house of prayer to strengthen our faith.

From *Sermons on the Gospel of Matthew*, Chapters 19–24 (Luther's Works 68:91)

"The kingdom of heaven is like leaven that a woman took and hid in three measures of flour, till it was all leavened." MATTHEW 13:33

The New Leaven

 he Gospel, the new leaven, once it has been mixed into the human race (that is, the dough), will not cease working until the end of the world but will permeate the whole lump of those who are to be saved and will extend to all who are worthy, even if all the gates of hell resist [see Matthew 16:18]. And just as it is impossible for the leaven to be separated from the dough once it has been mixed in with the dough (inasmuch as it has changed the nature of the dough), even so it is impossible for Christians to be snatched from Christ, for Christ is the leaven in them that has been made part of them in such a way that they are one body, one lump, one loaf, one bread, etc. (see Romans 12:3–4; 1 Corinthians 12:12–13; Ephesians 4:6). It is therefore in vain that the devil drives the Church from the world and persecutes it—that is, separates Christ from the faithful, the leaven from the dough. For it is as impossible for the devil to separate Christ from His Church as it is for human beings to separate leaven from dough. The dough has been leavened; the devil shall not separate the leaven from the dough. Even if he cooks or roasts it, or even grills it and burns it, Christ the leaven is in it and shall remain in it until the Last Day so that it may all become thoroughly leavened and none of the dough be left unleavened.

From *Annotations on Matthew* (Luther's Works 67:206)

May 21

Your word is a lamp to my feet and a light to my path.

PSALM 119:105

Living in the Light

t is a great gift of God to live in the light of the Word and the divine calling. For this is the golden and round crown that shines around the heads of the saints, as they are commonly depicted, namely, the Word, which directs the course of life day and night. Thus David says in Psalm 119:105: "Thy Word is a lamp to my feet," and 2 Peter 1:19 says: "You do well to pay attention to the Word as to a lamp shining in a dark place, until the day dawns, etc." Reason is in darkness. Therefore it has need of the light of the Word as a leader and guide. . . . We must note this carefully in order that we may know that nothing should be done, considered, and carried out rashly, but only when we have the Word of God, whether it is written in a book or, if anything special is to be undertaken, has been handed down by parents or magistrates. Consequently, we should do nothing contrary to the obedience and reverence we owe to God. One should not invite the devil as a guest.

From *Lectures on Genesis* (Luther's Works 8:83)

"The bread of God is He who comes down from heaven and gives life to the world." JOHN 6:33

The Bread of Life

hus the Lord declared above: "He who believes in Me has eternal life" and: "I am the bread of life." These words greatly offended the Jews. It annoyed them to think that this Man should have the power to save, to bestow eternal life, and also to deliver us from death, sin, and all evil. After all, He did not give that appearance. He was a poor man, the son of a poor carpenter and of a poor mother, devoid of all power. Therefore it sounded unreasonable to hear Him say: "He who believes in Me will have eternal life." But I have told you that whoever would remain a Christian and be saved must not follow his eyes or judge by appearances, confer with reason, or employ his other senses in this matter; he must hear solely what is preached to him and must turn his ear to the lips of this Man. Whoever fails to do this, but surrenders and forsakes God's Word, is lost. Christ swears an oath attesting this: "Truly, truly, I say to you, he who believes in Me has eternal life. This is the only way to eternal life and the only redemption from sin, death, and devil, namely, your faith in Me; for I am the Way and the Life (John 14:6). If you can obtain this bread and permit Me to feed you, that is, if you believe in Me, then you are healthy. Then sin, death, and hell cannot harm you, and you are rid of all your enemies."

From *Sermons on the Gospel of John*, Chapters 6–8 (Luther's Works 23:109–10)

"The righteous shall live by faith."

ROMANS 1:17

Only by Christ's Work

 isten to this: For Christ alone it is proper to help and save others with His merits and works. The works of others are of benefit to no one, not to themselves either; for the statement stands: "The just shall live by faith" (Romans 1:17). For faith grounds us on the works of Christ, without our own works, and transfers us from the exile of our sins into the kingdom of His righteousness. This is faith; this is the Gospel; this is Christ.

From *Judgment of Martin Luther on Monastic Vows* (WLS, p. 922, no. 2891)

We rejoice in our sufferings.

ROMANS 5:3

Christian Boasting

 aul shows what true Christian boasting is, namely, to boast, rejoice, and be proud in suffering, shame, weakness, etc. The world not only regards Christians as the most despicable of men; but with vehemence and what it regards as righteous zeal it hates, persecutes, condemns, and kills them as a dangerous menace to both the spiritual and the earthly realm, in other words, as heretics and revolutionaries. But because they are not suffering on account of murder, stealing, and other such crimes, but on account of Christ, whose blessings and glory they proclaim, they glory in their afflictions and in the cross of Christ. With the apostles they "rejoice that they are counted worthy to suffer dishonor for the name of Christ" (Acts 5:41).

From *Lectures on Galatians* (1535) (Luther's Works 27:133)

"Honor your father and your mother."

EXODUS 20:12

Standing in God's Place

We must, therefore, impress this truth upon the young that they should think of their parents as standing in God's place. They should remember that however lowly, poor, frail, and strange their parents may be, nevertheless, they are the father and the mother given to them by God. Parents are not to be deprived of their honor because of their conduct or their failings. Therefore, we are not to consider who they are or how they may be, but the will of God, who has created and ordained parenthood. . . . Learn, therefore, what is the honor towards parents that this commandment requires. (a) They must be held in distinction and esteem above all things, as the most precious treasure on earth. (b) In our words we must speak modestly toward them. Do not address them roughly, haughtily, and defiantly. But yield to them and be silent, even though they go too far. (c) We must show them such honor also by works, that is, with our body and possessions. We must serve them, help them, and provide for them when they are old, sick, infirm, or poor. We must do all this not only gladly, but with humility and reverence, as doing it before God.

From the *Large Catechism* (*Concordia*, p. 371)

Ask for the Gospel

ecause the promise was made . . . that the Gospel would come, therefore prepare for it, and do not merely wait for it but also ask for it. For now it is time to ask for the true spring rain so that you may not be hindered by men's teaching and the works of the Law and be found unprepared for this rain. It will surely come; but it wants to be accepted and not despised; instead, it wants to be desired and received with careful attention. If you act in this way, then enough rain will come for the growing of all the good fruits of the Spirit. Christ Himself speaks very much like this text in Matthew 9:36ff.: "When He saw the crowds, He had compassion on them, because they were harassed and helpless, like sheep without a shepherd. Then He said to His disciples, 'The harvest is plentiful, but the laborers are few; pray therefore the Lord of the harvest to send out laborers into His harvest.' " These laborers are the preachers . . . . And so the prophets, too, were ready and prepared to give the true rain. And the rain is called a "spring rain," which comes when the grain has sprouted and is shooting forth, and when the soil is dry from the heat. And so the Gospel also comes when the consciences have become hot and thirsty because of the Law.

From *Lectures on Zechariah* (German text) (Luther's Works 20:299)

Therefore let those who suffer according to
God's will entrust their souls to a faithful Creator
while doing good.

1 PETER 4:19

Trusting Our Creator

 hat is, those whom God afflicts with suffering which they themselves have not sought and chosen should entrust their souls to Him. They do well, continue in good works, do not withdraw because of the suffering, and entrust themselves to their Creator, who is faithful. This is a great comfort for us. God created your soul without any trouble and assistance on your part. He did so before you came into being. Accordingly, He is surely able to preserve it. Therefore entrust it to Him, but in such a way that it is done with good works. You must not think: "Ah, I will die with no concern!" You must see to it that you are a good Christian, and you must prove your faith with your works.

From *Sermons on 1 Peter* (Luther's Works 30:130–31)

Brothers, if anyone is caught in any transgression,
you who are spiritual should restore him in a spirit
of gentleness.

Galatians 6:1

In Our Weakness, We Sin

t sometimes happens that the saints may lapse and gratify the desires of their flesh. Thus David, in a great and horrible lapse, fell into adultery and was responsible for the murder of many when he had Uriah die in battle (2 Samuel 11). Thereby he gave his enemies an excuse to be boastful against the people of God, to worship their idol, and to blaspheme the God of Israel. Peter also lapsed horribly when he denied Christ. But no matter how great these sins were, they were not committed intentionally; they were committed because of weakness. In addition, when they had been admonished, these men did not persist stubbornly in their sins but returned to their senses. . . . Paul commands that such men be received, instructed, and restored, saying: "If a man is overtaken, etc." Those who sin because of weakness, even if they do it often, will not be denied forgiveness, provided that they rise again and do not persist in their sins; for persistence in sin is the worst of all.

From *Lectures on Galatians* (1535) (Luther's Works 27:80)

"[The devil] is a liar and the father of lies."

JOHN 8:44

The Devil Underfoot

ou will also have the devil about you. You will not entirely tread him underfoot, because our Lord Christ Himself could not entirely avoid him. Now, what is the devil? Nothing other than what the Scriptures call him, a liar and a murderer. He is a liar, to lead the heart astray from God's Word and to blind it, so that you cannot feel your distress or come to Christ. He is a murderer, who cannot bear to see you live one single hour. If you could see how many knives, darts, and arrows are every moment aimed at you, you would be glad to come to the Sacrament as often as possible. But there is no reason why we walk about so securely and carelessly, except that we neither think nor believe that we are in the flesh and in this wicked world or in the devil's kingdom.

From the *Large Catechism* (*Concordia*, p. 440)

There shall come forth a shoot from the stump of Jesse,
and a branch from his roots shall bear fruit. And the
Spirit of the LORD *shall rest upon Him, the Spirit*
of wisdom and understanding, the Spirit of counsel
and might, the Spirit of knowledge and the fear
of the LORD. ISAIAH 11:1–2

The Visitation
(Three-Year Lectionary)

 saiah calls [Christ] a "Shoot" (Isaiah 11:1) and says that He sprouts forth like an outstanding and excellent young plant (Isaiah 53:2). With this expression Isaiah indicates that Christ's kingdom is always growing. You see, the Spirit and Christ's Word are always in a state of growing. They move forward constantly, and as a consequence they bear greater fruit. The world sets itself against it with might and main to cause this branch to wither and dry. It attacks the branch with death, disgrace, poverty, and every evil. God, however, always causes it to grow. He supplies it with enough moisture so that it still grows and flourishes even in the burning summer sun.

From *Lectures on Zechariah* (Latin text) (Luther's Works 20:40)

*"Baptizing them in the name of the Father
and of the Son and of the Holy Spirit."*

MATTHEW 28:19

Instituted by God

 ince Baptism is a divine act in which God Himself participates and since it is attended by the three exalted Persons of the Godhead, it must be prized and honored. One must agree that Baptism was not invented by any man but was instituted by God. It is not plain water but has God's Word in it and with it; and this transforms such water into a soul bath and into a bath of rejuvenation. . . . We have discoursed amply on . . . the glory of Baptism. We have emphasized that it must not be viewed as plain water which any cow or horse might drink but that the dear Trinity, together with all His beloved angels, is present. It is a divine and heavenly water in which God Himself is at work, cleansing us from sin, saving us from eternal death, and giving us life eternal. This is the way true and pious Christians view Baptism, and no one can take it away from them.

From *Sermons on the Gospel of John*, Chapters 1–4 (Luther's Works 22:174, 181)

He has commanded His covenant forever.

PSALM 111:9

The Covenant of Grace

hristendom can err and make mistakes, but it does not remain in error and sin. Against this it has the covenant of grace, in which Christ has become its Throne of Grace (Romans 3:25) and continually offers forgiveness of sin. This is something that Christendom accepts by faith, as the article of the Creed says: "I believe in the forgiveness of sin." And in the Our Father it seeks and obtains it when saying: "Forgive us our debts." Christendom on earth as a whole is not entirely without spot or wrinkle, but it shall become so, as St. Paul declares (Ephesians 5:27). Nor is it in itself so holy that it is without sin; but in Christ it is holy, and in itself it is still full of sin, as St. Paul so emphatically teaches (Romans 7:18) that in his flesh there is no good thing. In Paul's flesh there is no good thing; thus he is a captive slave of sin, yet one of the best and holiest members of Christendom. Why, then, should not Christendom also have sin and serve sin in its lesser members? All saints must pray Psalm 19:12: "Who knows all errors? Lord, cleanse me of those that are hidden"; and Psalm 25:11: "For Thy name's sake, Lord, be gracious toward my sin; for it is great."

From *Commentary on Psalm 111* (Luther's Works 13:382–83)

"I have chosen him, that he may command his children and his household after him to keep the way of the LORD by doing righteousness and justice, so that the LORD may bring to Abraham what He has promised him." GENESIS 18:19

The Most Valuable Work

ut this at least all married people should know. They can do no better work and do nothing more valuable either for God, for Christendom, for all the world, for themselves, and for their children than to bring up their children well. . . . If we want to help Christendom, we most certainly have to start with the children, as happened in earlier times. . . . False natural love blinds parents so that they have more regard for the bodies of their children than they have for their souls. . . . Therefore, it is of the greatest importance for every married man to pay closer, more thorough, and continuous attention to the health of his child's soul than to the body which he has begotten, and to regard his child as nothing else but an eternal treasure God has commanded him to protect, and so prevent the world, the flesh, and the devil from stealing the child away and bringing him to destruction. For at his death and on the Day of Judgment he will be asked about his child and will have to give a most solemn account.

From *Sermon on the Estate of Marriage* (Luther's Works 44:12–13)

Jesus said to him, " 'If You can'! All things are possible
for one who believes."

MARK 9:23

God's Will Toward Us

 ou must rather, without any wavering or doubt, realize His will toward you and firmly believe that He will do great things also to you, and is willing to do so. Such a faith has life and being; it pervades and changes the whole man; it constrains you to fear if you are mighty, and to take comfort if you are of low degree. And the mightier you are, the more must you fear; the lowlier you are, the more must you take comfort. This no other kind of faith is able to effect. How will it be with you in the hour of death? There you must believe that He has not only the power and the knowledge but also the desire to help you. For it requires indeed an unspeakably great work to deliver you from eternal death, to save you and make you God's heir. To this faith all things are possible, as Christ says (Mark 9:23); it alone abides; it also comes to experience the works of God and thus attains to the love of God and thence to songs and praise of God, so that man esteems Him highly and truly magnifies Him.

From *The Magnificat* (Luther's Works 21:306–7)

"I am the way, and the truth, and the life. No one
comes to the Father except through Me."

JOHN 14:6

The Only Way

 he entire Gospel of John . . . always points out that
Christ is God's Son and sent by the Father. Whoever
does not believe that He is true God is already lost,
as He says, "If you do not believe that I am He, you will die
in your sins" (John 8:24). Likewise: "In Him was life, and the
life was the light of men" (John 1:4). Likewise: "I am the way
and the truth and the life" (John 14:6). . . . No one has the
right to make his own way to God through his own devotion
or works. It does not help when you call on God like the
Jews and the Turks do; you must come to Him through the
Seed of Abraham and be blessed through Him, according
to the wording of the testament of God. He will not make a
special one for you and for the sake of your service tear up
His testament. You must abandon your own affairs and cling
to this Seed, flesh and blood, or you are lost with all the skill
and wisdom which you know from God, for He says, "No one
comes to the Father except through Me" (John 14:6).

From the *Church Postil*, sermon for the Sunday after Christmas on
Galatians 4:1–7 (Luther's Works 75:382–83)

[Christ] gave Himself for our sins to deliver us
from the present evil age, according to the will
of our God and Father.

GALATIANS 1:4

Gazing upon Christ

s Christ does in the Gospel of John, here Paul] calls us back to the will of the Father, so that in [Christ's] words and works we are to look, not at Him but at the Father. For Christ came into the world so that He might take hold of us and so that we, by gazing upon Christ, might be drawn and carried directly to the Father. As we have warned you before, there is no hope that any saving knowledge of God can come by speculating about the majesty of God; this can come only by taking hold of Christ, who, by the will of the Father, has given Himself into death for our sins. When you have grasped this, then all wrath stops, and fear and trembling disappear; and God appears as nothing by the merciful One who did not spare His own Son but gave Him up for us all (Romans 8:32).

From *Lectures on Galatians* (1535) (Luther's Works 26:42)

"But the Helper, the Holy Spirit, whom the Father will send in My name, He will teach you all things."

JOHN 14:26

The Proper Touchstone

ur whole quarrel with all these factions revolves about their claim that they have the Holy Spirit and that therefore they should be believed. It is our lot to be constantly locked in combat with the devil and false spirits. But if we view this verse and others aright, we can judge properly and refute everything that opposes it. Let them advance whatever doctrine they will; I know well what my Lord Christ says and what I must believe. If someone comes with a doctrine allegedly taught and revealed by the Holy Spirit, I cling to this Word and apply it to his doctrine as the proper touchstone. If I see that it agrees with the words of Christ, I consider it true and good. But if it deviates from them and presents something else, I declare: "You are not the Holy Spirit; you are the devil! For the true Spirit comes in the name of no one else than Christ, and He teaches nothing but what Christ said."

From *Sermons on the Gospel of John*, Chapters 14–16 (Luther's Works 24:176–77)

This is His commandment, that we believe in the
name of His Son Jesus Christ and love one another,
just as He has commanded us.

1 JOHN 3:23

The Narrow Heart

 uman frailty has a heart too narrow to grasp this grace, namely, that the Son of God died for us. The principal commandment is this, that we should believe in the name of His Son. The second part of this is that we should love. Accordingly, the sum and substance is belief in the name of the Son of God and love for one's brother. . . . In the end those people are wise who do the will of God, that is, believe in the name of the Son of God and love one another . . . . They do not love the world. No, they exercise themselves with the fruits of the love for God, and they do not pass away. For just as the will of God does not pass away, so those who do the will of God do not pass away either but abide forever [1 John 2:17].

From *Lectures on 1 John* (Luther's Works 30:282, 251)

"Everyone who has left houses or brothers or sisters or father or mother or children or lands, for My name's sake, will receive a hundredfold and will inherit eternal life." MATTHEW 19:29

For His Name's Sake

isunderstanding of this passage has given rise to so many sects and schisms among Christians. It does not mean, as you have heard, that we are supposed to run away from our [family, etc.,] of our own volition. God's commandment is that I obey my father and mother, stay with my wife, stay with my husband, stay with and provide for my children—which cannot happen without a house and yard and other possessions. However, if it comes to the point of renouncing either my Savior or my father and mother, etc., yes, even my own soul—in other words, losing life and limb—then I should say: "Farewell and good night, dear father, dear mother, dear brother, dear sister, dear lord and prince. I would like to stay and live here with you, but since you are pressing me to renounce my Lord Christ, you shall no longer be my father. I would rather be separated from you here in time than from my Lord in eternity."

From *Sermons on the Gospel of Matthew*, Chapters 19–24 (Luther's Works 68:60–61)

We know that for those who love God all things work
together for good.

ROMANS 8:28

Making Evil Good

his is the work and skill of God, to . . . make evil matters good when we have spoiled and harmed matters. . . . Certainly, I have often done many things imprudently and foolishly, concerning which I was much disturbed later. Nor was I able to see how I might work my way out and extricate myself from matters that were being hampered by my folly. But the Lord found a means and a way that the error might be corrected. . . . God so governs His saints that even though they err and stray, the outcomes are nevertheless salutary or without great loss. For all things work together for good to the elect and those who believe (see Romans 8:28), even errors and sins, and this is absolutely certain. For God is accustomed to make all things out of nothing, and so He can call forth and produce good from evil.

From *Lectures on Genesis* (Luther's Works 6:58–59)

"Whoever has seen Me has seen the Father."

JOHN 14:9

The Revealed God

od says to you: "Behold, you have My Son. Listen to Him, and receive Him. If you do this, you are already sure about your faith and salvation." "But I do not know," you will say, "whether I am remaining in faith." At all events, accept the present promise and the predestination, and do not inquire too curiously about the secret counsels of God. If you believe in the revealed God and accept His Word, He will gradually also reveal the hidden God; for "He who sees Me also sees the Father," as John 14:9 says. He who rejects the Son also loses the unrevealed God along with the revealed God. But if you cling to the revealed God with a firm faith, so that your heart is so minded that you will not lose Christ even if you are deprived of everything, then you are most assuredly predestined, and you will understand the hidden God.

From *Lectures on Genesis* (Luther's Works 5:46)

Now that you have come to know God, or rather
to be known by God, how can you turn back again
to the weak and worthless elementary principles of
the world, whose slaves you want to be once more?

GALATIANS 4:9

Do Not Be Misled

 herefore, do not be misled by the hypocrites who despise faith, who place your salvation far away from you, and who urge you to get it by works. No, dear friend, it is within you; everything has already been done, as Christ says, "The kingdom of God is within you" (Luke 17:21). Therefore, the rest of life after Baptism is nothing more than a looking forward to, a waiting, and a longing for the revelation of what is in us, so that we may take hold of what has taken hold of us, as St. Paul says, "I pursue it to take hold of it, because Christ Jesus has taken hold of me" (Philippians 3:12), that is, that I may see what good things have been put into the shrine of faith. He is curious to see his treasure, which Baptism has given and sealed to him in faith. So he goes on to say, "Our citizenship is already in heaven, and from it we await a Savior, Jesus Christ, who will transform our lowly body to be like His glorious body" (Philippians 3:20–21).

From the *Church Postil*, sermon for the Second Day of Christmas on Titus 3:4–8 (Luther's Works 75:237)

Devote yourself to the public reading of Scripture,
to exhortation, to teaching. 1 TIMOTHY 4:13

Certain Knowledge

n Romans 15:4 it is Paul's wish "that by steadfastness and by the encouragement of the Scriptures we might have hope." In us we have fear, trembling, and darkness. Yet in such great darkness we must believe that we have life. Therefore John wants us to know and no longer to doubt or tremble but to have the certain knowledge that we live and grow in faith. . . . For in the last chapter of his Gospel, John speaks as follows: "These are written that you may believe" (John 20:31). Accordingly, we should know that God's testimony does not come to us except through the spoken Word or through Scripture. "All Scripture is inspired by God and profitable," as 2 Timothy 3:16 says; and (v. 15) "from childhood you have been acquainted with the Sacred Writings which are able to instruct you through faith." Likewise in 1 Tim. 4:13: "Attend to reading." . . . Listen to Christ, who says in John 17:20: "I do not pray for these only but also for those who are to believe in Me through their Word." Certainly through the spoken or written Word, not through the internal Word. Above all, therefore, one must listen to and read the Word, which is the vehicle of the Holy Spirit. When the Word is read, the Holy Spirit is present; and thus it is impossible either to listen to or to read Scripture without profit.

From *Lectures on 1 John* (Luther's Works 30:321)

*"Will not God give justice to His elect, who cry
to Him day and night? Will He delay long over them?
I tell you, He will give justice to them speedily."*

LUKE 18:7–8

When God's Help Begins

n earnest and fervent prayer, which does not cease and does not become tired but keeps on waiting up to the last moment, eventually forces its way through heaven and earth, and it is impossible for it not to be heard. For it is a sacrifice most pleasing to God when we pray in such a way that the prayer surpasses our comprehension and understanding, as is stated in the Epistle to the Ephesians: "Who is able to do far more abundantly than all that we ask or think" (3:20). When the situation is hopeless and all plans and efforts are in vain, then be courageous, and beware of giving up; for God calls all things from the dead and from nothing. When no resource or hope at all is left, then at last God's help begins. And so these are perfect prayers. Meanwhile weak prayers and those of weak people should nevertheless not be despised. But the former are presented to us in their highest grade and by a perfect example, in order that we may try to imitate them.

From *Lectures on Genesis* (Luther's Works 4:361–62)

He has caused His wondrous works to be remembered;
the LORD is gracious and merciful.

PSALM 111:4

The Names of God

e does not simply put down His name as only "God and Lord" but as "the gracious and merciful Lord." The names "God" and "Lord" contain something terrifying, for they are the names of majesty. But the surnames "gracious and merciful" contain pure comfort and joy. I do not know if God anywhere in the Scriptures lets Himself be called by lovelier names. So anxiously does He want to impress on our heart with sweet words that we really ought to accept and honor His remembrance with joy and love, with praise and thanks. . . . Do not give Him a different name in your heart or make Him anything else in your conscience. You would do Him an injustice and a great wrong, and yourself the greatest harm.

From *Commentary on Psalm 111* (Luther's Works 13:374–75)

*"When you pray, do not heap up empty phrases
as the Gentiles do, for they think that they will be
heard for their many words."*

MATTHEW 6:7

Our Father Knows

 here are those who think that it is a prayer if they put forth many words in their praying (as though God were a boy needing to be instructed and informed about our affairs, as if He knew nothing about them). . . . In praying it is needful above all to know that it is indeed certain that we are heard and that God knows [what we need] and intends [to do it] even before our prayer, etc., but that we should not stipulate the time, measure, person, or place for Him in advance. This is what Christ means when He says "for your Father knows," as if to say, "Do not teach Him when you pray, but be certain that He Himself knows those things." But do this: hope, trust, [and] be certain of His grace. He hears you in accord with His will; in accord with His time, not in accord with yours; in accord with His measure, not in accord with yours. Cast all of these things upon His will, and do not measure by your own feelings.

From *Annotations on Matthew* (Luther's Works 67:37–38)

Resist the devil, and he will flee from you.

JAMES 4:7

No Other Word Than This

When you hear the Word of Christ, therefore, you must listen to it as nothing else than the Word of God, and look at it as though there were no other word in heaven or on earth than this. The sweet and delightful Word that is pronounced over me on earth is spoken over me also in heaven. Therefore I must not suppose that God is angry with me. For here I hear His Word, which speaks of nothing but grace, love, consolation, help, and bliss, to preserve me from despair and fear. This serves not only to afford me the comforting assurance that I am safe before God and that there is nothing but grace with Him; it also enables me to resist the devil when he wants to tempt and try me with terror and sorrow or perhaps with a different doctrine. Then I can tell him to shut his lying and blasphemous mouth, and I can say: "Here I have the Word God speaks in heaven before all the angels and on earth before all creatures and men; to this I will hold, and I will listen to no other word." . . . Such a conviction helps immeasurably to produce cheerfulness, boldness, and courage over against all sorts of trials as well as against the devil and the world.

From *Sermons on the Gospel of John*, Chapters 14–16 (Luther's Works 24:166)

While we are still in this tent, we groan,

being burdened.

2 CORINTHIANS 5:4

The Earthly Tent

 t. Peter calls his body a tent in which the soul dwells [2 Peter 1:13]. . . . Thus Saint Paul also says in 2 Corinthians 5:1–2, 4: "For we know that if the earthly tent we live in is destroyed, we have a building from God, a house not made with hands, eternal in the heavens. Here indeed we groan, and long to put on our heavenly dwelling . . . for while we are still in this tent we sigh with anxiety, etc." Likewise (vv. 6, 8): "So we are always of good courage; we know that while we are at home in the body, we are away from the Lord . . . We would rather be away from the body and at home with the Lord." Here the apostle Paul also calls the body a house and designates two homes and two pilgrimages. Thus here Peter calls the body a tent in which the soul rests. He speaks disparagingly enough of this and does not want to call it a house; he calls it a hut and a barn such as is used by shepherds. The treasure is great, but the box in which it lies and dwells is small.

From *Sermons on 2 Peter* (Luther's Works 30:161)

*They were bringing children to Him that He might
touch them, and the disciples rebuked them. But when
Jesus saw it, He was indignant and said to them, "Let
the children come to Me; do not hinder them, for to
such belongs the kingdom of God."* MARK 10:13–14

Jesus Blesses the Children

nterpret these words of Christ as you please, we
have [to conclude] that children are to be brought
to Christ and are not to be hindered; when they
are brought to Him, then He compels us to believe that He
blesses them and gives them the kingdom of heaven, as He
does for these children. It is proper for us to act and believe
in no other way, as long as the words stand: "Let the little
children come to Me and do not hinder them" [Matthew
19:14]. No less is it proper for us to believe that when they
are brought to Him, He will embrace them, lay His hands on
them, bless them, and give them heaven, as long as this text
stands that He blessed and gave heaven to the children who
were brought to Him. Who can ignore this text? Who, on the
other hand, will be so bold as not to allow little children to
come to Baptism or not to believe that He blesses them when
they come to Him? He is just as present in Baptism now as
He was then. Because we Christians certainly know this, we
dare not keep Baptism away from children. So also we dare
not doubt that He blesses all who come to Him, just as He
blessed those [children].

From the *Church Postil*, sermon for Epiphany 3 on Matthew 8:1–13
(Luther's Works 76:262)

Love covers a multitude of sins.

1 PETER 4:8

The Good and the Bad

e love to beautify and decorate ourselves and to see what is good in us, tickling ourselves with it as if it belonged to us. In order to maintain our exclusive claim to beauty, we ignore and leave out of sight the good there is in our neighbor. If we notice the least little pimple on him, we fill our eyes with it and so magnify it that on its account we see nothing good, though the man may have eyes like a hawk and a face like an angel. That would be like seeing someone in a garment all of gold except perhaps for a seam or a white thread drawn through it, and then acting shocked, as if it were worthless on that account. Meanwhile I would be precious in my own sight on account of the gold patch sewn on my shabby smock frock. So it is that we overlook our own vices, which are all over us, while we fail to see anything good about other people. Now, once this natural inclination appears among Christians, then the judging begins. Then I am ready to despise and condemn a man as soon as he stumbles a little or makes some other mistake. He treats me the same way, giving me the same measure I give him, as Christ says here. He searches out and he criticizes the worst things he can find about me. By such behavior love is suppressed, and all that remains is a biting and a devouring back and forth, until they have consumed each other and lost their Christianity.

From *The Sermon on the Mount* (Luther's Works 21:214–15)

Jacob said, "I will not let You go unless You bless me."

Genesis 32:26

The Spirit's Strength

 uch examples teach us that faith should not yield or cease urging or pressing on even when it is already feeling God's wrath and not only death and sin. This is the power and strength of the Spirit. . . . We should not immediately cast aside courage and all hope at the first blow but press on, pray, seek, and knock. Even though He is already thinking of leaving, do not cease but keep on following Him just as the Canaanite woman did, from whom Jesus could not conceal Himself . . . . Even if He hides Himself in a room in the house and does not want access to be given to anyone, do not draw back but follow. If He does not want to listen, knock at the door of the room; raise a shout! For this is the highest sacrifice, not to cease praying and seeking until we conquer Him.

From *Lectures on Genesis* (Luther's Works 6:139–40)

Rejoice in hope, be patient in tribulation,
be constant in prayer.

ROMANS 12:12

Twofold Joy

 o not rejoice over things of the present, or things you have experienced and know. For joy is twofold. The first kind has to do with things that are visible, that is, things that are known in some way or other either inwardly or outwardly. This kind is vain, because it is transitory. The other kind has to do with invisible things, that is, things that are unknown but simply accepted in faith; and this is true joy, eternal, firm, and without this kind of hope there is no joy in the other. For who can rejoice in the former if he despairs or doubts that he will receive future joy? And thus the apostle wants Christians to rejoice to the full, but not because of any earthly thing but because of their hope.

From *Lectures on Romans* (Luther's Works 25:457)

"Give us this day our daily bread."

MATTHEW 6:11

What Is Daily Bread?

 hat does this mean? God gives daily bread, even without our prayer, to all wicked people; but we pray in this petition that He would lead us to realize this and to receive our daily bread with thanksgiving. *What is meant by daily bread?* Everything that belongs to the support and needs of the body, such as food, drink, clothing, shoes, house, home, field, cattle, money, goods, a pious spouse, pious rulers, good government, good weather, peace, health, discipline, honor, good friends, faithful neighbors, and the like.

From the *Small Catechism* (*Concordia*, p. 335)

And [John] looked at Jesus as He walked by and said,
"Behold, the Lamb of God!"

JOHN 1:36

Nativity of St. John the Baptist

 he general tenor of John the Baptist's message [is that] he diverted the attention of all from himself and toward Christ. For this reason he is fittingly called a teacher "rich in grace," a preacher of grace, who proclaims the gracious and merciful message that Christ is our Light, with no reference to his locusts or to his garment of camel's hair. In a similar manner we still bear witness to Christ today when we declare that He is the only Savior of the world, the Lamb of God, yes, our Shepherd, our Abbot, our Bridegroom, and our Messiah. That proclamation is the sum and substance of our testimony.

From *Sermons on the Gospel of John*, Chapters 1–4 (Luther's Works 22:53)

The LORD *is my rock and my fortress and my deliverer,*
my God, my rock, in whom I take refuge, my shield,
and the horn of my salvation, my stronghold. I call
upon the LORD, *who is worthy to be praised, and I am*
saved from my enemies. PSALM 18:2–3

A Mighty Fortress

A mighty fortress is our God,
A trusty shield and weapon;
He helps us free from ev'ry need
That hath us now o'ertaken.
The old evil foe now means deadly woe;
Deep guile and great might
Are his dread arms in fight;
On earth is not his equal.

With might of ours can naught be done,
Soon were our loss effected;
But for us fights the valiant One,
Whom God Himself elected.
Ask yes, Who is this? Jesus Christ it is,
Of Sabaoth Lord,
And there's none other God;
He holds the field forever.

From *A Mighty Fortress Is Our God* (*LSB* 656:1–2)

*"Blessed are those who have not seen
and yet have believed."*

JOHN 20:29

On This Foundation

 aith, which is given by God's grace to the ungodly and by which they are justified, is the substance, foundation, fountain, source, chief, and the firstborn of all spiritual graces, gifts, virtues, merits, and works. "No other foundation can anyone lay" (1 Corinthians 3:11). Of this fountain the Lord says, John 4:13–14: "If anyone will drink of the water that I shall give him, it will become in him a spring of living water welling up to eternal life." Faith is the prerequisite before everything. If one has faith, all other things gush forth from it, like water from the rock and stone. And this is said in Psalm 1:1–3, that the blessed man is a tree planted by the running waters, namely, because his will is in the law of the Lord. But his will is not in the Law except through the grace of faith. Otherwise it will be his unwillingness and hatred in the law of the Lord. But Christ grants this willingness. Therefore, "blessed is the man whose strength is in Thee and whose help is from Thee, namely, of grace."

From *First Lectures on the Psalms* (Luther's Works 11:146)

No unbelief made [Abraham] waver concerning
the promise of God, but he grew strong in his faith
as he gave glory to God.

ROMANS 4:20

Cling and Be Content

 t is necessary to know that not all [apparitions] are
to be believed, but only if they are of the analogy
of faith (Romans 12:6). I shall cling to the Word of
God and be content with that. By it I shall die, and by it I
shall live. . . . For if God sent an angel to say: "Do not believe
these promises!" I would reject him, saying: "Depart from
me, Satan, etc." (see Matthew 16:23). Or, if God Himself
appeared to me in His majesty and said: "You are not worthy
of My grace; I will change My plan and not keep My promise
to you," I would not have to yield to Him, but it would be
necessary to fight most vehemently against God Himself. It is
as Job says: "Though He slay me, yet will I hope in Him" (see
Job 13:15). . . . Therefore I want to see and hear nothing else,
but I shall live and die in this faith, whether God or an angel
or the devil says the contrary.

From *Lectures on Genesis* (Luther's Works 6:131)

"Flesh and blood has not revealed this to you,
but My Father who is in heaven."

MATTHEW 16:17

Taught by God

 od is hidden in the flesh, so that no man can recognize Him unless he has been enlightened by God's spiritual grace. Hence blessed Peter, who had been thus converted and said, "You are Christ, the Son of the living God," heard Him say: "Blessed are you, Simon, Bar-Jona. Flesh and blood has not revealed this to you, but My Father who is in heaven" (Matthew 16:16–17). And in John 6:45 we read: "They shall all be taught by God"; and in Matthew 11:25: "Thou hast revealed these things to the little ones and hidden them from the wise and prudent." . . . Therefore no one can be converted to God unless he has first been converted to Christ, as He says (John 14:6): "No one comes to the Father, but by Me." Consequently the prophet, who sees that many, indeed almost all, of his people could go astray, be offended, and be turned away from Christ, prays that they might be converted. And that happens through the knowledge of Christ or God incarnate.

From *First Lectures on the Psalms* (Luther's Works 11:156–57)

*The saying is trustworthy and deserving of full
acceptance, that Christ Jesus came into the world
to save sinners, of whom I am the foremost. But I
received mercy for this reason, that in me, as the foremost, Jesus Christ might display His perfect patience
as an example to those who were to believe in Him
for eternal life.* 1 TIMOTHY 1:15–16

Too Great a Sinner?

 would gladly believe if I were like St. Peter, Paul,
and others who are righteous and holy, but I am
too great a sinner. Who knows whether I am elect?"
Answer: Look at the words! Look at how and about whom
He is speaking: "God so loved the world" and "so that all who
believe in Him" [John 3:16]. Now, "the world" does not mean
only St. Peter and Paul, but the entire human race together,
and here no one is excluded. God's Son was given for all, all
are to believe this, and all who believe will not be lost, etc.
. . . Therefore, beware of excluding yourself by permitting
thoughts such as: "Who knows whether it has also been given
to me?" That would be calling God a liar in His Word. Rather,
make a cross before yourself and repeat these words: "Even
if I am not St. Peter or Paul, I am still a part of the world. If He
had wanted to give it only to the worthy, then He would have
had to send this preaching only to the angels, who are pure
and without sin. Yes, He would even have had to withhold it

from St. Peter, David, and Paul, for they were sinners as well as I am. No matter who I am, I know that God's Word is true, and if I do not accept it, then, on top of all other sins, I am also committing this one, that I regard God's Word and truth as lies and am slandering them."

From the *Church Postil*, sermon for Pentecost Monday on John 3:16–21 (Luther's Works 77:375–76)

To the one who does not work but believes in Him who
justifies the ungodly, his faith is counted
as righteousness.

ROMANS 4:5

The Principal Doctrine

he issue here is nothing trivial for Paul; it is the principal doctrine of Christianity. When this is recognized and held before one's eyes, everything else seems vile and worthless. For what is Peter? What is Paul? What is an angel from heaven? What is all creation in comparison with the doctrine of justification? Therefore if you see this threatened or endangered, do not be afraid to stand up against Peter or an angel from heaven. For this cannot be praised highly enough.

From *Lectures on Galatians* (1535) (Luther's Works 26:106)

"On this rock I will build My church, and the gates of hell shall not prevail against it." MATTHEW 16:18

The True Dwelling of God

We must learn this and be informed as to who and what constitutes Christendom and what we have in Christ. Then our hope of eternal life will be ever more solidly based, especially in our last hour; then we shall remain cheerful and undaunted by the world and by the devil, with his evil suggestions; then we are confident that Christ will remain our Guest, and we His inn and dwelling . . . . Since we have Him, we certainly have everything and will be able to cope with the devil, death, and hell. Hence even though we die now, we shall still live; and even though we go to hell, we are still in heaven. Even though the devil consumes and devours us, his belly will burst with his eternal mockery and mischief, and will disgorge us alive. For he will surely be compelled to leave undevoured this Lord who dwells in us, and to leave His church and dwelling undestroyed. For this Lord also wants to have a tabernacle and castle. He has erected it on a solid rock and mountain, and no power of hell will prevail against it (Matthew 16:18). This is the true dwelling of God that is typified in the Old Testament by the Ark of the Covenant and the temple, namely, the little group of Christians, who believe and confess the Word of Christ.

From *Sermons on the Gospel of John*, Chapters 14–16 (Luther's Works 24:159–60)

When Elizabeth heard the greeting of Mary, the baby
leaped in her womb. And Elizabeth was filled with
the Holy Spirit, and she exclaimed with a loud cry,
"Blessed are you among women, and blessed is the
fruit of your womb! And why is this granted to me that
the mother of my Lord should come to me? . . . Blessed
is she who believed that there would be a fulfillment of
what was spoken to her from the Lord." LUKE 1:41–45

The Visitation
(One-Year Lectionary)

s that not surprising that the Creator was in the world, dwelt among men, and still passed unrecognized by His creatures? This was particularly true during the days before He inaugurated His ministry and performed miracles. Then there was no one who knew of Him. And yet, at that time there were several pious people in the world who knew Him—to be sure, not by reason but by power from above, by revelation from the Holy Spirit. Among these were Zacharias, Elizabeth, Simeon, the prophetess Anna, the shepherds, Mary, Joseph, and others. Elizabeth, full of the Holy Spirit, addressed Mary, the mother of the Lord, when she visited her: "Blessed are you among women, and blessed is the Fruit of your womb" (Luke 1:42). And: "The babe John in my womb leaped for joy" (Luke 1:44).

From *Sermons on the Gospel of John*, Chapters 1–4 (Luther's Works 22:76)

*"My soul magnifies the Lord, and my spirit
rejoices in God my Savior."*

LUKE 1:46–47

Mary's Hymn of Praise

his word "magnifies" is used by Mary to indicate what her hymn of praise is to be about, namely, the great works and deeds of God, for the strengthening of our faith, for the comforting of all those of low degree, and for the terrifying of all the mighty ones of earth. We are to let the hymn serve this threefold purpose; for she sang it not for herself alone but for us all, to sing it after her. Now, these great works of God will neither terrify nor comfort anyone unless he believes that God has not only the power and the knowledge but also the willingness and hearty desire to do such great things. In fact, it is not even enough to believe that He is willing to do them for others but not for you. This would be to put yourself beyond the pale of these works of God, as is done by those who, because of their strength, do not fear Him, and by those of little faith who, because of their tribulations, fall into despair. . . . You must rather, without any wavering or doubt, realize His will toward you and firmly believe that He will do great things also to you, and is willing to do so.

From *The Magnificat* (Luther's Works 21:306)

"He has shown strength with His arm;
He has scattered the proud in the thoughts
of their hearts."

LUKE 1:51

The Arm of God

 hese words ["He has shown strength"] . . . are not bound to any one time, but are intended to set forth in general the works of God that He always has done, always does, and always will do. Hence the following would be a fair translation: "God is a Lord whose works are of such a nature that He mightily scatters the proud and is merciful to those who fear Him." In the Scriptures, the "arm" of God means God's own power, by which He works without the medium of any creature. This work is done quietly and in secret, and no one becomes aware of it until all is accomplished; so that this power, or arm, can be known and understood only by faith.

From *The Magnificat* (Luther's Works 21:339)

"Behold, your relative Elizabeth in her old age has also conceived a son, and this is the sixth month with her who was called barren."

Signs and Promises

t is the custom of Holy Scripture to add signs to promises. Thus in Baptism and in the Lord's Supper there is not only the Word of promise but also a sign or work or ceremony. Therefore after Abraham has become more intimate with God and has been encouraged by Him, he has the courage to ask for a sign. At any other time this would be the sin of putting God to the test. Putting God to the test is linked with doubting. Therefore the Virgin Mary seems to have acted more properly when she believed the promise without exacting a sign. Of his own accord the angel gives her the sign concerning Elizabeth (Luke 1:36).

From *Lectures on Genesis* (Luther's Works 3:29)

*Because you are sons, God has sent the Spirit of His
Son into our hearts, crying, "Abba! Father!"*

GALATIANS 4:6

The Calling in Your Heart

 e certainly know that we are poor sinners, but here
we must not look at what we are and do, but at what
Christ is and has done and still does for us. . . . If you
think it is a big thing that you are God's child, do not think
it is a small thing that God's Son was born of a woman, born
under the Law, so that you could become such a child [of
God]. What God does is altogether something great, which
gives us great joy and courage and makes spirits undaunted, which are afraid of nothing and can do everything. . . .
Therefore, cling firmly to this text. You must feel the calling
of the Spirit in your heart. Since it is the calling of your own
heart, how could you not feel it? . . . "The Spirit of God bears
witness to our spirit that we are children of God" (Romans
8:16). How, then, should our hearts not feel such calling,
groaning, and witness? Temptation and suffering serve this
purpose beautifully! They promote such calling out and
awaken our spirit. . . . If you do not perceive that calling out,
then think and do not rest from praying until God grants it.

From the *Church Postil*, sermon for the Sunday after Christmas on
Galatians 4:1–7 (Luther's Works 75:392–93)

[The LORD] is wonderful in counsel and excellent
in wisdom.

ISAIAH 28:29

Our Active God

 herefore let us learn this rule and order which God is wont to employ in governing His saints. For I, too, have often attempted to prescribe to God definite methods He should use in the administration either of the church or of other matters. "Ah, Lord," I have said, "I would like this to be done in this order, with this result!" But God would do the very opposite of what I had sought. Then the thought would come to me: "Nevertheless, my plan is not disadvantageous to the glory of God; but it will contribute very much toward the hallowing of Thy name, the gathering and increasing of Thy kingdom, and the propagation of the knowledge of Thy Word. In short, it is a very fine plan and excellently thought out." But the Lord undoubtedly laughed at this wisdom and said: "Come now, I know that you are a wise and learned man; but it has never been My custom for Peter, Dr. Martin, or anyone else to teach, direct, govern, and lead Me. I am not a passive God. No, I am an active God who is accustomed to do the leading, ruling, and directing."

From *Lectures on Genesis* (Luther's Works 7:104)

"Whoever believes in Me, though he die,

yet shall he live."

John 11:25

Amazing Help

 he right hand of God mightily lifts the heart and comforts it in the midst of death, so that it can say: "Though I die, I die not. Though I suffer, I suffer not. Though I fall, I am not down. Though I am disgraced, I am not dishonored." This is the consolation. Furthermore, the psalmist says of the help: "I shall live." Isn't this an amazing help? The dying live; the suffering rejoice; the fallen rise; the disgraced are honored. It is as Christ says: "He who believes in Me, though he die, yet shall he live" (John 11:25). Paul speaks in a similar manner: "We are afflicted in every way, but not crushed; perplexed, but not driven to despair" (2 Corinthians 4:8). These are all words that no human heart can comprehend. And here you see that this comfort and help is eternal life, which is the true, everlasting blessing of God.

From *Commentary on Psalm 118* (Luther's Works 14:86)

We walk by faith, not by sight.

2 CORINTHIANS 5:7

The Purpose of Baptism

What is the purpose of Baptism? "So that we might become heirs of eternal life" [Titus 3:7]. Not so that we might possess the sort of treasure that greedy people [would like], but an eternal treasure that shall be yours eternally. . . . This [Baptism] takes place to make you a son or daughter, an heir of eternal life, certain that you will not die forever. Therefore, be grateful to God, thank and praise Him, because you have a Savior who is and always will be kind and loving toward humanity; His kindness and love for humanity endure to the end of the world. If you fall, repent; even if everything turns out badly, you will [still] be an heir of eternal life. [We possess this] not by sight, but in hope [see Romans 8:24; 2 Corinthians 5:7]. We possess this inheritance, but only in hope, and therefore we live [in hope], that He will at last come and free us. "This is certainly true" [Titus 3:8]. To this, let everyone say, "Amen!"

From *Sermon for the First Sunday after Epiphany* (Luther's Works 58:396)

*"Fear not, little flock, for it is your Father's good
pleasure to give you the kingdom."*

LUKE 12:32

Have Courage to Believe

 his consolation has always been necessary for all believers; for if a man looks about him, he stumbles at the idea of eternal life. Our primary impression is that we are sinners, but it is a sublime thing to believe that God has prepared eternal life. He raises the poor up from the dirt and leads him from sin and death; He crowns the unworthy. Thus He says in John (John 14:1–2): "Let not your heart be troubled. In My Father's house, do not doubt. Eternal life is promised to you. It is a grand thing, but do not fear. You are a little flock, but you should have the courage to believe; for it has pleased the Father. Besides, if dwelling places were not prepared, I would prepare them for you now."

From *Lectures on Titus* (Luther's Works 29:12)

[They] will turn away from listening to the truth
and wander off into myths.

2 TIMOTHY 4:4

Too Soon Forgotten

f the world does actually tolerate it for a while and gives ear to the Word, this lasts about as long as it takes to stroll to High Mass. Then the world casts the Word aside again and quickly becomes sated. When it constantly hears this one theme, faith in Christ, dinned into its ears, it thinks to itself: "After all, what is faith?" But let some schismatic spirit come along with a novel doctrine, which is not light but sheer human fabrication and darkness, the world is ready to rally around it. Birds of a feather flock together. The world likes to be wheedled and cajoled; it acts gentle and grunts with pleasure, like a sow when you scratch her ears. And then it turns its ears from the truth and toward fables (2 Timothy 4:4). But the light dazzles their eyes. This they do not want to permit.

From *Sermons on the Gospel of John*, Chapters 1–4 (Luther's Works 22:36)

"I am your brother, Joseph, whom you sold
into Egypt."
GENESIS 45:4

The Unexpected Change

e may not look at this manifestation of Joseph only in passing but may consider the great affection of the heart by which both Joseph and his brothers were benumbed. I would not know how I should have reacted when he said: "I am Joseph." Nor do they know. What will happen, then, when our Lord and Savior Jesus Christ comes, who also disciplines us in various ways in this life and allows us to be troubled, scourged, killed, etc.? What great joy there will be after that sudden and unexpected change, since we previously felt that He was a very harsh tyrant who wanted to destroy everyone in a trice! Then He will say: "I am Joseph; I am your Savior."

From *Lectures on Genesis* (Luther's Works 8:15)

You may be sure of this, that everyone who is sexually immoral or impure, or who is covetous (that is, an idolater), has no inheritance in the kingdom of Christ and God. EPHESIANS 5:5

Sustained by Trust

t is a great error to attribute justification to a love that does not exist or, if it does, is not great enough to placate God; for, as I have said, even the saints love in an imperfect and impure way in this present life, and nothing impure will enter the kingdom of God (Ephesians 5:5). But meanwhile we are sustained by the trust that Christ, "who committed no sin and on whose lips no guile was found" (1 Peter 2:22), covers us with His righteousness. Shaded and protected by this covering, this heaven of the forgiveness of sins and this mercy seat, we begin to love and to keep the Law. As long as we live, we are not justified or accepted by God on account of this keeping of the Law. But "when Christ delivers the kingdom to God the Father after destroying every authority" (1 Corinthians 15:24), and when "God is everything to everyone" (1 Corinthians 15:28), then faith and hope will pass away, and love will be perfect and eternal (1 Corinthians 13:8).

From *Lectures on Galatians* (1535) (Luther's Works 27:64)

He Who Bears All Sins

his is our highest comfort, to clothe and wrap Christ this way in my sins, your sins, and the sins of the entire world, and in this way to behold Him bearing all our sins. When He is beheld this way, He easily removes all the fanatical opinions of our opponents about justification by works. For the Papists dream about a kind of faith "formed by love." Through this they want to remove sins and be justified. This is clearly to unwrap Christ and to unclothe Him from our sins, to make Him innocent, to burden and overwhelm ourselves with our own sins, and to behold them, not in Christ but in ourselves. This is to abolish Christ and make Him useless. For if it is true that we abolish sins by the works of the Law and by love, then Christ does not take them away, but we do. But if He is truly the Lamb of God who takes away the sins of the world, who became a curse for us, and who was wrapped in our sins, it necessarily follows that we cannot be justified and take away sins through love. For God has laid our sins, not upon us but upon Christ, His Son. If they are taken away by Him, then they cannot be taken away by us. All Scripture says this, and we confess and pray the same thing in the Creed when we say: "I believe in Jesus Christ, the Son of God, who suffered, was crucified, and died for us."

From *Lectures on Galatians* (1535) (Luther's Works 26:279–80)

You prepare a table before me in the presence

of my enemies.

PSALM 23:5

A Wonderful Victory

 ow highly blessed David exalts and praises the dear Word, namely, by telling us that by means of it the believers gain the victory over the devil, the world, the flesh, sin, conscience, and death. When one has the Word and in faith clings to it firmly, these enemies, who otherwise are invincible, must all yield and let themselves be taken captive. It is, however, a wonderful victory and power, also a very proud and haughty boast on the part of the believers, that they may compel and conquer all of these horrible and, as it were, almighty enemies—not by raging, biting, resisting, striking back, avenging, seeking counsel and help here and there, but by eating, drinking, rejoicing, sitting, being happy, and resting. All of this, as we have said, is accomplished through the Word. For in Scripture "eating and drinking" means believing and clinging firmly to the Word; and from this proceeds peace, joy, comfort, strength, and the like.

From *Commentary on Psalm 23* (Luther's Works 12:172–73)

The LORD *has disciplined me severely,*
but He has not given me over to death.

PSALM 118:18

We Shall Not Die, But Live

 e should recognize this verse as a masterpiece. How mightily the psalmist banishes death out of sight! He will know nothing of dying and of sin. At the same time he visualizes life most vividly and will hear of nothing but life. But whoever will not see death, lives forever, as Christ says: "If anyone keeps My Word, he will never see death" (John 8:51). He so immerses himself in life that death is swallowed up by life (1 Corinthians 15:55) and disappears completely, because he clings with a firm faith to the right hand of God. Thus all the saints have sung this verse and will continue to sing it to the end. We note this especially in the case of the martyrs. So far as the world is concerned, they die. Yet their hearts say with a firm faith: "I shall not die, but live."

From *Commentary on Psalm 118* (Luther's Works 14:87)

He spoke, and it came to be;
He commanded, and it stood firm.

PSALM 33:9

When God Speaks

ut what or in what manner will He speak? Here we must observe the Hebrew way of expression. For when Scripture says that God speaks, it understands a word related to a real thing or action, not just a sound, as ours is. For God does not have a mouth or a tongue, since He is a Spirit, though Scripture speaks of the mouth and tongue of God: "He spoke, and it came to be" (Psalm 33:9). And when He speaks, the mountains tremble, kingdoms are scattered, then indeed the whole earth is moved. That is a language different from ours. When the sun rises, when the sun sets, God speaks. When the fruits grow in size, when human beings are born, God speaks. Accordingly the words of God are not empty air, but things very great and wonderful, which we see with our eyes and feel with our hands. For when, according to Moses (Genesis 1), the Lord said: "Let there be a sun, let there be a moon, let the earth bring forth trees," etc., as soon as He said it, it was done. No one heard this voice, but we see the works and the things themselves before our eyes, and we touch them with our hands.

From *Commentary on Psalm 2* (Luther's Works 12:32)

"No one is able to snatch them out
of the Father's hand."

John 10:29

Our Faithful Shepherd

hrist our dear Lord is such a faithful Guardian and true Bishop and Shepherd (for it is the same office and name). He has this name above all others, with all honor, for our eternal comfort, both at the right hand of God—where He unceasingly intercedes with the Father for us, prays for us, and shows His wounds—and then here below on earth, where through His Word, Sacraments, and the power of the Holy Spirit He rules, sustains, cares for, and protects the little flock that believe in Him. If He were not Himself present and watching, the devil would long ago have torn us all away and blotted us out, along with God's Word and Christ's name. That is how it happens when God is angry and turns away His eyes to punish the world and [its] ingratitude. Then immediately everything is in the devil's power. But wherever true doctrine, faith, confession, and the use of the Sacraments still remain, that is due only to the keeping and watching of this dear Shepherd and Bishop.

From the *Church Postil*, sermon for Easter 2 on 1 Peter 2:20–25 (Luther's Works 77:171)

All Scripture is breathed out by God and
profitable for teaching, for reproof, for correction,
and for training in righteousness.

2 TIMOTHY 3:16

The Purpose of Scripture

 he purpose of the whole Scripture is this: to teach, reprove, correct, and train in righteousness, so that the man of God may be perfect for every good work, as Paul says in 2 Timothy 3:16–17. Those who fail to observe this purpose, even if they create the impression of erudition among the unlettered by their divinations, nevertheless are ignorant of the true essence of Scripture.

From *Lectures on the Song of Solomon* (Luther's Works 15:194)

"I do not ask that You take them out of the world, but that You keep them from the evil one." John 17:15

One Little Word

 or the sake of the Word we must endure misfortune and evil in this world from both tyrants and sects, who press in upon us on every side with clenched fist and false doctrine, with cunning and force, in order to take the Word from us. Moreover, we must be surrounded by devils and stand like a lone sheep amid wolves, yes, amid raging, roaring lions (as St. Peter says in 1 Peter 5:8) that have sharpened their teeth for us and intend to tear us to pieces and devour us. Tell me, who is it that holds us here, so that we remain and endure against so many abominable enemies without despairing at every moment and losing both faith and the Word from our hearts? Who has protected us to this hour against our tyrants and all devils, even though they have made so many plans and contrived so much secret treachery against us? . . . I answer: It is surely not any human might or wisdom. But here stands one little Word that accomplishes it. Above us there sits One who remembers this prayer and says, "My Christ once prayed for them. Therefore, they shall be protected and preserved." This is our comfort, our bulwark and defense—that they cannot do to us what they desire, even though they swell to bursting with malice and anger until they wear themselves out persecuting and pursuing us, and God will snatch us out of their teeth and they shall come to ruin.

From *Sermons on the Gospel of John*, Chapters 17–20 (Luther's Works 69:89)

"Father, I desire that they also, whom You have given Me, may be with Me where I am, to see My glory that You have given Me because You loved Me before the foundation of the world." JOHN 17:24

The Supreme Consolation

ere is the supreme consolation. If a man could believe it were true, he would be little concerned about this temporal life and all the world's possessions and honor. Indeed, he would gladly forsake everything on earth. For what harm can the world do us by taking from us possessions, honor, body, and life?—except to require us to come to Christ and see His glory, compared with which all the possessions and glory of the world are nothing at all. But we are too cold and hesitant to believe this. We do not feel the comfort, strength, and savor that the words possess. Moreover, the glory of the matter is too great (as has been said) to enter our heart. For it is too far beyond our senses and too high above human understanding that this poor, stinking sack of worms is to come to see such matchless, divine glory eternally and ever before its eyes. Yes, and through that glory my body and yours, after they have been corrupted in the earth and destroyed by worms, shall become brighter than the sun and stars [Daniel 12:3]. For the vision of glory includes all this, together with everything that we shall possess and enjoy in eternal life and bliss, which no human tongue can express nor thought attain.

From *Sermons on the Gospel of John*, Chapters 17–20 (Luther's Works 69:115)

*A thorn was given me in the flesh, a messenger of
Satan to harass me, to keep me from becoming
conceited.* 2 CORINTHIANS 12:7

A Thorn in the Flesh

 he prophet David confesses that he, too, had to
learn the same thing: "I said in my prosperity: 'I
shall never be defeated.' But when You hid Your
face, I was terrified" (Psalm 30:6–7). St. Paul laments the
great suffering he endured in Asia when he says: "We do
not want you to be ignorant, dear brothers, of the affliction we encountered in Asia. We were so utterly burdened
beyond our strength that we gave up on life itself, and we
had concluded that we had to die. But that happened so
that we would not place our trust on ourselves but on God,
who raises the dead" (2 Corinthians 1:8–9). He says that a
thorn was given him in the flesh, a messenger of Satan to
beat him with fists, to keep him from becoming conceited
because of the high revelation. God did not want to take that
away from him, even though he pleaded three times about
it, but he had to cling to the comfort of God's words that he
should be satisfied with His grace and through it overcome
his weakness (2 Corinthians 12:7–9). Therefore, this testing of
the saints is necessary, and even more necessary than eating
and drinking, so that they may remain in fear and humility
and learn to cling only to God's grace.

From the *Church Postil*, sermon for Epiphany 1 on Luke 2:41–52
(Luther's Works 76:198)

[Christ] gave Himself for us to redeem us from all lawlessness and to purify for Himself a people for His own possession who are zealous for good works. TITUS 2:14

Never Doubt Redemption

gain a great light shines forth and teaches us how Christ, God's Son, has redeemed us from death which, after the creation, had become our lot through Adam's fall and in which we would have perished eternally. Now think: just as in the First Article you were to consider yourself one of God's creatures and not doubt it, now you must think of yourself as one of the redeemed and never doubt that. Emphasize one word above all others, for instance, Jesus Christ, *our* Lord. Likewise, suffered for *us*, died for *us*, arose for *us*. All this is ours and pertains to us; that *us* includes *yourself,* as the Word of God declares.

From *A Simple Way to Pray* (Luther's Works 43:210–11)

Against You, You only, have I sinned.

PSALM 51:4

This Is the Victory

he Law awakens sin so that it becomes alive and gives death power and might over us. Thus, then, we come into death and hell. . . . How are we freed from all of this? Who will remove from our hearts the Law, the handwriting that was against us (Colossians 2:14), or our evil conscience? No human being is able to do this. Indeed, no creature in heaven or earth can take away the evil conscience or sin that the conscience feels. But this is what does it, he says: "Thanks be to God, who has given us the victory through our Lord Jesus Christ" [1 Corinthians 15:57]. We have the victory through Jesus Christ, who, for us men and for our salvation, came down from heaven and was made man, suffered death on the cross for us, descended into hell, rose from the dead, and ascended into heaven; destroyed sin, death, and hell in His body; fulfilled the Law perfectly and entirely and stopped its mouth so that it must stop accusing and condemning us. This is the victory: that death has lost its sting. The Law can no longer awaken sin, nor can sin any longer make death strong, for Christ has atoned for our sin and has erased the handwriting, the Law, setting it aside and nailing it to the cross (Colossians 2:14).

From *Eastertide Sermons on 1 Corinthians 15* (Luther's Works 58:159)

[Isaac said,] "Behold, the fire and the wood, but where is the lamb for a burnt offering?" Abraham said, "God will provide for Himself the lamb for a burnt offering, my son." GENESIS 22:7–8

Let Your Faith Be Firm

 he nature and manner of faith are to picture and mirror the goodness of Christ thus in the heart of man. Therefore the Epistle to the Hebrews says, in 11:1: "Faith is the substance of things hoped for," that is, of something good, the grace and goodness of God. . . . However good and genuine faith may be, it falls back when it comes to a battle, unless it has been well-disciplined and has grown strong. Therefore you should not imagine it is enough if you have commenced to believe; but you must diligently watch that your faith continue firm, or it will vanish; you are to see how you may retain this treasure you have embraced; for Satan concentrates all his skill and strength on how to tear it out of your heart. Therefore the growth of your faith is truly as necessary as its beginning, and indeed more so; but all is the work of God. The young milk-faith is sweet and weak; but when long marches are required and faith is attacked, then God must strengthen it, or it will not hold the field of battle.

From the *Church Postil*, sermon for Trinity 21 on John 4:46–54
(Luther's Works 79 (Lenker) 5:255–56)

Cast me not away from Your presence,
and take not Your Holy Spirit from me.

PSALM 51:11

A Pure Dwelling Place

Because David asks for these things from the Lord, he clearly shows us that it is not up to our doing or our powers to preserve these gifts, but that we are in danger of being rejected. This rejection takes place when the Lord leaves us to ourselves and withdraws His Spirit, as Scripture says, "He gave them up into their own desires" (Psalm 81:12; Romans 1:24). When this happens, we immediately fall. Either we indulge our lusts, as David did in his adultery, or we fall into presumption or despair. Hence he says: "Cast me not away; that is, do not desert me with Thy sanctifying Spirit, for when this happens, I am truly cast away and I perish. And take not Thy Holy Spirit from me." He confesses that he has the Holy Spirit, but not perfectly or totally. These are only the firstfruits of the Spirit (Romans 8:23). After this life it will come to pass that we shall attain the fullness of the Spirit, and shall be as He is (1 John 3:2). Thus these two things should be combined, that through the Holy Spirit we might be saved from all iniquities, inwardly and outwardly, in the spirit and in the flesh, that our hearts might become a pure dwelling place (Ephesians 2:22), in which no entrance is open for the return of the unclean spirit, as Christ teaches in the Gospel (Luke 11:24).

From *Commentary on Psalm 51* (Luther's Works 12:382)

"I chose you and appointed you that you should go
and bear fruit and that your fruit should abide."

JOHN 15:16

Building an Eternal House

o support or protect a poor, pious pastor is an act that makes no show and looks like a small thing. . . . Meanwhile my pastor, who does not glitter, is practicing the virtue that increases God's kingdom, fills heaven with saints, plunders hell, robs the devil, wards off death, represses sin, instructs and comforts every man in the world according to his station in life, preserves peace and unity, raises fine young folk, and plants all kinds of virtue in the people. In a word, he is making a new world! He builds not a poor, temporary house, but an eternal and beautiful Paradise, in which God Himself is glad to dwell. A pious prince or lord who supports or protects such a pastor can have a part in all this. Indeed, this whole work and all the fruits of it are his, as though he had done it all himself, because without his protection and support the pastor could not abide. Therefore no mountain of gold or silver in a land can be compared with this treasure.

From *Commentary on Psalm 82* (Luther's Works 13:52–53)

We have the prophetic Word made more sure.

2 PETER 1:19

Glorious Promises

e, too, have been called, and we have promises that are much clearer and more glorious than those the fathers had. Thus Peter praises this good fortune of ours when he says (2 Peter 1:19): "And we have the prophetic Word made more sure. You will do well to pay attention to this as to a lamp shining in a dark place." Grace and eternal life have been promised and offered to us in a much more glorious way than to them. For the Son has come, and all the promises have been fulfilled. We hear the Son Himself; we have the Sacraments and Absolution; and day and night the Gospel proclaims to us: "You are holy. You are holy. Your sins have been forgiven you. You are blessed, etc." But what do we do? We still tremble, and we cling to our weakness throughout our life. But why are we not aroused by the example of the patriarchs, who believed to complete perfection? I reply that they, too, were weak, just as we are, although we have richer promises than they had. But it comes to pass as God's voice says to Paul: "My power is made perfect in weakness" (2 Corinthians 12:9). For God could not retain and fulfill His promises in us if He did not kill that stupid, proud, and smug flesh in us.

From *Lectures on Genesis* (Luther's Works 5:255–56)

The Lord disciplines the one He loves, and chastises
every son whom He receives.

HEBREWS 12:6

Noble and Necessary Chastisement

ith supreme benefit He chastises His own with much greater love than earthly fathers. Thus you see that the Lord's chastening is distinguished by many features, namely, that it is paternal, that it is applied in moderation, and that it is for the purpose of implementing the remission of sins, because it leads a man to call upon God. "Call upon Me in the day of trouble; I will deliver you" (Psalm 50:15). He speaks thus so that we may more easily forgive others. We groan and sigh to God always, and thus spirit, faith, and love grow. Thus the forgiveness of sins follows and is put into effect. Thus you see how noble and necessary God's chastening is. For through the Word the forgiveness of sins is proclaimed, through faith it is received, and through the cross it is put into effect.

From *Lectures on Isaiah* (Luther's Works 16:215)

"Whoever is of God hears the words of God."

JOHN 8:47

Our New Motivation

herefore a new creation is not a change in clothing or in outward manner, . . . but a renewal of the mind by the Holy Spirit; this is then followed by an outward change in the flesh, in the parts of the body, and in the senses. For when the heart acquires new light, a new judgment, and new motivation through the Gospel, this also brings about a renewal of the senses. The ears long to hear the Word of God instead of listening any longer to human traditions and notions. The lips and the tongue do not boast of their own works, righteousness, and monastic rule; but joyfully they proclaim nothing but the mercy of God, disclosed in Christ. These changes . . . produce a new mind, a new will, new senses, and even new actions by the flesh, so that the eyes, the ears, the lips, and the tongue not only see, hear, and speak otherwise than they used to, but the mind itself evaluates things and acts upon them differently from the way it did before.

From *Lectures on Galatians* (1535) (Luther's Works 27:140)

"Jesus, remember me when You come into
Your kingdom."

LUKE 23:42

God Will Preserve His Church

 e may fare poorly as earthly citizens as we face the enmity of the devil, who molests us in his kingdom, the world. What are we to do about this? It does not matter much. We must put up with it if the devil murders us through the pope, the Turk, or a pestilence. God will not forsake us, and we will receive an eternal refuge and home in heaven instead. God will preserve His church. This church may be narrow and small, but some Christians will always survive.

From *Sermons on the Gospel of John*, Chapters 1–4 (Luther's Works 22:209)

Moses said, "The Lord will raise up for you a prophet
like me from your brothers. You shall listen to Him
in whatever He tells you."

ACTS 3:22

God's Will, Christ's Purpose

 verywhere in the Gospel Christ Himself relates all His words and deeds to the Father's will and counsel. He does so in order to bring about the realization and the belief that everything He said and did flowed from the Father's command and from the Father Himself. Just as His divine essence is also from the Father from eternity, so He shows that He did not assume or devise His own office on His own authority, but that it resulted from the Father's premeditated and firm counsel. And, as has been stated repeatedly, He does this for the purpose of drawing us to the Father, in order that we may seek, or think of, no other god than Christ or fear the Father as though the Father and Christ were not of one mind. No, we are to believe and know that the Father is just as graciously disposed toward us as Christ, who mercifully and willingly dies for us because this is the Father's will and command.

From *Sermons on the Gospel of John*, Chapters 14–16 (Luther's Works 24:403)

[Christ] is the propitiation for our sins, and not for
ours only but also for the sins of the whole world.

1 JOHN 2:2

Our Savior Defined

 know why I define Christ so strictly from the words
of Paul. For Christ is not a cruel master; He is the
Propitiator for the sins of the whole world. If you are
a sinner, therefore—as indeed we all are—do not put Christ on
a rainbow as the Judge; for then you will be terrified and will
despair of His mercy. No, grasp the true definition of Him,
namely, that Christ, the Son of God and of the Virgin, is not
One who terrifies, troubles, condemns us sinners or calls us
to account for our evil past but One who has taken away the
sins of the whole world, nailing them to the cross (Colossians
2:14) and driving them all the way out by Himself.

From *Lectures on Galatians* (1535) (Luther's Works 26:37–38)

"Whoever kills you will think he is offering service to God."

JOHN 16:2

False Saintliness

he world appeared to itself most holy and most righteous; it assumed that it had adequate reasons for persecuting Noah, especially so far as the First Table and the worship of God were concerned. To be sure, the Second Table likewise gives rise to pretense and hypocrisy; but there is no comparison with the First. An adulterer, a thief, and a murderer can remain hidden for a time, but not forever. But the sins against the First Table usually remain hidden under the guise of saintliness until God reveals them. Ungodliness never wants to be considered and actually to be ungodliness; it strives to be praised for piety and godliness. It embellishes its forms of worship to such a degree that in comparison with them the true forms of worship and true godliness are filthy.

From *Lectures on Genesis* (Luther's Works 2:59)

"Behold, I am the one who has laid as a foundation in Zion, a stone, a tested stone, a precious cornerstone, of a sure foundation . . . ." ISAIAH 28:16

The True Center of Salvation

ou also know the true center and foundation of your salvation from whom you are to seek comfort in this and all troubles, namely, Jesus Christ, the cornerstone. He will not waver or fail us, nor allow us to sink or perish, for He is the Savior and is called the Savior of all poor sinners, and of all who are caught in tribulation and death, and rely on Him, and call on His name. [Christ] says: "Be of good cheer; I have overcome the world." If He has overcome the world, surely He has also overcome the sovereign of this world with all his power. But what else is [the devil's] power but death, by which he has made us subject to himself, [and] held us captives on account of our sin? But now that death and sin are overcome, we may joyfully and cheerfully listen to the sweet words: "Be of good cheer; I have overcome the world." We certainly are not to doubt that these words are indeed true.

From Luther's May 20, 1531, letter to his mother, Margaret (Luther's Works 50:17)

God has taken His place in the divine council;
in the midst of the gods [that is, earthly rulers] He
holds judgment. PSALM 82:1

The Purpose of Government

rom this we see how high and how glorious God will have rulers held, and that men ought to obey them as His officers and be subject to them with all fear and reverence, as to God Himself. Whoever resists them or is disobedient to them or despises them, whom God names with His own name and calls "gods," and to whom He attaches His own honor—whoever, I say, despises, disobeys, or resists them is thereby despising, disobeying, and resisting the true Supreme God, who is in them, who speaks and judges through them, and calls their judgment His judgment. . . . All this is written because it is God's will to establish and maintain peace among the children of Adam for their own good. . . For where there is no government, or where government is not held in honor, there can be no peace.

From *Commentary on Psalm 82* (Luther's Works 13:44–45)

"She has done a beautiful thing to Me."

MATTHEW 26:10

What Is a Good Work?

e teach that reconciling God, making righteous, and wiping away sin is such a lofty, great, glorious work that Christ, God's Son, alone must do it, and that it is properly, purely, simply, and uniquely a work of the one true God and of His grace, in relation to which our work is and can do nothing. But to say that, because of this, good works should be nothing or be worth only a groschen—who has ever taught or heard this, except now, from the lying mouth of the devil? I would not give a single one of my sermons, one of my lectures, one of my writings, one of my Our Fathers—indeed, whatever small work I have ever done or will do—in exchange for all the goods of the world. In fact, I hold one of these to be of more worth than my bodily life, which is and should be of more worth to each person than the whole world. For if it is a good work, then God has done it through and in me. If God has done it and it is God's work, what is the whole world in comparison with God and His work? Even though I do not become righteous through such a work (for this must already have happened through Christ's blood and grace, without works), it has still been done to the praise and honor of God, for the help and well-being of my neighbor. None of these things can be paid for or compared with the world's goods.

From Luther's preface to Justus Menius, *The Doctrine and Secret of the Anabaptists, Refuted from Scripture* (Luther's Works 59:270–71)

"Whoever feeds on My flesh and drinks My blood has eternal life, and I will raise him up on the last day."

JOHN 6:54

The Chief Doctrine

 f you apprehend Christ as your Head, hold His flesh and blood in high esteem, that is, grant them the power and the honor they deserve, namely, that they are a flesh and blood which impart life, banish hell, mightily drive away and expel devil and sin, then you have the true chief doctrine of the Christian faith. This you must find in the word "My," that this flesh and blood have the power to abolish sin and death, to bestow life and righteousness, and to break down all the gates of heaven and earth.

From *Sermons on the Gospel of John*, Chapters 6–8 (Luther's Works 23:140–41)

The testimony of the LORD is sure,
making wise the simple.

PSALM 19:7

A Simple Explanation

 hrist's kingdom is established . . . not with human force, wisdom, counsel or power, but with the Word and the Gospel preached by infants and sucklings. . . . Christ founds, strengthens, and fortifies His kingdom only through the oral Word. By "infants" He does not mean young children who cannot talk (for if they are to speak and preach the Word, they must be able to talk), but plain, simple, unsophisticated people, who are like infant children in that they set aside all reason, grasp and accept the Word with simple faith, and let themselves be led and directed by God like children. Such people are also the best scholars and pupils in Christ's kingdom, as He Himself says in Matthew 11:25: "I thank Thee, Father, Lord of heaven and earth, that Thou hast hidden these things from the wise and under-standing and revealed them to babes." In Psalm 19:7 David says: "The testimony of the Lord makes wise the simple." And Psalm 119:130: "The unfolding of Thy words gives light; it imparts understanding to the simple."

From *Commentary on Psalm 8* (Luther's Works 12:108)

In Him you also, when you heard the word of truth,
the gospel of your salvation, and believed in Him, were
sealed with the promised Holy Spirit. EPHESIANS 1:13

Joyful News

 say here again, once and for all, that you should understand the Gospel as nothing other than the divine promise of His grace and the forgiveness of sins. For that is why it happened that previously Paul's Epistles were not understood and could not be understood, because they did not know what the Law and the Gospel really mean. For they regarded Christ to be a lawmaker, and the Gospel a mere doctrine of new laws. That is nothing else than locking up the Gospel and concealing all things. The word "Gospel" [*Evangelium*] is Greek and signifies "joyous news," because it proclaims the wholesome doctrine of life by divine promise and offers grace and forgiveness of sin. Therefore, works do not belong to the Gospel, for it is not Law; rather, only faith [belongs to the Gospel], for it is altogether a promise and an offer of divine grace. Whoever now believes the Gospel receives grace and the Holy Spirit. This causes the heart to rejoice and find delight in God, and [the heart] then keeps the Law voluntarily, gratuitously, without fear of punishment, without seeking reward, since the heart is perfectly satisfied with God's grace, by which the Law has been fulfilled.

From the *Church Postil*, sermon for Advent 3 on Matthew 11:2–10
(Luther's Works 75:145–46)

August 9

[Jesus] gave them authority over unclean spirits.

MATTHEW 10:1

Harmless Noise

 he devil has often raised a racket in the house and has tried to scare me, but I appealed to my calling and said: I know that God has placed me into this house to be lord here. Now if you have a call that is stronger than mine and are lord here, then stay where you are. But I well know that you are not lord here and that you belong in a different place—down in hell.—And so I fell asleep again and let him be angry, for I well knew that he could do nothing to me.

From the *House Postil*, third sermon for Easter on Luke 24:36–47 (WLS, p. 404, no. 1192)

*There is therefore now no condemnation for those
who are in Christ Jesus.* ROMANS 8:1

In God's Hands

 e learn here that the saints must wrestle with the devil and fight with death, whether by persecution or pestilence or other sickness and mortal danger. In that conflict nothing is better and more vital for victory than learning to sing this little song of the saints, that is, to look away from self and to cling to the hand of God. Thus the devil is defrauded and made to miss the boat. It works like this: I am nothing. The Lord is all my strength, as stated above. I am stripped of everything, of myself and all that is mine. I can say: "Devil, what are you fighting? If you try to denounce my good works and my holiness before God, why, I have none. My strength is not my own; the Lord is my Strength. You can't squeeze blood out of a turnip! If you try to prosecute my sins, I have none of those either. Here is God's strength—prosecute it until you have had enough. I know absolutely nothing about either sins or holiness in me. I know nothing whatever except God's power in me."

From *Commentary on Psalm 118* (Luther's Works 14:85)

We have this treasure in jars of clay.

2 CORINTHIANS 4:7

Treasure in Weak Vessels

 atan is raging so ferociously, filling everything with turmoil and scandals, and stirring up the whole world against us. Therefore someone may say that it would have been better to be silent [about the doctrine of justification], and that then none of these evils would have arisen. We ought to set greater store by the favor of God, whose glory we proclaim, than by the rage of the world, which persecutes us. For what are the pope and the whole world in comparison with God, whom we surely should praise and to whom we should give preference over all creatures? In addition, the wicked increase the uproar and the scandals which Satan arouses in order to crush or at least to distort our teaching. We, on the other hand, emphasize the comfort and the inestimable fruit of this doctrine; this we vastly prefer to all those turmoils, sects, and scandals. We, of course, are small and weak; and we are carrying a heavenly treasure in earthen vessels (2 Corinthians 4:7). But though the vessels may be weak, the treasure is infinite and incomprehensible.

From *Lectures on Galatians* (1535) (Luther's Works 27:19)

*Many Samaritans from that town believed in Him be-
cause of the woman's testimony . . . . And many more
believed because of His word.* JOHN 4:39, 41

The Pure, Clear Word

 f only God would grant that my interpretation and that of all teachers perish and that every Christian himself would take for himself the pure Scripture and the clear Word of God! You can see from my babbling how immeasurably different God's Word is from human words, and how no man with all his words is able sufficiently to attain to and elucidate a single Word of God. It is an infinite Word that must be grasped and contemplated with a quiet spirit, as the psalmist says, "I will hear what God Himself speaks in me" (Psalm 85:8). No one but such a quiet, contemplating spirit grasps it. Whoever could arrive at this without glosses and interpretations would have no need of my glosses and those of other men; indeed, they would only be in his way. Therefore, go in, go in, dear Christians, and let my interpretation and that of other teachers be only a scaffold for the true building, so that we may grasp and taste the pure, clear Word of God and remain there, for there alone God dwells in Zion. Amen.

From the conclusion of the 1522 and 1525 editions of the *Church Postil* (Luther's Works 76:137 n. 134)

"We have found this man a plague, one who stirs up riots among all the Jews throughout the world."

ACTS 24:5

Was It Better Before?

his is the reason for the general complaint and cry that the Gospel is causing so much conflict, strife, and disturbance in the world and that everything is worse since it came than it was before, when things moved along smoothly, when there was no persecution, and when the people lived together like good friends and neighbors. . . . So this is what I say in reply to these idle talkers and grumblers: "Things neither can nor should run peacefully and smoothly. How could things run smoothly, when the devil is in charge and is a mortal enemy of the Gospel? . . . Do not hope for any peace and quiet so long as Christ and His Gospel are in the midst of the devil's kingdom. And woe upon the peaceful and smooth situation that used to be, and upon those who would like to have it back! This is a sure sign that the devil is ruling with all his might and that no Christ is there. I am worried that it may be this way again and that the Gospel may be taken away from us . . . all too soon, which is just what these rioters are struggling for now."

From *The Sermon on the Mount* (Luther's Works 21:51–52)

If food makes my brother stumble,
I will never eat meat, lest I make my brother stumble.
1 CORINTHIANS 8:13

Responsibility to Others

n keeping with Christ's example, your strength should take [your brothers'] weakness upon itself until they, too, become strong. For if we live by the spirit and in love, we do not live for ourselves; then we live for our brothers. Therefore we shall do what is serviceable and necessary for them." "Owe no one anything," says Paul, "except to love one another" (Romans 13:8); and in 1 Corinthians 8:13 he says: "If food is a cause of my brother's falling, I will never eat meat." Why? Because I love my brother, and his salvation is incomparably more important to me than my freedom, by which I am free to do what he does not yet understand to be permitted. Thus if my righteousness, wisdom, capacity, or any action whatever that is entirely permissible to me causes my brother to fall, I must give it up and render service to love.

From *Lectures on Galatians* (1519) (Luther's Works 27:384)

[There is] one God and Father of all,
who is over all and through all and in all.

EPHESIANS 4:6

True Equality

All outside of Christ are condemned, one like the other; each needs Christ as much as the other. But when we are converted, each one receives the same Baptism, the same Sacrament, the same faith, the same Christ, the same Spirit, the same Gospel—in short, the same God as the other [see Ephesians 4:4–6]. Here in this wilderness manna is distributed equally [Exodus 16:16–17]. Then how can it possibly be right for one to claim to be more spiritual than another, more a priest than another? What can he have that is better than Christ? Nevertheless, each has the same Christ, and Christ receives each one unreservedly.

From the *Church Postil*, sermon for Advent 2 on Romans 15:4–13 (Luther's Works 75:81)

You shall not steal.

EXODUS 20:15

A Broad Interpretation

 et the commandment not be understood too narrowly. But let it apply to everything that has to do with our neighbors. Briefly, in summary . . . this is what is forbidden: (a) To do our neighbor any injury or wrong (in any conceivable manner, by impeding, hindering, and withholding his possessions and property), or even to consent or allow such injury. Instead, we should interfere and prevent it. (b) It is commanded that we advance and improve his possessions. When they suffer lack, we should help, share, and lend both to friends and foes [Matthew 5:42].

From the *Large Catechism* (*Concordia*, p. 387)

You guide me with Your counsel,
and afterward You will receive me to glory.

PSALM 73:24

The Flesh Is Weak

s often as we are afflicted and tempted, . . . let us stoutly resist the flesh when it rages and is angry. Let us say: "Why God neglects me in this way, I do not know, but I have no doubts about the excellent, wise, and most useful plan of the Father, although the flesh does not see but murmurs and struggles against the Spirit. Nevertheless, the cross must be borne and overcome by faith and patience, for in the saintly fathers I see the wonderful plans of God by which they are ruled." . . . The flesh is indeed weak; it groans, howls, and complains, but God says: "You know nothing; you are a fool! Wisdom belongs to Me, and from this cross of yours I will bring forth the greatest good."

From *Lectures on Genesis* (Luther's Works 6:352)

"But I say to you who hear, Love your enemies, do good to those who hate you, bless those who curse you, pray for those who abuse you." LUKE 6:27–28

When Pity Is Wrong

t is necessary carefully to distinguish the teaching that pertains universally to each individual person from the teaching that pertains to persons in an office, whether it be spiritual or secular, whose task it is to punish and to resist evil. Therefore, even though personally they may be gentle, yet administering justice and meting out punishment is their official work; and it has to go on. It would be wrong if their pity moved them to neglect this; for that would be tantamount to helping, strengthening, and encouraging the evil. It is as if I were to say to our enemies . . . who are persecuting the Gospel and trampling its poor adherents underfoot: "Gentlemen, may the dear God reward you! You are pious people and holy fathers"; or as if I were to keep quiet, pay them homage, or kiss their feet. No, dear brother, this is what I ought to say: "I am a preacher. I have to have teeth in my mouth. I have to bite and salt and tell them the truth. And if they refuse to hear, then in the name of God I have to excommunicate them, lock them out of heaven, consign them to the fire of hell, and turn them over to the devil."

From *The Sermon on the Mount* (Luther's Works 21:123–24)

August 19

Are we to continue in sin that grace may abound?

By no means!

ROMANS 6:1–2

No Sin Allowed

 t is godless reasoning to say: "If our sin praises the mercy of God, then let us sin." For God does not want or permit this. Nor does He prescribe for you a rule according to which you may sin with impunity. He does not say that He does good for the sake of sin. It is one thing to do good for the sake of sin; it is another thing to give help and assistance on account of sin. God certainly detests and hates sin. Yet He sets forth the promise: "He who has fallen should not despair." He does not give orders to commit sin; He forbids it. But after sin has been committed and the Law accuses and terrifies the conscience so that sin becomes "sinful beyond measure," as Romans 7:13 says . . . then He does not want death to reign, as the prophet testifies: "I do not want the death of the sinner, but that he should be converted and live" (see Ezekiel 18:23).

From *Lectures on Genesis* (Luther's Works 8:329)

Note then the kindness and the severity of God: severity toward those who have fallen, but God's kindness to you, provided you continue in His kindness. ROMANS 11:22

Take the High Road

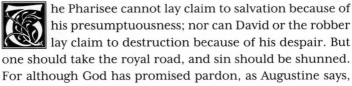he Pharisee cannot lay claim to salvation because of his presumptuousness; nor can David or the robber lay claim to destruction because of his despair. But one should take the royal road, and sin should be shunned. For although God has promised pardon, as Augustine says, yet He does not promise that you will be sure to return after a fall. Thus Saul and Judas do not return. It is not in our power to take hold of grace; nor do you know whether you are able to accept the remission that is offered. Therefore one should fear God. He hates both presumption and despair.

From *Lectures on Genesis* (Luther's Works 8:329)

For the word of the LORD *is upright,*
and all His work is done in faithfulness.

PSALM 33:4

God Is True

he fact that He promised us the Son was the sheer mercy of God. And so He Himself, in His coming, is Mercy, that is, the result of God's mercy that He promised. But the fact that God sent Him was the truth and faithfulness of God. And so He is Himself the Truth, that is, the realization of the truth of God offering the promise. Therefore what God the Father promised was Mercy; and what He sent was Truth. And so they are wonderfully mingled and brought together. The fact that God is true in the things promised is His mercy, not our merit. But the fact that He has mercy is His truth. And so, when He has mercy, He becomes true [that is, He keeps faith and promise], and when He keeps faith or remains true, He has mercy. And both are in Christ.

From *First Lectures on the Psalms* (Luther's Works 11:165)

What we proclaim is not ourselves,
but Jesus Christ as Lord.
2 CORINTHIANS 4:5

Setting an Example

 t. Paul says: "We do not want to lord it over your faith" (2 Corinthians 1:24) and "What we proclaim is not ourselves, but Jesus Christ as Lord, with ourselves as your servants" (2 Corinthians 4:5). Likewise: "You should not domineer over them" (1 Peter 5:3), as if it were your inheritance. They preached the pure faith to us and also offered their example and let it serve us for this alone: that Christ might rule in us and faith remain pure, so that we don't receive their word and work as if it were their own, but that we learn Christ in both their words and works.

From the *Church Postil*, sermon for Advent 1 on Matthew 21:1–9 (Luther's Works 75:59–60)

I am not aware of anything against myself, but I am
not thereby acquitted. It is the Lord who judges me.

1 CORINTHIANS 4:4

The Spirit Giveth Life

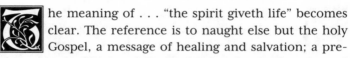he meaning of . . . "the spirit giveth life" becomes clear. The reference is to naught else but the holy Gospel, a message of healing and salvation; a precious, comforting word. It comforts and refreshes the sad heart. It wrests it out of the jaws of death and hell, as it were, and transports it to the certain hope of eternal life, through faith in Christ. When the last hour comes to the believer, and death and God's judgment appear before his eyes, he does not base his comfort upon his works. Even though he may have lived the holiest life possible, he says with Paul (1 Corinthians 4:4): "I know nothing against myself, yet am I not hereby justified." These words imply being ill pleased with self, with the whole life; indeed, even the putting to death of self. Though the heart says, "By my works I am neither made righteous nor saved," which is practically admitting oneself to be worthy of death and condemnation, the Spirit extricates from despair, through the Gospel faith . . . .

From the *Church Postil,* sermon for Trinity 12 on 2 Corinthians 3:4–11 (Luther's Works 79 (Lenker) 8:243)

As for the one who is weak in faith, welcome him . . . .

ROMANS 14:1

The Christian Law

No outward rule can maintain itself without an inward gentleness (though the hand be stern), much less the government of the church. Away with those who are out to set forth the Christian life in perfection! But the Christian law is that the strong must bear the weak. They, on the contrary, cry, "Whoever does not do what he should is under the curse." Don't you know, you ungodly man, that there are bones and flesh in the body? So it is in the church. It is like a hospital, where there are the strong and the weak, bones and flesh. One bears another's burden. The Christian life, therefore, is a mixture of strength and weakness. One supports the other. This is indeed a comforting situation.

From *Lectures on Isaiah*, Chapters 40–66 (Luther's Works 17:66)

The people wander like sheep;
they are afflicted for lack of a shepherd.

ZECHARIAH 10:2

Beware of False Shepherds

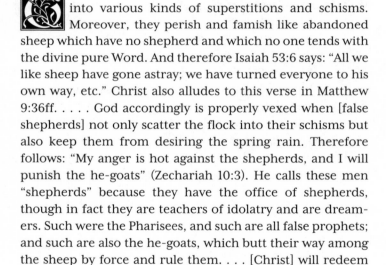 he people] are driven away and scattered like a flock into various kinds of superstitions and schisms. Moreover, they perish and famish like abandoned sheep which have no shepherd and which no one tends with the divine pure Word. And therefore Isaiah 53:6 says: "All we like sheep have gone astray; we have turned everyone to his own way, etc." Christ also alludes to this verse in Matthew 9:36ff. . . . . God accordingly is properly vexed when [false shepherds] not only scatter the flock into their schisms but also keep them from desiring the spring rain. Therefore follows: "My anger is hot against the shepherds, and I will punish the he-goats" (Zechariah 10:3). He calls these men "shepherds" because they have the office of shepherds, though in fact they are teachers of idolatry and are dreamers. Such were the Pharisees, and such are all false prophets; and such are also the he-goats, which butt their way among the sheep by force and rule them. . . . [Christ] will redeem His flock from the he-goats and will Himself be their shepherd and visit them with mercy.

From *Lectures on Zechariah* (German text) (Luther's Works 20:301–2)

*The word of the cross is folly to those who are perish-
ing, but to us who are being saved it is the power
of God.* 1 CORINTHIANS 1:18

The Lofty and the Lowly

 t. Paul says in 1 Corinthians 2:1–2, "I decided when I
was with you not to be clever, like some of the lofty
spirits, and did not claim to know anything except
Jesus Christ and Him crucified." Is this the sublime apostle
who was so exceptionally enlightened, and yet he knows of
nothing more glorious and precious to extol against the false
prophets and nothing loftier to preach than the poor, crucified God? What, then, are those haughty spirits doing when
they seek after great revelations and think that one must
ascend up much higher and soar in spirit? . . . For the devil
also delights in beautiful and sublime thoughts. He is able to
make a mask in the heart as if he were God and to disguise
himself in sheer splendor and majesty, as he did when he
appeared to Christ, in Matthew 4:8. In sum, so far as great
wisdom, holiness, and majesty are concerned, he is the
world's master and god. . . . He is still unable to change his
nature; he always seeks to be honored in majesty in the place
of God. Therefore, God played a trick on him by descending
here into the depths and concealing Himself in the lowliest
of forms, as in the lap of the Virgin, and does not want to be
found in any other way. The devil cannot follow there, for he

is a proud, vainglorious spirit, even though he can simulate the appearance of the greatest humility. Therefore, no one can deceive him any better than by binding himself to the stake to which God nailed [Christ].

From *Sermons on the Gospel of John*, Chapters 17–20 (Luther's Works 69:67–68)

"When a woman is giving birth, she has sorrow because her hour has come, but when she has delivered the baby, she no longer remembers the anguish, for joy that a human being has been born into the world. So also you have sorrow now, but I will see you again, and your hearts will rejoice, and no one will take your joy from you." JOHN 16:21–22

In the Hour at Hand

or [a woman in labor] the hour of endurance is now at hand. . . . Everything is concentrated on the moment when the child is born into the world. In that moment the anguish is immediately forgotten because of the happy sight of the newborn child. A change like this is also experienced here in this Christian life. Sadness will not last forever; it will turn into joy. Otherwise our condition would be hopeless and helpless. But Christ has helped by saying that we will not be subjected to the eternal spectacle of the devil with his horns and claws, but that our hearts will again see Christ and rejoice in Him. Thus here on earth Christians experience an ever-recurring alternation of "a little while and again a little while." Now it is dark night; soon it is day again. Therefore the lamenting does not have to last forever, even though it seems and feels that way when we are in it. But even though we cannot see or determine the end, Christ has already done so. He points out to us in advance that we must bear this suffering, no matter how bad and unpleasant the devil makes it. Even though we do not see the end, we must wait for Him who says: "I will put an end to it and will again comfort you and give you joy."

From *Sermons on the Gospel of John*, Chapters 14–16 (Luther's Works 24:382)

Out of my distress I called on the
LORD; *the* LORD *answered me and set me free.*

PSALM 118:5

Learning to Call

We read: "I called upon the Lord." You must learn to call. Do not sit by yourself or lie on a couch, hanging and shaking your head. Do not destroy yourself with your own thoughts by worrying. Do not strive and struggle to free yourself, and do not brood on your wretchedness, suffering, and misery. Say to yourself: "Come on, you lazy bum; down on your knees, and lift your eyes and hands toward heaven!" Read a psalm or the Our Father, call on God, and tearfully lay your troubles before Him. Mourn and pray, as this verse teaches . . . . It is His desire and will that you lay your troubles before Him. He does not want you to multiply your troubles by burdening and torturing yourself. He wants you to be too weak to bear and overcome such troubles; He wants you to grow strong in Him. By His strength He is glorified in you. Out of such experiences men become real Christians.

From *Commentary on Psalm 118* (Luther's Works 14:60–61)

Be still before the LORD and wait patiently for Him;
fret not yourself over the one who prospers in his way,
over the man who carries out evil devices!

PSALM 37:7

When the Wicked Succeed

t is as if [the psalmist] were saying: "It will tend to vex you when you encounter misfortune in a righteous cause, while they get along very well in their wickedness and do not disappear, as you wish they would. You see the wicked man succeed so well in all his evil devices that a proverb has been coined about it: 'The greater the scoundrel, the greater his success.' But be wise, dear child, and do not let that get you down. Cling to God, and your heart's desire will come—in abundance! But it is not yet time; the scoundrel's success must pass by and have its appointed time before it is all over. Meanwhile you must commit it to God, take your pleasure in Him, and find satisfaction in His will, so that you do not hinder His will in you or in your enemy. For that is what happens when people will not stop raging; either they ram their cause through headfirst, or they smash it to bits." He uses a fine Hebrew word here: "Be still before the Lord, and wait patiently for Him." Just as an embryo in the mother's womb lets God form it, so in this case you have been conceived in God, and He will form you in the correct shape if you will only be still.

From *Four Psalms of Comfort* (Luther's Works 14:213–14)

August 30

For it has been granted to you that for the sake
of Christ you should not only believe in Him
but also suffer for His sake.

PHILIPPIANS 1:29

Take up Your Cross

 e need to have a definition of what "taking up one's cross" is. "Taking up one's cross" is willingly taking on and bearing the hatred of the devil, the world, the flesh, sin, death, etc., for the sake of the Word and faith. Here there is no need to choose the cross. Just begin with the first part of [this] life and deny yourself, that is, denounce the righteousness of your works and confess the righteousness of faith, and the second part will straightaway be present, that is, the cross, which you are then to accept, just as Christ accepted His own. But since the hypocrites condemn the first part and defend their own righteousness, they not only do not take the cross upon themselves, but they even become the crucifiers and killers of the godly—those who are bearing the cross.

From *Annotations on Matthew* (Luther's Works 67:293)

*Finally, then, brothers, we ask and urge you in the
Lord Jesus, that as you received from us how you
ought to walk and to please God, just as you are
doing, that you do so more and more.*

1 THESSALONIANS 4:1

On Godly Behavior

n this Epistle lesson, you see that the apostle writes
nothing about faith, but rather about godly behavior in good works toward our own person and
toward our neighbor. . . . As a proper apostle and preacher,
[Paul] exhorts the [Thessalonians] concerning their calling,
that they should consider that they have been baptized and
acknowledge that they have received great grace and mercy
from the Lord, who has redeemed them, not that they
might live wantonly, but rather that they should be dead
to sin and live honorably. For this reason he speaks in such
a pleasant manner, beseeching and exhorting, not merely
[on his own authority] but in the name of the Lord. "Know
then," [he says], "what [Christ], who has liberated you from
death, should mean to you: He is called the Savior, who has
liberated His people from sin to righteousness. Therefore,
Christians should not remain in sin but be intent on living in
chastity and holiness, with kindness toward their neighbor."

From *Sermon for Lent 2 on 1 Thessalonians 4:1–7* (Luther's Works
58:20)

Do the work of an evangelist, fulfill your ministry.

2 TIMOTHY 4:5

The Sheep of Christ

n spiritual sheepherding, that is, in the kingdom of Christ, one should, therefore, preach to the sheep of Christ . . . not the Law of God, much less the ordinances of men, but the Gospel, which the prophet with metaphorical words calls a rod of comfort and a staff of comfort. For through the Gospel, Christ's sheep obtain strength in their faith, rest in their hearts, and comfort in all kinds of anxieties and perils of death. Those who preach this way conduct the office of a spiritual shepherd properly, feed the sheep of Christ in a green pasture, lead them to the fresh water, restore their souls, keep them from being led astray, and comfort them with Christ's rod and staff. Where men hear such preachers, they should believe for certain that they are hearing Christ Himself. They should also acknowledge such preachers as right shepherds, that is, as servants of Christ and stewards of God (1 Corinthians 4:1), and pay no attention at all to the fact that the world proclaims and damns them as heretics and seducers. Those who preach something else than the Gospel . . . are horrible wolves and murderers that do not spare the flock of Christ, but scatter, torture, and slaughter it not only spiritually but also bodily . . . .

From *Commentary on Psalm 23* (Luther's Works 12:171)

September 2

"Save us, Lord; we are perishing."

MATTHEW 8:25

The Calm after the Storm

ere, in this final moment, there glimmers yet one little spark of faith, which is unaware of itself, because it says, "We are perishing!" For if it were aware of itself, it would not say, "We are perishing!" But it perceives nothing but destruction, forgetting that it has survived up to this point and is still burning. For it would not have been aware of anything if it were not still alive and burning. But, behold, Christ does not reject this spark, this smoldering wick, this trembling reed [Isaiah 42:3; Matthew 12:20], but He so increases it that it becomes a blaze by which the winds and seas are calmed. This is what He does for all of us who tremble in fear, if only we groan, sigh, and say with nothing more than a single tremor of the heart: "O Jesus Christ, bring help or there is no hope of my salvation!" Soon, relief will be felt, because Christ is moved through this groaning to rebuke the winds and the sea. And thus there is a great calm, that is, joy and peace, followed by praise and thanksgiving.

From *Annotations on Matthew* (Luther's Works 67:51)

Not that I have already obtained this or am already
perfect, but I press on to make it my own, because
Christ Jesus has made me His own.

PHILIPPIANS 3:12

On Becoming a Christian

or there is really nothing more destructive to the believer than this presumptuousness, as if he had already taken hold of it and there were no need to seek it. It is from this that many slide backward and wither away in their security and laziness. . . . Therefore, whoever has begun to be a Christian, this is what remains: to consider that he has not yet become a Christian and to seek to become a Christian . . . . For a Christian is not in having become, but in becoming . . . . Therefore whoever is a Christian is not a Christian; that is, whoever thinks that he has already become a Christian when he is only becoming a Christian is nothing. For we are headed toward heaven; we are not yet in heaven. And just as he who thinks he is already in heaven will never enter heaven, so he who is headed to heaven is already in heaven since God reckons him as if he were in heaven already. . . . That is how wondrous the works of this kingdom are.

From *Annotations on Matthew* (Luther's Works 67:212–13)

"I am the living bread that came down from heaven.
If anyone eats of this bread, he will live forever.
And the bread that I will give for the life of the world
is My flesh." JOHN 6:51

Eternal Food

hrist wanted to avert our harm and doom by . . . exhorting us to turn our attention to the eternal food [that is, the Gospel], for this food does not perish. But if it is taken away, you must die forever. How eagerly you should strive for this food and not despise it but esteem it above everything as an enduring food that gives eternal life! You must go in quest of this food; for when the perishable food vanishes, you will be saved forever and have eternal life. The disciples of the Gospel are such as seek this eternal food and these eternal possessions. St. Peter and the dear apostles, as well as other pious Christians, understood and remembered this sermon well. Thus St. Peter exclaimed . . . : "You have the words of eternal life" (John 6:68), that is, words that give eternal life.

From *Sermons on the Gospel of John*, Chapters 6–8 (Luther's Works 23:9–10)

"Let the one who boasts, boast in the Lord."

1 CORINTHIANS 1:31

Concerning Knowledge and Power

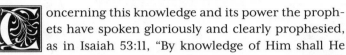 oncerning this knowledge and its power the prophets have spoken gloriously and clearly prophesied, as in Isaiah 53:11, "By knowledge of Him shall He (My Servant, the Righteous One) make many just or righteous." This means: "He will redeem them from sins and snatch them from the devil's jaws solely through this: that they know Him and who He is." Likewise, Jeremiah 9:23–24 says: "Let no one boast of his wisdom nor of his might nor of his riches"—in short, let no one boast at all—"but if anyone wants to boast, let him boast in this, that he knows Me and knows who I am: the Lord, who does good and establishes righteousness and justice on earth."

From *Sermons on the Gospel of John*, Chapters 17–20 (Luther's Works 69:35–36)

[Know] this first of all, that no prophecy of Scripture
comes from someone's own interpretation.

2 PETER 1:20

Fight Powerfully

he kind of study useful to battle is that one is learned in Scripture, as Paul says [Titus 1:9]. It means to fight powerfully and with many clear passages, as with a drawn and naked sword, without any glosses and interpretations. This was the significance of the golden spears in Solomon's temple. Thus the opponent, overcome by the bright light, must see and confess that God's sayings stand alone and need no human interpretation. The foe who does not believe clear Scripture will certainly not believe the glosses of any of the fathers either.

From *Answer to Emser* (Luther's Works 39:165)

For freedom Christ has set us free; stand firm there-fore, and do not submit again to a yoke of slavery.

GALATIANS 5:1

The Yoke of Christ

ut the yoke of Christ is a summons to [take] the cross, to put the old man to death. Now, His cross is easy once the burden of the Law—that is, sin and death—has been lifted. For if you believe that you are righteous and alive before God, that you are a son and heir of heaven, soon you will say: "If God is for me, who can be against me? (Romans 8:31). Death, where is your sting? Where is your victory and boasting? (1 Corinthians 15:55)." "For who," Peter says, "is there to harm you if you are zealous for the good?" (1 Peter 3:13). What can do any harm when God is so beneficent and gentle? Look at the martyrs, how they laugh at their punishments. Why? Because of the confidence and freedom of their heart. . . . How wonderful is Christ's power in His saints (see Psalm 68:35 [67:36 Vg]), that in the hearts of human beings, through faith, He changes death into laughter, punishment into joy, hell into heaven. For all who believe in Him laugh at and scorn all these evils while the world and the flesh flee them with dread and hate them. That is what Christ calls the easy yoke and the light burden: that is, bearing the cross with joy.

From *Annotations on Matthew* (Luther's Works 67:146–47)

I am a worm and not a man.

PSALM 22:6

The Obedient Christ

hrist not only subjected Himself to people but also to sin, death, and the devil, and bore all of that for us. Moreover, [He bore] that death which is most disgraceful of all, namely, death on a cross, not as a man but as a worm (Psalm 22:6), even as the chief evildoer of all evildoers. He even lost the favor, thanks, and honor of the form of a servant which He took on, so that He became nothing at all. . . . He certainly did not do all of that because we were worthy of it or had deserved it, for who could be worthy of such service from such a person? Rather, [He did all of that] because He was obedient to the Father [Philippians 2:8]. Here St. Paul opens up heaven with a word and makes room for us to see the abundance of the divine majesty and to gaze on the inexpressibly gracious will and love of the Father's heart toward us, so that we would feel that God from eternity has been pleased with what Christ, the glorious person, would do and now has done for us. Whose heart does not melt for joy at this?

From the *Church Postil*, sermon for Palm Sunday on Philippians 2:5–11 (Luther's Works 76:421–22:)

The Fulfillment of the Law

 nly Christ takes away the Law, kills my sin, destroys my death in His body, and in this way empties hell, judges the devil, crucifies him, and throws him down into hell. In other words, everything that once used to torment and oppress me Christ has set aside; He has disarmed it and made a public example of it, triumphing over it in Himself (Colossians 2:14–15), so that it cannot dominate any longer but is compelled to serve me.

From *Lectures on Galatians* (1535) (Luther's Works 26:160–61)

Keep a close watch on yourself and on the teaching.

Persist in this.

1 TIMOTHY 4:16

Divine Righteousness

his is our glory to know for certain that our righteousness is divine in that God does not impute our sins. Therefore our righteousness is nothing else than knowing God. Let the Christian who has been persuaded by these words cling firmly to them, and let him not be deceived by any pretense of works or by his own suffering. . . . It is, however, the office of Christ to bear our sins. Hence we must conclude from this text: "If Christ bears my iniquities, then I do not bear them." All teachings which say that our sins must be borne by us are ungodly. Thus from such a text countless thunderbolts have come forward against an ungodly self-righteousness. So Paul by this article of justification struck down every kind of self-righteousness. Therefore we must diligently observe this article. I see that there are many snorers treating this article. They are the ones who consider these words the way a man does who looks at his face in a mirror (as James says, 1:23f.). The moment they come upon another object or business, they are overwhelmed, and they forget the grace of God. For that reason you must most diligently consider this article and not allow yourself to be led astray by other teachings, occupations, or persecutions.

From *Lectures on Isaiah*, Chapters 40–66 (Luther's Works 17:230–31)

"When they persecute you in one town,
flee to the next."
MATTHEW 10:23

The Gospel Is Public

I t is impossible to keep the Gospel from anyone. No power in heaven or on earth can do this, for it is a public teaching that moves about freely under the heavens and is bound to no one place. . . . It is true, of course, that the rulers may suppress the Gospel in cities or places where the Gospel is, or where there are preachers; but you can leave these cities or places and follow the Gospel to some other place. It is not necessary, for the Gospel's sake, for you to capture or occupy the city or place; on the contrary, let the ruler have his city; you follow the Gospel. Thus you permit men to wrong you and drive you away; and yet, at the same time, you do not permit men to take the Gospel from you or keep it from you. Thus the two things, suffering and not suffering, turn out to be one. . . . The Gospel needs no physical place or city in which to dwell; it will and must dwell in hearts.

From *Admonition to Peace* (Luther's Works 46:36)

Beloved, never avenge yourselves,
but leave it to the wrath of God.

ROMANS 12:19

To Live as a Christian

here people do not want to tolerate nor forgive and forget, hatred and envy must certainly follow. They cause only quarrels and strife, so that we have no peace and rest among one another, but bite and scratch one another, and so make our lives oppressive and bitter. There is so much displeasure, strife, and war on earth, and this is all the fault of the vile evil of having no love among one another, but letting that vile hatred move us to wrath and personal revenge whenever anyone does anything against us. . . . Now, if you want to live as a Christian and have peace in the world, then you must strive not to make room, like others, for your own wrath and vengefulness, but to conquer and suppress the hatred through love, so that you can overlook and tolerate it, even if there is great injustice and pain. Then you will be an excellent man who can accomplish much good through gentleness and patience, calm and take away hostility and strife, and thus even improve and convert others.

From the *Church Postil*, sermon for the Sunday after Ascension on 1 Peter 4:7–11 (Luther's Works 77:301–2)

Godliness with contentment is great gain.

1 TIMOTHY 6:6

The Promise of Godliness

he eagerness, or desire, for money extends more widely than greed. It extends to all other things, to the desire for power, pleasure, gold, or silver. . . . The man who is involved with greed has the source of every evil. One evil after another wells up for him. . . . On the other hand, "there is great gain in godliness with contentment" (1 Timothy 6:6). Also, an enthusiasm for generosity is the source of all good things. We have heard Paul's admonition against greed, which he describes as the "root of all evils." He means of this life, so that we say nothing about the life which is to come. You see, the greedy man deprives himself of eternal life, because his heart is swollen with many concerns. Because he has all these worries, he is forced to fear the dangers of fire and of water. As many worries threaten him as there are grains of sand on the seashore. Thus he destroys this life as well as that which is to come, just as "godliness has the promise" (see 1 Timothy 4:8). Greed is the worship of idols. You see, greed worships money, but godliness worships God.

From *Lectures on 1 Timothy* (Luther's Works 28:371–72)

September 14

The LORD *has laid on Him the iniquity of us all.*

ISAIAH 53:6

Why Is Christ Punished?

 hese words must not be diluted but must be left in their precise and serious sense. For God is not joking in the words of the prophet; He is speaking seriously and out of great love, namely, that this Lamb of God, Christ, should bear the iniquity of us all. But what does it mean to "bear"? The sophists reply: "To be punished." Good. But why is Christ punished? Is it not because He has sin and bears sin? That Christ has sin is the testimony of the Holy Spirit in the Psalms. Thus in Psalm 40:12 we read: "My iniquities have overtaken Me"; in Psalm 41:4: "I said: 'O Lord, be gracious to Me; heal Me, for I have sinned against Thee!' "; and in Psalm 69:5: "O God, Thou knowest My folly; the wrongs I have done are not hidden from Thee." In these psalms the Holy Spirit is speaking in the Person of Christ and testifying in clear words that He has sinned or has sins. . . . Therefore Christ not only was crucified and died, but by divine love sin was laid upon Him. When sin was laid upon Him, the Law came and said: "Let every sinner die! And therefore, Christ, if You want to reply that You are guilty and that You bear the punishment, you must bear the sin and the curse as well." Therefore Paul correctly applies to Christ this general Law from Moses: "Cursed be everyone who hangs on a tree." Christ hung on a tree; therefore Christ is a curse of God. And this is our highest comfort, to clothe and wrap Christ this way in my sins, your sins, and the sins of the entire world, and in this way to behold Him bearing all our sins.

From *Lectures on Galatians* (1535) (Luther's Works 26:278–79)

*No longer walk as the Gentiles do, in the futility of their
minds. They are darkened in their understanding,
alienated from the life of God because of the ignorance
that is in them, due to their hardness
of heart.* EPHESIANS 4:17–18

Blind Human Nature

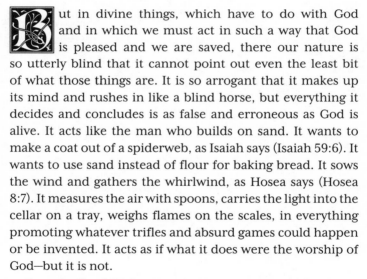

ut in divine things, which have to do with God and in which we must act in such a way that God is pleased and we are saved, there our nature is so utterly blind that it cannot point out even the least bit of what those things are. It is so arrogant that it makes up its mind and rushes in like a blind horse, but everything it decides and concludes is as false and erroneous as God is alive. It acts like the man who builds on sand. It wants to make a coat out of a spiderweb, as Isaiah says (Isaiah 59:6). It wants to use sand instead of flour for baking bread. It sows the wind and gathers the whirlwind, as Hosea says (Hosea 8:7). It measures the air with spoons, carries the light into the cellar on a tray, weighs flames on the scales, in everything promoting whatever trifles and absurd games could happen or be invented. It acts as if what it does were the worship of God—but it is not.

From the *Church Postil*, sermon for Epiphany on Isaiah 60:1–6 (Luther's Works 76:55)

"Truly, I say to you, unless you turn and become like children, you will never enter the kingdom of heaven."

MATTHEW 18:3

Have Faith Like Children

ow often does Christ tell us that we must become children and fools? How often does He condemn reason? Likewise, tell me what kind of reason the little children had whom Christ embraced and blessed and to whom He gave heaven? Were they not still without reason? Why, then, does He command them to be brought to Him and bless them? Where did they get the faith, which makes them children of the kingdom of heaven? Yes, just because they are without reason and foolish, they are better adapted for faith than adults and the wise, for whom reason is always in the way and refuses to push its big head through the narrow door.

From the *Church Postil*, sermon for Epiphany 3 on Matthew 8:1–13 (Luther's Works 76:263)

"The Spirit of truth . . . will not speak on His own authority, but whatever He hears He will speak, and He will declare to you the things that are to come."

JOHN 16:13

The Spirit of Truth

 ere Christ makes the Holy Spirit a Preacher. He does so to prevent one from gaping toward heaven in search of Him, as the fluttering spirits and enthusiasts do, and from divorcing Him from the oral Word or the ministry. One should know and learn that He will be in and with the Word, that it will guide us into all truth . . . . For I, too, am a half-baked theologian. This I say lest I exalt myself over the great minds who have long ago ascended into the clouds beyond all Scripture and have nestled under the wings of the Holy Spirit. But experience has taught me all too often that whenever the devil catches me outside Scripture and sees that my thoughts are rambling and that I, too, am fluttering toward heaven, he brings me to the point of not knowing where God is or where I am. The Holy Spirit wants this truth, which He is to impress into our hearts to be so firmly fixed that reason and all one's own thoughts and feelings are relegated to the background. He wants us to adhere solely to the Word and to regard it as the only truth. And through this Word alone He governs the Christian Church to the end.

From *Sermons on the Gospel of John*, Chapters 14–16 (Luther's Works 24:362)

September 18

For still the vision awaits its appointed time; it hastens
to the end—it will not lie. If it seems slow, wait for it;
it will surely come; it will not delay.

HABAKKUK 2:3

Waiting for God

od's nature is always like Himself and will never change on our account. It is His nature to be long-suffering, to try and to discipline His own in a wonderful manner, and gradually to lead them all the way until death comes, but, on the other hand, when the crisis of life has been reached, to be present at once and to assist them in their trials. Therefore God must be awaited, as the examples and exhortations in the psalms and the prophets remind us. Besides, He is the kind of God who not only makes everything out of nothing but makes nothing out of everything, just as He first reduced Joseph to nothing. And when it seemed that Joseph was ruined and lost, He makes everything out of him, that is, the greatest man in the world. . . . We see, then, what a godly and heroic heart is, namely, a heart that retains trust in God in the utmost poverty and in trials of every kind but, on the other hand, is not puffed up by prosperity but fears the Lord. Such men are surely able to rule the world. They attend to all their duties in such a spirit that they are not content with the good things of this life but hope and wait for another kingdom.

From *Lectures on Genesis* (Luther's Works 8:19–20)

Everyone who goes on ahead and does not abide in the
teaching of Christ, does not have God. Whoever abides
in the teaching has both the Father and
the Son. 2 JOHN 9

To Know God

 he Turks, Jews, and all the heathen] imagine that He
is a God who has neither a Son nor a Holy Spirit in
His Godhead, and thus what they esteem and worship as God is nothing but an empty dream. Indeed, they
extol lies and blasphemies as the knowledge of God because
they presume, without divine revelation (that is, without
the Holy Spirit), to know God and to come to Him without a
mediator (which must be God's only Son). And thus, at bot-
tom, they are without God. For, in truth, there is no other
God than the one who is the Father of our Lord Jesus Christ,
both of whom reveal Themselves through the Holy Spirit to
His Church and who work and rule in the hearts of the faithful. As 2 John 9 says, "Whoever does not believe and abide in
the doctrine of Christ does not have God." And Christ says in
John 5:23: "Whoever does not honor the Son does not honor
the Father as well," or John 14:6: "No one comes to the Father
except through Me."

From *Four Sermons Preached at Eisleben* (Luther's Works 58:414–15)

September 20

"Blessed are those who mourn,
for they shall be comforted."

MATTHEW 5:4

The Purpose of Need

 his is the right kind of sacrifice, one that pleases God, . . . namely, a soul that has no comfort among creatures and is even forsaken and persecuted by itself, so that it looks for nothing but the pure grace of God. Those who weep are blessed, for they shall be comforted (Matthew 5:4). . . . Those who are illustrious and exalted and dwell in the light of men do not want to be troubled and sad. They have comfort and joy in the present life and in the works of their own strength, wisdom, and righteousness; they do not need God. But I, who am so poor in these things, know of no other comfort than this, that God in times past has permitted all His saints to experience need and has never sustained anyone through his own works, abilities, knowledge, or piety. Thus Psalm 44:1–3: "O God, we have heard, our fathers have told us, what deeds Thou didst perform in their days, how Thou didst drive out and afflict the heathen, that Thou mightest plant them in their land. For indeed, not with their swords did they possess the land, nor did their own power help them, but Thy power and the gracious light of Thy countenance; for it pleased Thee to do this even though they did not deserve it."

From *Seven Penitential Psalms* (Luther's Works 14:198–99)

Behold, I am against the prophets, declares the LORD,
who use their tongues and declare, "declares the
LORD*." Behold, I am against those who prophesy lying*
dreams, declares the LORD, *and who tell them and*
lead My people astray by their lies and their reckless-
ness, when I did not send them or charge them. So
they do not profit this people at all, declares the LORD.

JEREMIAH 23:31–32

Who Is an Apostle?

or who can preach unless he is an apostle? But who is an apostle except one who brings the Word of God? And who can bring the Word of God except one who has listened to God? But the man who brings his own dogmas or those that rest on human laws and decrees, or those of the philosopher—can he be called an apostle? Indeed, he is one who comes as a thief, a robber, and a destroyer and slayer of souls. . . . To put it clearly, this means that as often as the Word of God is preached, it renders consciences joyful, expansive, and untroubled toward God, because it is a Word of grace and forgiveness, a kind and sweet Word. As often as the word of man is preached, it renders the conscience sad, cramped, and full of fear in itself, because it is a word of the Law, of wrath and sin; it shows what a person has failed to do and how deeply he is in debt.

From *Lectures on Galatians* (1519) (Luther's Works 27:164)

September 22

*Faith comes from hearing, and hearing through
the word of Christ.*

ROMANS 10:17

When Salvation Begins

ur salvation begins, not with any work of ours but with the hearing of the Word of life. Hence also the Law precedes, to humble, to reveal sin, and to teach that we can do nothing by our own strength. Romans 4:15: "The Law brings wrath," and brings it so completely that the people not only do not do the Law but will not even hear it, for it kills them. For this reason they seek another Word, one which can make us alive before we do any works, as you have seen here. Through the hearing of the Word the Holy Spirit is given; by faith He purifies the heart. Romans 10:17: "Faith comes from what is heard," not indeed to all who hear but to whom God wills. For the Spirit blows where *He* wills (John 3:8), not where *we* will. But when the Holy Spirit is received by faith, then we are justified by Him without any work of our own, only by the gift of God, and we experience peace and a good conscience toward God (Romans 5:1), and joyfully and confidently we cry: "Abba, Father" (Romans 8:15). Now there is no more fear or slavish flight from the face of the wrath of God; there is childlike access to God through grace, in which we stand and boast (Romans 5:2–3).

From *Lectures on Deuteronomy* (Luther's Works 9:184)

September 23

Commit your way to the LORD; *trust in Him,*
and He will act.

PSALM 37:5

Trust in God

herefore it is best to trust in God, even though we cannot be without tears, sorrow, and pain. What can we do against this? Our flesh is such that it is impossible for it not to sob, weep, grieve, and complain. Indeed, even cattle express their pain by their bellowing when they are slaughtered; and lifeless things, like timber, are not cut down and broken up without a crash. But let us sustain ourselves with the Word and faith, and let us not doubt that it has already been determined by God that He wants to turn these pains, troubles, and brief crosses . . . into everlasting and supreme joy. With this confidence and hope we shall very easily lighten our troubles and cares. "He will act" (Psalm 37:5).

From *Lectures on Genesis* (Luther's Works 8:47)

In Christ Jesus you are all sons of God, through faith.

GALATIANS 3:26

The Time for Rescue

o human being can endure [the devil's attacks] without God's special help and strength. . . . For [the devil] takes for himself a piece of truth which one cannot deny and with it increases the cutting edge of his lies so that a person cannot defend himself. . . . At this point, then, the time is ripe for rescue and help from heaven above; either a brother will stand by you with a spoken word of God, or the Holy Spirit Himself will be in your heart, reminding you of such a spoken word and saying: "You have confessed and not denied, for the devil has made you admit that you have sinned and been justly condemned, like Judas. But now like St. Peter turn back to Christ, and look at what He has done for you. . . . Because you are in Christ and call upon Him, your answer of 'Yes' has in turn become a 'No,' and you can defy the devil and make your boast in opposition to him: 'If I am truly a sinner, I am nevertheless not a sinner. I am a sinner in and by myself apart from Christ. Apart from myself and in Christ I am not a sinner, for He has blotted out my sin with His holy blood; I do not doubt that. [As proof] of this I have Baptism and Absolution and the Sacrament as sure seals and letters.' "

From *The Private Mass* (Luther's Works 38:157–58)

The Jesus said to him, "Be gone, Satan!"

MATTHEW 4:10

God Is Unchangeable

hrist manifested Himself in the flesh to snatch us from death, from the power of the devil. From this knowledge must come great joy and delight that God is unchangeable, that He works in accordance with unchangeable necessity, and that He cannot deny Himself (2 Timothy 2:13) but keeps His promises. . . . One must refrain from debates and say: "I am a Christian; that is, the Son of God was made flesh and was born; He has redeemed me and is sitting at the right hand of the Father, and He is my Savior." Thus you must drive Satan away from you with as few words as possible and say: "Be gone, Satan! (Matthew 4:10.) Do not put doubt in me. The Son of God came into this world to destroy your work (1 John 3:8) and to destroy doubt." Then the trial ceases, and the heart returns to peace, quiet, and the love of God.

From *Lectures on Genesis* (Luther's Works 5:48–49)

*I did not shrink from declaring to you anything that
was profitable, and teaching you in public and
from house to house.*

Acts 20:20

There Is No Secret Salvation

hrist says and bears witness in clear words that everything necessary for salvation has been made known to us. For this is how He addresses those who are His in John 15:27: "The Spirit will bear witness to Me." And in John 16:13: "He will guide you into all the truth." Likewise in John 15:15: "All that I have heard from My Father I have made known to you." And in Acts 20:20, 27 Paul says: "You know that I did not shrink from declaring to you anything that was profitable, and teaching you in public and from house to house. I did not shrink from declaring to you the whole counsel of God." With this very statement Paul teaches at the same time that all Scripture has been fulfilled.

From *Lectures on 1 John* (Luther's Works 30:307)

*"Let your light shine before others, so that they may
see your good works and give glory to your Father
who is in heaven."*

MATTHEW 5:16

A Chosen Race

What is this "holy adornment," these priestly garments that adorn the Christians so that they become His holy priesthood? Nothing else than the beautiful, divine, and various gifts of the Holy Spirit, as St. Paul (Ephesians 4:11, 12) and St. Peter (1 Peter 4:10) say, which were given to Christendom to advance the knowledge and the praise of God, a function which is carried out preeminently by the ministry of preaching the Gospel. For St. Paul says that these gifts exist "for the common good" of Christendom (1 Corinthians 12:7), which means that our preaching and confessing serve the purpose of bringing people to the knowledge of God so that He will be honored thereby. This is the reason why we are God's servants and are called priests. Whatever we do, our teaching and our life ought to shine like a beacon of light to the greater knowledge, honor, and praise of God, as Christ also says (Matthew 5:16). And St. Peter says (1 Peter 2:9): "But you are a chosen race, a royal priesthood, a holy nation, God's own people, that you may declare the wonderful deeds of Him who called you out of darkness into His marvelous light."

From *Commentary on Psalm 110* (Luther's Works 13:294–95)

September 28

Behold, angels came and were ministering to [Jesus].

MATTHEW 4:11

Feast of St. Michael and All Angels

his was written for our comfort, so that we would know how many angels serve us when one devil attacks us, if we fight valiantly. And if we stand firm, God does not let us suffer scarcity, but angels must first come from heaven and become our bakers, cellarers, and cooks and serve us in all our needs. This was not written for Christ's sake, for He does not need it. If the angels served Him, then they can and should serve us too.

From the *Church Postil*, sermon for Lent 1 on Matthew 4:1–11 (Luther's Works 76:374)

The prayer of a righteous person has great power as it is working. JAMES 5:16

What to Pray For

We usually press for small and trivial things and do not consider with what a great Majesty we are speaking when we pray. For if God wanted to give only small and trivial things, He would not have prescribed such a great and magnificent form of prayer (Matthew 6:9ff.): "Our Father who art in heaven, hallowed be Thy name. Thy kingdom come, etc." . . . He puts before us and offers us immense riches and the best gifts in heaven and on earth. These He wants us to ask for and to expect; for in every petition—"Hallowed be Thy name. Thy kingdom come. Thy will be done. Give us this day our daily bread, etc."—heaven and earth and everything that is in them are comprised. For what does it mean that His name is hallowed, that His kingdom comes, and that His will is done? It means to overthrow countless devils and to swallow the entire world with one prayer. But our courage is small, and our faith is weak. Therefore we should . . . learn how God is not content with a little, even though we ask for very little; but He gives more than we understand or have the courage to ask for (Ephesians 3:20).

From *Lectures on Genesis* (Luther's Works 4:364)

He fills you with the finest of the wheat. PSALM 147:14

God's Goodness

hen we see a whole field or one grain, we should recognize not only God's goodness but also His power and say to ourselves: "O lovely grain! God gives you to us in abundance out of His great goodness. And with what great power He protects you! What dangers have you not survived from the hour when you were sown until you are put on the table! With what mighty power has He not torn you from the devil's fingers and hands, which clutch and snatch to destroy you and starve us!" . . . A devout and believing heart understands well how useless all our plowing, sowing, and the like would be without the help of God's gifts. Although we are to do such work with diligence and seek our nourishment from the soil (Genesis 3:19), we are not to depend solely on this as though it could be done with our hands. More than our hands is necessary. God must bless and prosper it, and then mightily defend it against all devils.

From *Commentary on Psalm 147* (Luther's Works 14:122–23)

"Whoever feeds on My flesh and drinks My blood abides in Me, and I in him."

JOHN 6:56

These Great Things

 ou must not view these words with your physical eyes as you begin to discuss topics such as the conquest of death, devil, and hell, the forgiveness of sins, and eternal life. These demand other thoughts. . . . This doctrine of the flesh and blood of Christ is the power and the strength to rise from the dead. Therefore His flesh and blood must not be regarded as common flesh and blood but as endued with the power over all misery in heaven and on earth, namely, over sin, death, devil, world, and whatever else is cruel and terrifying. These great things are the concern of this flesh and blood.

From *Sermons on the Gospel of John*, Chapters 6–8 (Luther's Works 23:141)

"Look at the birds of the air: they neither sow nor reap nor gather into barns, and yet your heavenly Father feeds them. Are you not of more value than they?"

MATTHEW 6:26

You Can Trust God

hrist says: "Every day you see before your very eyes how the heavenly Father feeds the little birds in the field, without any concern on their part. Can you not trust Him to feed you as well, since He is your Father and calls you His children? Shall He not be concerned about you, whom He has made His children and to whom He gives His Word and all creatures, more than about the little birds, which are not His children but your servants? And yet He thinks enough of them to feed them every day, as if they were the only thing He is concerned about. And He enjoys it when they fly around and sing without a care in the world, as if they were saying: 'I sing and frolic, and yet I do not know of a single grain that I am to eat. My bread is not baked yet, and my grain is not planted yet. But I have a rich Master who takes care of me while I am singing or sleeping. He can give me more than all my worries and the worries of all people could ever accomplish.' " Now, since the birds have learned so well the art of trusting Him and of casting their cares from themselves upon God, we who are His children should do so even more.

From *The Sermon on the Mount* (Luther's Works 21:198)

Feed me with the food that is needful for me.

PROVERBS 30:8

Bearing Witness to God

hrist bears witness everywhere that He does the will of His Father, and He teaches others to do the same thing, as He says in John 4:34: "My food is to do the will of My Father." To cling to God is to be freed from the world and all creatures; to bear the image of Christ is to live according to the love and the example of Christ. "He who says that he loves God, and does not keep His commandments is a liar," says 1 John 2:4. But since these divine blessings are invisible, incomprehensible, and deeply hidden, nature cannot attain or love them unless it is lifted up through the grace of God. For the same reason it happens that the spiritual man can be judged, known, and seen by no one, not even by himself; for he remains in the deepest darkness of God. David learned this and bears witness to it when he says in Psalm 31:20: "Thou shalt hide them in the covert of Thy presence" (that is, in the covert which is before Thee). To be sure, this begins in this life; but it will be completed in the life to come. Therefore it is a great thing to be a Christian and to have one's life hidden . . . in the invisible God Himself, namely, to live amid the things of the world and to be nourished by what appears nowhere except by means of ordinary verbal indication and hearing alone, as Christ says in Matthew 4:4: "Man does not live by bread alone but by every word."

From *Lectures on Hebrews* (Luther's Works 29:216)

October 4

I called out to the LORD, *out of my distress,
and He answered me.* JONAH 2:2

God Hears and Answers

e must feel that our crying to God is of a nature that God will answer, that we may glory with Jonah in the knowledge that God answers us when we cry to Him in our necessity. That means nothing else but to cry to God with the heart's true voice of faith; for the head cannot be comforted, nor can we raise our hands in prayer, until the heart is consoled. . . . The heart finds solace when it hastens to the angry God with the aid of the Holy Spirit and seeks mercy amid the wrath, lets God punish and at the same time dares to find comfort in His goodness. Take note what sharp eyes the heart must have, for it is surrounded by nothing but tokens of God's anger and punishment and yet beholds and feels no punishment and anger but only kindness and grace; that is, the heart must be so disposed that it does not want to see and feel punishment and anger, though in reality it does see and feel them, and it must be determined to see and feel grace and goodness, even though these are completely hidden from view. Oh, what a difficult task it is to come to God. Penetrating to Him through His wrath, His punishment, and His displeasure is like making your way through a wall of thorns, yes, through nothing but spears and swords. The crying of faith must feel in its heart that it is making contact with God . . . .

From *Lectures on Jonah* (German text) (Luther's Works 19:73–74)

October 5

Mercy triumphs over judgment.

JAMES 2:13

Remain in the Kingdom

 remain in the kingdom of grace when I do not despair of God's mercy, no matter how great my sin may be, but resolutely pin mind and conscience to the belief that there is still grace and forgiveness for me, even if the wrath of God and that of all creatures would threaten to consume me and even if my conscience would bear out this wrath and say that the supply of mercy is exhausted and that God will not forgive me. That is elevating God's grace above everything else, praising and extolling it and with it defying all anger and judgment, joining in the words of the Epistle of James (2:13): "Mercy triumphs over judgment," that is, mercy asserts itself and proves stronger than all wrath and every sentence and judgment of God. And whoever believes that can therewith defy all the anger and every judgment of God. He who is unable to do that bids judgment to challenge grace. And grace must perish and judgment hold sway alone to produce death and damnation. Conversely, where grace defies judgment, judgment must vanish and grace alone prevail to produce eternal life and bliss.

From *Lectures on Jonah* (German text) (Luther's Works 19:47–48)

*But even if you should suffer for righteousness' sake,
you will be blessed. Have no fear of them, nor be
troubled, but in your hearts honor Christ the Lord
as holy, always being prepared to make a defense to
anyone who asks you for a reason for the hope that is
in you.* 1 PETER 3:14–15

Rely on Christ Alone

he world is defiant and courageous when its
moneybags and bins are full. Then there is such
pride and defiance that the devil could not get along
with a rich peasant. . . . One who has a little more power,
honor, knowledge, favor, money, or goods refuses to yield to
another person. But if we look at this aright, we find nothing
but a foolish or childish reliance, without any stability. . . .
Christians have nothing to rely on but Christ, their Lord and
God. They willingly surrender all things for His sake and say:
"Before I deny or forsake my Christ, I will bid farewell to
neck and belly, honor and goods, house and home, wife and
child, and everything!" Therefore this courage cannot be a
sham or a delusion; it must be genuine and real. Its comfort
is not rooted in earth's temporal or transient things, for the
sake of which it would be willing to suffer this. No, it pins its
hopes solely on the Lord Christ, who was crucified and died
for us. . . . Whatever a Christian does and suffers in faith in
the Lord Christ is absolute truth, proper, and right; and he

October 7

can boast truthfully and joyfully that it is approved by God and all the angels. A Christian is sure of his position and fears neither the devil nor the world; neither is he intimidated by any threat or terror.

From *Sermons on the Gospel of John*, Chapters 14–16 (Luther's Works 24:118–19)

Let no one pass judgment on you . . . . Let no one
disqualify you.
COLOSSIANS 2:16, 18

Keep the Goal in Sight

 ow you can see, I think, what the correct gloss on St. Paul is and what he is teaching when he says to the Colossians in the second chapter: "Therefore, let no one pass judgment on you . . . ." Have these people not disgracefully "diverted us from our goal" [Colossians 2:18]? We were forced to do nothing but run astray in vain, with so much singing, praying, fasting, keeping vigil, and working. They set no other goal for these works than to attain grace and life through them. By doing so, they caused us to lose sight of Christ, who alone was and is the right goal, in whom through true faith we are meant to win the race and obtain such grace and life, making use of the works mentioned above to chastise our flesh so that we become fit to serve our neighbor. Without this faith, such works do nothing but create "puffed-up hearts," as St. Paul says here.

From Luther's afterword to *The Papacy with Its Members* (Luther's Works 59:147–48)

"Whoever receives you receives Me, and whoever receives Me receives Him who sent Me."

MATTHEW 10:40

This Is God's Kingdom

et us not think that heaven is closed, except to cows and pigs, that is, to creatures of the flesh. But where Christ is, there heaven stands open. We know that Christ baptizes, administers the Sacraments, and absolves, so that we Christians might have cause to live chaste and holy lives, for heaven is open, the Holy Trinity is all around us, the angels sing as they did on Christmas night, etc. But even if God abandons us and we suffer persecution, God is still with us, for this happens so that you might retain your faith that God is looking after you, whether you believe it or not. If you are a Christian, heaven and earth must pass away before anyone harms a hair of your head. "Who touches you, touches the apple of My eye" [Zechariah 2:8]. "Whoever receives you, receives Me" [Matthew 10:40]. But faith is required here. We do not see that Christ baptizes, the Father absolves, the Holy Spirit hovers above us, or that He is not only in heaven but also stands in the Jordan. But I say this to Christians, who must have this knowledge. This is God's kingdom where Christ rules inwardly, God speaks to us without ceasing, and the Holy Spirit hovers above us.

From *Sermon for Epiphany 1 on Matthew 3:13–17* (Luther's Works 58:74)

October 9

*"If I do not go away, the Helper will not come to you.
But if I go, I will send Him to you."*

Jᴏʜɴ 16:7

Our Comfort and Joy

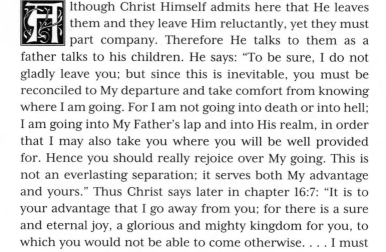

lthough Christ Himself admits here that He leaves them and they leave Him reluctantly, yet they must part company. Therefore He talks to them as a father talks to his children. He says: "To be sure, I do not gladly leave you; but since this is inevitable, you must be reconciled to My departure and take comfort from knowing where I am going. For I am not going into death or into hell; I am going into My Father's lap and into His realm, in order that I may also take you where you will be well provided for. Hence you should really rejoice over My going. This is not an everlasting separation; it serves both My advantage and yours." Thus Christ says later in chapter 16:7: "It is to your advantage that I go away from you; for there is a sure and eternal joy, a glorious and mighty kingdom for you, to which you would not be able to come otherwise. . . . I must be crucified and then glorified, in order that the Holy Spirit may be sent and it may become known that I have been placed at the right hand of My Father and have occupied My kingdom. This should be your comfort and joy.

From *Sermons on the Gospel of John*, Chapters 14–16 (Luther's Works 24:186–87)

"All things have been handed over to Me by My Father,
and no one knows the Son except the Father, and no
one knows the Father except the Son and anyone to
whom the Son chooses to reveal Him." MATTHEW 11:27

True God and True Man

 e who says "all things" leaves nothing as an exception. Therefore, He is the true God. What is in Psalm 8:6 agrees with this: "You have put all things under His feet." On the other hand, the fact that He says "have been handed over" means that He truly is a man, since He has received from the Father. For neither would God hand over all things to one who was merely a human being nor would one who was merely God receive anything from anyone, for neither can a mere human being be above all things nor can one who is merely God be below God. Therefore, in this one person true God and man come together.

From *Annotations on Matthew* (Luther's Works 67:139)

From among your own selves will arise men speaking
twisted things, to draw away the disciples after them.
Therefore be alert . . . . Acts 20:30–31

The Active Word of God

f there were no such sects through which the devil awakened us, we would become too lazy and would sleep and snore ourselves to death. Further, both faith and the Word would become dull and rusty among us until everything were destroyed. But instead such sects are our whetting stone and burnisher that sharpen and hone our faith and doctrine, so that they shine bright and pure like a mirror; and [we] also become acquainted thereby with the devil and his intentions and become ready and skilled for battle against him. . . . In the second place, the Word itself will also in this way be brought to light before the world all the better and more brightly, so that many, who would not otherwise come to it, will learn of the truth through such controversy, or else will be strengthened in it. For the Word of God is an active thing [Hebrews 4:12], and so God gives it its work to do, hanging and harrowing both the world and the devil upon it, that His power and might may be revealed and the lies be put to shame.

From Luther's preface to Justus Menius, *The Doctrine and Secret of the Anabaptists* (Luther's Works 59:268)

October 12

We were buried therefore with Him by Baptism into death, in order that, just as Christ was raised from the dead by the glory of the Father, we too might walk in newness of life. ROMANS 6:4

Baptismal Gifts

aptism, then, signifies two things—death and resurrection, that is, full and complete justification. When the minister immerses the child in the water it signifies death, and when he draws it forth again it signifies life. . . . This death and resurrection we call the new creation, regeneration, and spiritual birth. This should not be understood only allegorically as the death of sin and the life of grace, as many understand it, but as actual death and resurrection. For baptism is not a false sign. Neither does sin completely die, nor grace completely rise, until the sinful body that we carry about in this life is destroyed, as the apostle says in the same passage [Romans 6:6–7]. For as long as we are in the flesh, the desires of the flesh stir and are stirred. For this reason, as soon as we begin to believe, we also begin to die to this world and live to God in the life to come; so that faith is truly a death and a resurrection, that is, it is that spiritual Baptism into which we are submerged and from which we rise.

From *Babylonian Captivity of the Church* (Luther's Works 36:67–68)

"But a Samaritan, as he journeyed, came to where he was, and when he saw him, he had compassion."

The Good Neighbor

ou do not need to ask what outward works you should do; look at your neighbor, and you will find [enough] to do even if there were a thousand of you! Only do not mislead yourself into thinking that you will reach heaven by praying and going to church, by [contributing to] endowments and memorials, if you pass your neighbor by on the other side [Luke 10:31–32]. If you pass him by here, then he will lie in your way there, so that you again must pass him by in front of the gates of heaven, just like the rich man who left Lazarus lying at his door [Luke 16:20].

From the *Church Postil*, sermon for Christmas Day on Titus 2:11–15 (Luther's Works 75:196)

For all have sinned and fall short of the glory of God.

ROMANS 3:23

We Are All Alike

No one can exclude himself or boast that he is better than another. All are alike before God, and all must admit that they are guilty and deserving of eternal death and damnation. In fact, all would have to remain in this state forever, without help from any creature, if God were to deal with us according to our deserts and His justice. In His boundless goodness He had compassion on us wretched beings and had to send His dear Son from heaven to relieve and help us, to take our sin and damnation upon Himself, and to make payment and reconcile God to us by sacrificing His body and blood. And God commanded that this be proclaimed throughout the world and that this Christ be made known to all men, that they should cling to Him in faith if they were to be free from sin, God's wrath, and eternal damnation, and to come into the kingdom of God, redeemed and reconciled. Thus this proclamation accomplishes two things. In the first place, it confronts all people with the fact that they are all under sin and God's wrath, and are condemned by the Law; and it demands that we acknowledge this. In the second place, it shows how we can be delivered from this and can obtain mercy from God, namely, only by accepting Christ in faith.

From *Sermons on the Gospel of John*, Chapters 14–16 (Luther's Works 24:342–43)

October 15

"Strive to enter through the narrow door. For many,
I tell you, will seek to enter and will not be able."

LUKE 13:24

The Narrow Door

 ell, why not? Because they do not know what the narrow door is. It is faith, which makes a person small, even nothing, so that he must despair of all his works and only cling to God's grace, abandoning everything for that. But the Cain-saints think that good works are the narrow door. For that reason they do not become small, they do not despair of their [works], but rather gather them together in big bags, hang them around [their necks], and want to go through [that door]. And they will go through, just like a camel with its large hump can go through the eye of a needle [see Matthew 19:24; Mark 10:25; Luke 18:25].

From the *Church Postil*, sermon for the Sunday after Christmas on Galatians 4:1–7 (Luther's Works 75:367)

Can wicked rulers be allied with You, those who frame injustice by statute? PSALM 94:20

No Compromise

Now, we have some smart alecks who want to patch things up, to remove the issue, and to mediate the quarrel by suggesting that both sides ought to yield. We shall let them try to do what they can. They are welcome to their efforts. But if they succeed, they will be the first to make the devil become godly and agree with Christ. For my part, I think that kind of patchwork is the same as trying to glue potsherds together, as Jesus Sirach also says (Ecclesiasticus 22:7). There have been a lot of cobblers at this business; but they have worked in vain, losing both the thread and the stitch. In matters where we may dispose, regarding ceremonies or other such external things, let us conciliate and patch whatever we can. But Christ wants no improvement or patching of matters concerning the faith of His kingdom, which would result in bending and twisting His scepter. Anyone who attempts to do this will only make things worse and lose the scepter. Like a ruler or a measure, this scepter must remain undamaged and straight, without breaks or gaps, as a guide to how a man should believe and live.

From *Commentary on Psalm 110* (Luther's Works 13:277)

October 17

In the hand of the LORD *there is a cup with foaming*
wine, well mixed, and He pours out from it.

PSALM 75:8

Lean Not on Your Understanding

 ll who want to study in the Bible and sacred letters should with extreme diligence take note of this verse for themselves: *In the hand of the Lord there is a cup of pure wine* (Psalm 75:8). That is to say, Scripture is not in our power nor in the ability of our mind. Therefore in its study we must in no way rely on our understanding, but we must become humble and pray that He may bring that understanding to us, since it is not given except to those who are bowed down and humble. . . . For God can remove Scripture or its meaning from those who do not know and do not pay attention and think that they still have it. . . . Thus it happens to all the proud and stubborn who rely on their own puffed-up idea that God tips the truth and the pure wine away from them toward others and leaves them the dregs, as long as they are ignorant. . . . The pure truth cannot stand at the same time with the pride of the heart.

From *First Lectures on the Psalms* (Luther's Works 10:461–62)

October 18

"My yoke is easy, and My burden is light."

MATTHEW 11:30

Christians Can Bear Everything

hatever there is of cross or suffering to be borne later on is easily sustained. The yoke that Christ lays upon us is sweet, and His burden is light (Matthew 11:30). When sin has been forgiven and the conscience has been liberated from the burden and the sting of sin, then a Christian can bear everything easily. Because everything within is sweet and pleasant, he willingly does and suffers everything. But when a man goes along in his own righteousness, then whatever he does and suffers is painful and tedious for him, because he is doing it unwillingly.

From *Lectures on Galatians* (1535) (Luther's Works 26:133)

October 19

*"Unless one is born of water and the Spirit,
he cannot enter the kingdom of God."* JOHN 3:5

Born of God

his birth is different from the one which occurs among men through the instrumentality of father and mother. Of course, when a man is born in the natural way, it is God's work too . . . . But since no human being can contribute anything to the birth of Christians, it must be, as we read in John 1:13, "not of blood nor of the will of the flesh nor of the will of man, but of God." . . . Christians are "born of God," through a new and heavenly birth, namely, of water and the Holy Spirit (John 3:5). . . . It is like the dew of heaven, which fructifies the earth, and the wind, which cools it. No one sees or experiences the dew or knows how and out of what it is made until the droplets lie on the earth, just as no one knows or feels whence the wind comes or where it goes, except that one hears it howl or blow. Thus it also happens in the case of a divine birth from water and the Spirit. You can see the water of Baptism as you can see the dew, and you can hear the external or spoken Word as you can hear the wind; but you cannot see or hear or understand the Spirit, or what He accomplishes thereby: that a human being is cleansed in Baptism and becomes a saint in the hands of the priest, so that from a child of hell he is changed into a child of God.

From *Commentary on Psalm 110* (Luther's Works 13:302–3)

October 20

Consider Him who endured from sinners such
hostility against Himself, so that you may not grow
weary or fainthearted.

HEBREWS 12:3

Christ's Kind Heart

 ress on through to look at [Christ's] kind heart, how it is full of love toward you, love which compels Him to the difficult task of carrying your conscience and your sin. In that way your heart delights in Him, and the confidence of your faith is strengthened. . . . When your heart has thus been established in Christ, and you have become an enemy of sin out of love and not out of fear of pain, then the suffering of Christ should further be an example for your whole life, and you should reflect on [that suffering] in a different way. . . . Christ's suffering must be dealt with not in words and pretense, but in our lives and in truth. Thus St. Paul admonishes us: "Consider Him who endured from sinners such opposition against Himself, so that you may not grow weary and faint in your minds" (Hebrews 12:3). St. Peter [writes]: "As Christ suffered in the flesh, arm yourselves with the same way of thinking" [1 Peter 4:1].

From *Meditation on the Holy Suffering of Christ* (Luther's Works 76:431–32)

October 21

When the fullness of time had come, God sent forth
His Son, born of woman, born under the law, to
redeem those who were under the law, so that we
might receive adoption as sons. GALATIANS 4:4–5

Christ for Us

 ee what superabundant riches Christian faith has!
All these works and the suffering of Christ are given
to [the Christian] to become his own, so that he may
rely on them as if he had done them himself and they were
his own. As was said, Christ did them not for Himself, but for
us. He had no need of them, but amassed the treasure for us,
so that we can cling to it, believe it, and possess it. Moreover,
such faith brings with it the Holy Spirit. What more should
God do? How could a heart refrain from being free, joyous,
eager, and willing in God and Christ?

From the *Church Postil*, sermon for the Sunday after Christmas on
Galatians 4:1–7 (Luther's Works 75:390)

And the peace of God, which surpasses all
understanding, will guard your hearts and your minds
in Christ Jesus.

PHILIPPIANS 4:7

The Peace That Comes from God

his peace of God is not to be understood as that peace in which God is quiet and content with Himself, but rather as that [peace] which He puts into our hearts so that we are content . . . . Reason knows of no peace except that [which comes] when evil ceases. . . . But those who rejoice in God are satisfied that they have peace with God. They remain bold in affliction, do not desire the peace that reason chooses, namely, the cessation of evil. Rather, they stand firm and await inner strength through faith. They do not ask whether the evil will be and remain short or long, temporal or eternal—they also do not think or care how it will end—but they let God be in charge. . . . This is the peace of the cross, the peace of God, the peace of conscience, Christian peace, which makes a person outwardly calm, satisfied with everyone, and upset about no one. . . . It is the work of God, with which no one is familiar except the person who has experienced it.

From the *Church Postil*, sermon for Advent 4 on Philippians 4:4–7
(Luther's Works 75:169–70)

We appeal to you not to receive the grace of God

in vain.

2 CORINTHIANS 6:1

Do Not Despair

 t is also a source of great comfort to us to see that even the greatest and best saints sin grievously against God and that we are not the only poor, miserable sinners. We observe that they, too, were human, that they had flesh and blood as we do, and now we, too, must not despair, even though we fall into sin. If only we do not defect from the kingdom of grace through false doctrine and superstition! . . . I remain the kingdom of grace when I do not despair of God's mercy . . . .

From *Lectures on Jonah* (Luther's Works 19:47)

"Do not give dogs what is holy, and do not throw your pearls before pigs." MATTHEW 7:6

Preserve the Gospel

he Gospel has to be a doormat for everybody, and the whole world walks all over it and tramples it underfoot, along with its preachers and pupils. Now, what are we going to do about it? "Do not throw it," Christ says, "before swine and dogs." "Yes, dear Lord, but they already have it. Since the proclamation is in public and is broadcast into the world, we cannot keep them from coming across the Gospel and taking it for themselves." But this still does not mean that they have it, and, thank God, we can keep them from getting at what is holy. They may perhaps get the shells and the husks, that is, the freedom of the flesh. But all of them—dogs or swine, bigwigs or misers or peasants—shall be prevented from getting a single letter of the Gospel, though they may read all the books and listen to all the sermons and get the idea that they know it thoroughly. . . . Anyone who has the Gospel correctly must certainly agree with us and be one with us, insofar as we are already sure that what we have is the true Gospel and the pearls. Certainly he will not trample us underfoot the way Squire Bigwig does, or condemn us the way the sectarians do, or despise us the way the peasants do in the cities and towns. He will hold in esteem both the clear Word and those who preach it and gladly listen to it.

From *The Sermon on the Mount* (Luther's Works 21:225)

In the day of my trouble I seek the LORD.

PSALM 77:2

The Habit of Prayer

etting ourselves to the point of praying causes us distress and anguish, and this requires the greatest skill. With our own concerns and thoughts we torture ourselves and stew over trying to pull this off our neck and to get rid of it. There is an evil and clever devil riding me and other people and frequently playing these tricks on me in my temptation or anxiety, whether it has to do with spiritual or with secular affairs. He immediately butts in and makes you start stewing over it. In this way he snatches us from our prayer and makes us so dizzy that we do not even think of praying. By the time you begin praying you have already tortured yourself half to death. He is well aware of what prayer achieves and can do. That is why he creates so many obstacles and disturbances, to keep you from getting around to it at all. Hence we ought to learn to take these words to heart. We should develop the habit, whenever we see anguish or need, to fall on our knees immediately and to spread the need before God, on the basis of this admonition and promise. Then we would find help and would not have to torture ourselves with our own ideas about looking for help. This is a very precious medicine, one that certainly helps and never fails, if you will only use it.

From *The Sermon on the Mount* (Luther's Works 21:232)

He saved us, not because of works done by us in righteousness, but according to His own mercy. TITUS 3:5

Daily Sin Means Daily Repentance

n this life on earth it is impossible for us to live without any sin and defect (even if we have already received grace and the Holy Spirit) because of our sinful, corrupt flesh and blood. This does not cease to be active in evil lusts and desires against God's Commandments until the grave, even in the saints, even though, after they have received grace, they refrain from and guard against sin and oppose the evil lusts, as repentance requires. Therefore, they also still daily need forgiveness, just as they also daily repent because of those remaining defects and weaknesses. They recognize that their life and works are still sinful and would merit God's wrath, if they were not forgiven and covered for Christ's sake. For that reason Christ has established His kingdom on earth which should be called an eternal kingdom of grace and always remain under the forgiveness of sins. Upon those who believe it, it is so powerful that, even though sin is still stuck and so deeply rooted in their flesh and blood that it cannot at all be swept out in this life, nevertheless it shall do no harm but shall be forgiven and not imputed, as long as we remain in the faith and daily work at suppressing the remaining evil lusts until they are entirely blotted out through death and decay in the grave with this old maggot sack, so that the man may rise completely new and pure to eternal life.

From the *Church Postil*, sermon for Easter Tuesday on Luke 24:36–47 (Luther's Works 77:98–99)

October 27

*[Abraham] did not weaken in faith when he
considered his own body, which was as good as dead
(since he was about a hundred years old), or when he
considered the barrenness of Sarah's womb.*

ROMANS 4:19

Faith Wins

 hus Abraham killed [reason] by faith in the Word of God, in which offspring was promised to him from Sarah, who was barren and past childbearing. Reason did not immediately assent to this Word in Abraham. Surely it fought against faith in him and regarded it as something ridiculous, absurd, and impossible that Sarah, who was not only ninety years old now but was also barren by nature, should give birth to a son. Faith certainly had this struggle with reason in Abraham. But faith won the victory in him; it killed and sacrificed God's bitterest and most harmful enemy. Thus all devout people enter with Abraham into the darkness of faith, kill reason, and say: "Reason, you are foolish. You do not understand the things that belong to God (Matthew 16:23). Therefore do not speak against me, but keep quiet. Do not judge; but listen to the Word of God, and believe it."

From *Lectures on Galatians* (1535) (Luther's Works 26:228)

For from Him and through Him and to Him are all
things. To Him be glory forever. Amen.

ROMANS 11:36

In Him We Live

 hy would we want to boast (Paul means to say) when "all things" that have being—obviously also all our wisdom and abilities—derive not from themselves, but they both have their beginning from Him, are preserved through Him, and must continue in Him? He says, "In Him we live and move and have our being" (Acts 17:28). Likewise: "He has made us, and not we ourselves" (Psalm 100:3). That is, what we are and can do, that we live and have peace and protection—in short, whatever good or evil happens to us—happens not by chance and accidentally, but everything comes from and through His divine counsel and good-pleasure. He cares for us as for His people and sheep; He rules us, gives us good things, helps us in danger, preserves us, etc. Therefore, all glory and praise are due to Him alone before all creatures.

From the *Church Postil*, sermon for Trinity on Romans 11:33–36
(Luther's Works 78:15)

October 29

Then they sweep by like the wind and go on, guilty men, whose own might is their god!" HABAKKUK 1:11

Scattered Like Dust

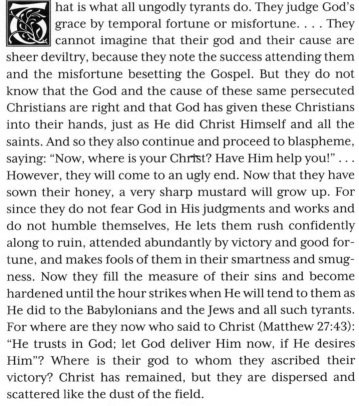 hat is what all ungodly tyrants do. They judge God's grace by temporal fortune or misfortune. . . . They cannot imagine that their god and their cause are sheer deviltry, because they note the success attending them and the misfortune besetting the Gospel. But they do not know that the God and the cause of these same persecuted Christians are right and that God has given these Christians into their hands, just as He did Christ Himself and all the saints. And so they also continue and proceed to blaspheme, saying: "Now, where is your Christ? Have Him help you!" . . . However, they will come to an ugly end. Now that they have sown their honey, a very sharp mustard will grow up. For since they do not fear God in His judgments and works and do not humble themselves, He lets them rush confidently along to ruin, attended abundantly by victory and good fortune, and makes fools of them in their smartness and smugness. Now they fill the measure of their sins and become hardened until the hour strikes when He will tend to them as He did to the Babylonians and the Jews and all such tyrants. For where are they now who said to Christ (Matthew 27:43): "He trusts in God; let God deliver Him now, if He desires Him"? Where is their god to whom they ascribed their victory? Christ has remained, but they are dispersed and scattered like the dust of the field.

From *Lectures on Habakkuk* (German text) (Luther's Works 19:176–77)

October 30

For we hold that one is justified by faith apart
from works of the law. ROMANS 3:28

Reformation Day

hrough faith in Christ, therefore, Christ's righteousness becomes our righteousness and all that He has becomes ours; rather, He Himself becomes ours. Therefore the apostle calls it "the righteousness of God" in Romans 1:17: For in the Gospel "the righteousness of God is revealed . . . as it is written, 'The righteous shall live by his faith.' " Finally, in the same Epistle, chapter 3:28, such a faith is called "the righteousness of God": "We hold that a man is justified by faith." This is an infinite righteousness, and one that swallows up all sins in a moment, for it is impossible that sin should exist in Christ. On the contrary, he who trusts in Christ exists in Christ; he is one with Christ, having the same righteousness as He. It is therefore impossible that sin should remain in him. This righteousness is primary; it is the basis, the cause, the source of all our own actual righteousness. For this is the righteousness given in place of the original righteousness lost in Adam. It accomplishes the same as that original righteousness would have accomplished; rather, it accomplishes more. It is in this sense that we are to understand the prayer in . . . [Psalm 31:1]: "In Thee, O Lord, do I seek refuge; let me never be put to shame; in Thy righteousness deliver me."

From *Two Kinds of Righteousness* (Luther's Works 31:298–99)

October 31

And the ransomed of the Lord *shall return and come
to Zion with singing; everlasting joy shall be upon their
heads; they shall obtain gladness and joy, and sorrow
and sighing shall flee away.* Isaiah 35:10

All Saints' Day

 t is stated in Luke 2:9 that when the angel came to the
shepherds, the brightness of the Lord shone round
about them. Such was also Christ's countenance
on Mt. Tabor (Matthew 17:2). Such will be our countenance
when on the Last Day we are raised for the glory which
Christ has gained for us. . . . Our faces will shine like the
sun at noon; no longer will there be those familiar wrinkles,
the contracted brow, and the watery eyes. But, as it is stated
in Revelation 21:4: "The Lord will wipe away all tears from
our eyes, so that no death, no sorrow, no laments, or any
hardships remain." Let us hold fast to this hope, and let us
live in the fear of God until, set free from this life fraught
with misery, we shall live that angelic and eternal life. Amen,
Amen.

From *Lectures on Genesis* (Luther's Works 1:236)

Consider the ancient generations and see:
who trusted in the Lord and was put to shame?

ECCLESIASTES 2:10

Weaknesses of the Saints

t is salutary for us to hear of the weaknesses of the saints, for these examples of weakness are more necessary for us and bring more consolation than the examples of that heroic and very great fortitude and other virtues. Thus the fact that David killed Goliath, a bear, a lion, etc., does not edify me much. For I cannot imitate such things, since they surpass my strength and all my thinking. Although they commend the saints in their strength and heroic fortitude, they do not concern us; for they are too sublime for us to be able to match or imitate them. But when examples of weakness, sins, trepidation, and trials are set forth in the saints—as when I read David's complaints, sobs, fears, and feelings of despair—they buoy me up in a wonderful manner and give great consolation. For I see how they, fearful and terrified though they were, did not perish but buoyed themselves up with the promises they had received; and from this I conclude that there is no need for me to despair either. . . . They are finally preserved and sustained by the Word.

From *Lectures on Genesis* (Luther's Works 5:254)

November 2

Oh give thanks to the LORD; *call upon His name;*
make known His deeds among the peoples!

PSALM 105:1

Honor God's Name

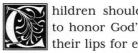hildren should be constantly urged and moved to honor God's name and to have it always upon their lips for everything that may happen to them or come to their notice [Psalm 8:2; 34:1; Matthew 21:16; Hebrews 13:15]. For that is the true honor of His name, to look to it and call upon it for all consolation [Psalm 66:2; 105:1]. Then—as we have heard in the First Commandment—the heart by faith gives God the honor due Him first. Afterward, the lips give Him honor by confession. This is also a blessed and useful habit and very effective against the devil. He is ever around us and lies in wait to bring us into sin and shame, disaster and trouble [2 Timothy 2:26]. But he hates to hear God's name and cannot remain long where it is spoken and called upon from the heart. . . . To confuse the devil, I say, we should always have this holy name in our mouth, so that the devil may not be able to injure us as he wishes.

From the *Large Catechism* (*Concordia*, p. 366)

Better is the little that the righteous has than the
abundance of many wicked.

PSALM 37:16

Treasures in Heaven

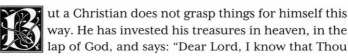ut a Christian does not grasp things for himself this way. He has invested his treasures in heaven, in the lap of God, and says: "Dear Lord, I know that Thou hast more. Thou hast more than it would ever be possible for Thee to distribute. With Thee I shall never suffer want, for if necessary, the heavens will have to rain down guldens. Be Thou my coffer and cellar and loft. In Thee I have my treasure. If I have Thee, I have enough." These are real Christians. . . . If we only could believe, there would be no want. Our Lord God is a good Goldsmith who can turn one gulden into more than a hundred thousand. It does not depend on cash reserves, and he who has an unbelieving heart will not get as far with a thousand guldens as he who trusts God will get with one gulden.

From *Commentary on Psalm 112* (Luther's Works 13:400–401)

"Behold, the days are coming, declares the LORD,
when I will raise up for David a righteous Branch,
and He shall reign as king and deal wisely, and shall
execute justice and righteousness in the land."

JEREMIAH 23:5

"The LORD *your God will raise up for you a prophet*
like me from among you, from your brothers—it is to
him you shall listen."

DEUTERONOMY 18:15

Two Ministries of the Word

 e have these two ministries of the Word which are necessary for the salvation of the human race: the ministry of the Law and the ministry of the Gospel, one for death and the other for life. They are indeed alike if you are looking at their authority, but most unlike if you are thinking about their fruit. The ministry of Moses is temporary, finally to be ended by the coming of the ministry of Christ, as he says here, "Heed Him." But the ministry of Christ will be ended by nothing else, since it brings eternal righteousness and "puts an end to sin," as it is said in Daniel 9:24.

From *Lectures on Deuteronomy* (Luther's Works 9:178)

November 5

"You shall not covet your neighbor's house; you shall not covet your neighbor's wife, or his male servant, or his female servant, or his ox, or his donkey, or anything that is your neighbor's." EXODUS 20:17

You Shall Not Covet

n whatever way such things happen, we must know that God does not want you to deprive your neighbor of anything that belongs to him, so that he suffer the loss and you gratify your greed with it. This is true even if you could keep it honorably before the world. . . . If it is not called stealing and cheating, it is still called coveting your neighbor's property, that is, aiming at possession of it, luring it away from him without his consent, and being unwilling to see him enjoy what God has granted him. . . . But we must gladly wish and leave him with what he has. Also, we must advance and preserve for him what may be for his profit and service, just as we wish to be treated [Matthew 7:12]. So these commandments are especially directed against envy and miserable greed. God wants to remove all causes and sources from which arises everything by which we harm our neighbor. Therefore, He expressed it in plain words, "You shall not covet," and so on. For He especially wants us to have a pure heart [Matthew 5:8] . . . .

From the *Large Catechism* (*Concordia*, pp. 394–95)

Take Refuge in the Lord

 his, too, is a word overflowing with comfort—that the Lord knows His people, that He keeps an eye on them, protects and watches over them, that they are His concern, as David says in the psalm (Psalm 121:4): "Behold, He who keeps Israel will neither slumber nor sleep." What greater comfort can one have in every adversity, every temptation, both temporal and spiritual, than that the Lord keeps an eye on him, that he is the Lord's concern? A conviction of this character overcomes sin, death, hell, and every temptation. We, then, must have this sort of conviction in temptation, no matter how great it may be, so that we may have a conviction of glory in the greatest dishonor, a conviction of fullness in the midst of hunger, a conviction of life in the greatest despair over all things, etc. This is what Psalm 1:6 says: "The Lord knows the way of the righteous."

From *Lectures on Nahum* (Luther's Works 18:288–89)

[Christ] Himself bore our sins in His body on the tree,
that we might die to sin and live to righteousness.
By His wounds you have been healed.

1 PETER 2:24

Christ Comes in Our Place

o Christ is now crucified and hangs on the cross as the worst thief, scoundrel, rebel, and murderer who has ever been on earth; and the innocent Lamb, Christ, must bear and pay for someone else's guilt. For it applies to us; those are our sins that burden His neck. We are this kind of sinners, thieves, scoundrels, rebels, and murderers; for even if we are not all so coarse as to carry them out in deed, we are still guilty of them before God. But now Christ comes in our place and bears our sins and pays for them so that through Him we are delivered. For if we believe in Him, not only will those of us who avoid gross outward sin be saved through Christ, but also those who fall into gross outward sin will be saved if they genuinely repent and believe in Christ. For many murderers are saved, as the histories of the Passion demonstrate when the malefactor on the right is converted and saved [Luke 23:39–43].

From *Sermons on the Gospel of John*, Chapters 17–20 (Luther's Works 69:256)

She said to herself, "If I only touch His garment,
I will be made well."

MATTHEW 9:21

Faith That Heals

 er faith was so strong that she believed she could obtain help, if only she could touch His garment. She did not deem it necessary to come to Him and with many words present her complaint and pray that He would have mercy on her and help her, nor did others pray for her; but she sought only to reach Him and touch Him, for she thought, if only she could do this, she would receive help. She neither doubted His power, nor His willingness to help. . . . Nor did her faith deceive her, for as soon as she touched the hem of His garment, the fountain of blood was stopped. . . . Hence you may see what faith, which clings to the person of Christ is and does, namely, a heart that regards Him as the Lord and Savior, the Son of God, through whom God reveals Himself and bestows upon us His grace, assuring us that through Him and for His sake, he will hear and help us.

From the *Church Postil*, sermon for Trinity 24 on Matthew 9:18–26 (Luther's Works 79 (Lenker) 5:349–50)

November 9

For when one says, "I follow Paul," and another,
"I follow Apollos," are you not being merely human?
What then is Apollos? What is Paul? Servants through
whom you believed. 1 CORINTHIANS 3:4–5

Faithful Teachers

our teachers should be content with the common honor of being a faithful teacher of God, teaching and baptizing rightly. What is the emperor or the king of France, even if he makes you a prince? He does not promise or give the remission of sins. But the office of Christ and [His] stewardship [do these things]. If [one minister has] a better voice [than another], nevertheless he does not [have] another Gospel to teach or another Baptism to administer. Every Christian ought to know this. For this reason there should be no division among the ministers. Therefore, Peter does not set himself above Paul. Neither does Paul do this. Neither should you. Afterward he says: "What is Peter? [What is] Paul? Stewards of Christ, through whom you believed [see 1 Corinthians 3:5]. Christ sent [them] out as His ministers, and they are discharging the office through which you are saved. All things are yours," [Paul says, "whether] Peter or Paul, through whom you believed and are saved; and you are Christ's. We are not your lords. [And] Christ is God the Father's" [1 Corinthians 3:21–23]. It is a magnificent sermon against sectarianism and schism.

From *Sermon for Advent 3 on 1 Corinthians 4:1–5* (Luther's Works 58:344)

Who is like the LORD our God, who is seated on high,
who looks far down on the heavens and the earth?

PSALM 113:5–6

Who Is Like the Lord?

 or since [God] is the Most High, and there is nothing above Him, He cannot look above Him; nor yet to either side, for there is none like Him. He must needs, therefore, look within Him and beneath Him; and the farther one is beneath Him, the better does He see him. The eyes of the world and of men, on the contrary, look only above them and are lifted up with pride, as it is said in Proverbs 30:13: "There is a people whose eyes are lofty, and their eyelids lifted up on high." This we experience every day. Everyone strives after that which is above him, after honor, power, wealth, knowledge, a life of ease, and whatever is lofty and great. And where such people are, there are many hangers-on; all the world gathers round them, gladly yields them service, and would be at their side and share in their exaltation. . . . On the other hand, no one is willing to look into the depths with their poverty, disgrace, squalor, misery, and anguish. From these all turn away their eyes. Where there are such people, everyone takes to his heels, forsakes and shuns and leaves them to themselves; no one dreams of helping them or of making something out of them. And so they must remain in the depths and in their low and despised condition. There is among men no creator

November 11

who would make something out of nothing . . . . Therefore to God alone belongs that sort of seeing that looks into the depths with their need and misery, and is near to all that are in the depths.

From *The Magnificat* (Luther's Works 21:299–300)

We are treated as . . . dying, and behold, we live.

2 CORINTHIANS 6:8–9

When Weakness Ends

He lets the godly become powerless and to be brought low, until everyone supposes their end is near, whereas in these very things He is present to them with all His power, yet so hidden and in secret that even those who suffer the oppression do not feel it but only believe. There is the fullness of God's power and His outstretched arm. For where man's strength ends, God's strength begins, provided faith is present and waits on Him. And when the oppression comes to an end, it becomes manifest what great strength was hidden underneath the weakness. Even so, Christ was powerless on the cross; and yet there He performed His mightiest work and conquered sin, death, world, hell, devil, and all evil. Thus all the martyrs were strong and overcame. Thus, too, all who suffer and are oppressed overcome. Therefore it is said in Joel 3:10: "Let the weak say, 'I am strong' "—yet in faith, and without feeling it until it is accomplished.

From *The Magnificat* (Luther's Works 21:340)

*Even if we or an angel from heaven should preach
to you a Gospel contrary to the one we preached
to you, let him be accursed.*

GALATIANS 1:8

Boast in the Gospel

 thank God that I cannot boast of my great knowledge, of my holiness, or of my life; for my life has been such that I dare not glory, and I have been a blasphemer. This is my boast—and, please God, let it strike emperor, pope, bishops, universities, doctors, or all the angels—that I am proud and stubborn in glorying in the Gospel. This I will not surrender, as St. Paul also says in Galatians 1:8: "Let anyone who preaches another Gospel than that which I have preached be accursed." This sounds haughty enough; he inflexibly defies all angels and men in heaven and on earth. This is the arrogance I must have, and no one shall keep me from it. It would be good if I could be unyielding and proud enough in this matter; for here I do not rest on myself but on One who is called Christ, in whose name I am baptized.

From *Sermons on the Gospel of John*, Chapters 6–8 (Luther's Works 23:329)

Now therefore, O kings, be wise; be warned, O rulers of the earth. Serve the LORD *with fear, and rejoice with trembling.* PSALM 2:10–11

Prayer for Protection

We see in the sacred histories, as well in all the histories of the Gentiles, how many and various are the stratagems and tricks through which the devil has always sought to rule at the courts of kings and princes (for he sees that from them issues the greatest and most wholesome benefits for the church and state), and striven to overturn everything. Thus, unless this prayer surrounds and encloses a prince—"May the name of the God of Jacob protect you; may He send you help from the sanctuary and give you support from Zion" [Psalm 20:1–2]—he will certainly not be able to carry his burden and to endure all by himself in the midst of so many dragons, serpents, wolves, foxes, and whatever worse monsters there be, the servants of the raging devil, that is, in the midst of deceitful counselors, faithless friends, traitorous servants, and rapacious nobles. And yet he is compelled to live and rule among them. . . . Wherefore let the church and everyone who wants to belong to Christ . . . with faithful and earnest prayers to God support them against their chief enemy, the devil. In this way we not only make a most agreeable offering to God but also bestow a necessary and salutary benefit upon ourselves. For who can express adequately in thought, much less in words, what a blessing it is to live under a good and beneficent prince who seeks, increases, and upholds the glory of God and the well-being of the commonwealth? These are the gifts and (as Scripture says) the most splendid blessings of God.

From Luther's preface to John Frederick II and John William of Saxony, *Declamations* (Luther's Works 60:314)

Have mercy on me, O God, according to Your
steadfast love; according to Your abundant mercy blot
out my transgressions.

PSALM 51:1

Have Mercy, Lord

 et all men sing this verse with David and acknowledge that they are sinners but that God is righteous, that is, merciful. This confession is a sacrifice
acceptable and pleasing to God, and David invites us to it.
He wants this to be a teaching for the whole world. When
the devil or our conscience accuses us because of our sins,
we can freely confess that our sins are many and great, but
not despair because of them. For though our sins are many
and great, nevertheless we are taught here that the mercies
of God are also many and great. With this argument all the
saints have defended themselves against Satan, that though
they were sinners, yet they are made holy by this knowledge,
according to Isaiah 53:11: "The knowledge of Christ will
justify many."

From *Commentary on Psalm 51* (Luther's Works 12:325–26)

Precious in the sight of the LORD *is the death*
of His saints.

PSALM 116:15

God Cares for His People

en should be individually certain about this, that they are the people of God, or members of the church. Above all things this faith is necessary which firmly apprehends the following syllogism. The whole people of God is blessed, holy, pleasing, and acceptable to God in such a way that it cannot be torn from the hands of God. We are the people of God. Therefore God exercises care for us. The major premise is eminently true, because even the death and blood of the saints are precious in the sight of the Lord (see Psalm 116:15); all they do and suffer is pleasing to God. On the contrary, their errors and lapses have been covered and forgiven, as Psalm 32:1 testifies.

From *Lectures on Genesis* (Luther's Works 6:9)

November 16

"If they have called the master of the house Beelzebul,
how much more will they malign those of His
household." MATTHEW 10:25

The Gospel Will Never Perish

 he fact that nowadays we still encounter offense need not surprise us, since Christ Himself meets with it. . . . I can expect to fare no better than my Lord Christ. Since He experienced apostasy, I might know that among us not everyone will stand either. In Matthew 10:25 we read: "If they have called the Master of the house Beelzebul, how much more will they malign those of His household!" Therefore let them proceed with their persecutions. This doctrine will not perish or crumble because of them. The Gospel will and must be constructed on a different foundation from that of might or of great, learned, and smart men. Let the angry princes or the ranting and raving bishops persecute the Gospel, let the learned people abandon it! It is necessary for the Gospel to be despised outwardly by the world, to be trodden underfoot and persecuted, yes, even for those who claim to be good Christians often to fall away from it entirely. There is, after all, another power which preserves this doctrine.

From *Sermons on the Gospel of John*, Chapters 6–8 (Luther's Works 23:158)

Serve the LORD *with fear, and glorify Him*
with trembling.

PSALM 2:11

Praise God at All Times

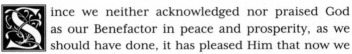

ince we neither acknowledged nor praised God as our Benefactor in peace and prosperity, as we should have done, it has pleased Him that now we should acknowledge and praise Him through the cross and adversity. We did not serve God with gladness in security, and so He is pleased that we serve Him with gladness in fear and rejoice with trembling. . . . This is the cross of Christ and the foolishness of preaching by which He saves the believers. Those who follow opinion, reason, wisdom, and knowledge are offended by all this and perish. This, then, is the meaning: When Christ the Lord reigns with His iron scepter and crushes the old man through the Word of the cross, according to the will and command of the Father, who has subjected everything to Him, you must recognize yourself as subjected to Him. However, you are subjected in fear, that you may bear His cross in patience and humility.

From *Labors on the Psalms* (Luther's Works 14:344)

November 18

"Why are you afraid, O you of little faith?"

MATTHEW 8:26

Our Lord Sustains Us

hen [Peter] walked on the sea and came to Christ, so long as he held to the Word, the water had to bear him up; but when he turned his eyes from Christ and he let go the Word, he saw the wind blowing and he began to sink. Therefore I said we must let go of everything and cling only to the Word; if we have laid hold of that, then let rage and roar the world, death, sin, hell and all misfortune. But if you let go the Word, then you must perish. This we see also in people who seek temporal nourishment. When they have sufficient, and their house and barn are full, they easily trust in God and say they have a gracious God; but when they have nothing they begin to doubt, then their faith vanishes; for they picture before their eyes that there is nothing at hand and no provision in store, and they do not know how they shall exist; thus care and worry drive faith out of the heart. But if they would lay hold of God's Word, they would think thus: My God lives, He assures me He will sustain my life; I will go forth and labor, He will make everything right, as Christ says, Matthew 6:33: "But seek ye first the kingdom of God and His righteousness; and all these things shall be added unto you." If I retained this Word and would cast the other out of my mind, I would not come into need.

From the *Church Postil*, sermon for Trinity 21 on John 4:6–54
(Luther's Works 79 (Lenker) 5:257–58)

November 19

The foolishness of God is wiser than men.

1 CORINTHIANS 1:25

The Weakness of God

e who believes in the Gospel must become weak and foolish before men so that he may be strong and wise in the power and wisdom of God, as 1 Corinthians 1:27, 25 tells us: "The weak and foolish things of the world God chose that He might confound the strong and wise. The weakness and foolishness of God is stronger and wiser than men." Therefore, when you hear that the power of God is soon rejected, you must recognize this as a manifestation of the power of men, or of the world and the flesh. Thus all power and wisdom and righteousness must be hidden and buried and not apparent, altogether according to the image and likeness of Christ, who emptied Himself so that He might completely hide His power, wisdom, and goodness and instead put on weakness, foolishness, and hardship.

From *Lectures on Romans* (Luther's Works 25:150–51)

November 20

"Come out of her, My people, lest you take part
in her sins."

REVELATION 18:4

Forsake All Sin

 his command about censuring sins concerns not only the teachers in the church and the officers in the state but also every citizen and every member of a household. Joseph reported his brothers' sins to his father and accused his brothers (Genesis 37:2). Thus citizens should not disregard the sins of others among themselves, and in the church a brother should reprove a brother in accordance with Christ's command, lest he have a part in the sins of others. And in the state it is not rare to find examples which show that ruin and terrible disasters of the people have followed whenever the government has either supported or defended manifest sins. Then, of course, one must flee, unless one wants to become a partaker of the sin of others and bring down upon one's own head punishment for the sin of others. Thus we are warned in Revelation 18:4 to depart from Babylon and forsake her . . . unless we want to perish with it.

From *Lectures on Genesis* (Luther's Works 3:280)

"Where two or three are gathered in My name,
there am I among them."

MATTHEW 18:20

Christian Friends

 ven if one's heart is well grounded by the Holy Spirit, it remains a great advantage to have a brother with whom one can converse about religion and from whom one can hear words of comfort. . . . I for my part consider the loss of all my possessions less important than that of a faithful friend. When Christ was wrestling with temptation in the garden (Matthew 26:37ff.), we see Him seeking comfort among His three disciples. When Paul, in Acts 28:15, saw the brethren coming to meet him, he took courage from the sight and experienced comfort. Loneliness distresses a person who is solitary and deprived of his intimate friends. He can exert himself and struggle against it, but he does not overcome it without great difficulty. Everything is less burdensome if you have a brother with you; for then the promise applies (Matthew 18:20): "Where two or three are gathered in My name, there am I in the midst of them." Therefore solitude should be shunned and the companionship of familiar people sought, especially in spiritual perils.

From *Lectures on Genesis* (Luther's Works 2:335)

November 22

"I tell you, none of those men who were invited shall taste My banquet."

LUKE 14:24

Christ's Banquet

 t is as if [Jesus] meant to say: "Well, My supper, too, is something and is surely better than their oxen, fields, and houses or wives, even though they now despise it and regard their fields, oxen, and houses as much more precious. The hour will come when they must leave their oxen, fields, and houses, and would gladly taste something from My supper. But then it will be said: 'Friend, I am not now at home, and I cannot now wait on the guests. Go to your fields, to your oxen, to your houses; they will certainly give you a better supper, because you have despised My supper so confidently and boldly. I have certainly cooked for you and spent much on it, but that is offensive to you. If now you have cooked something better, then eat and be cheerful—except that you will not taste My supper.' " . . . We, however, who accept it and with hearts frightened because of our sins do not decline the grace of God which is preached and offered to us in the Gospel through Christ, will receive grace instead of wrath, eternal righteousness instead of sin, and eternal life instead of eternal death.

From the *Church Postil*, sermon for Trinity 2 on Luke 14:16–24 (Luther's Works 78:95)

November 23

Oh give thanks to the LORD, *for He is good;*
for His steadfast love endures forever!

PSALM 118:1

God Provides Abundantly

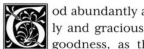 od abundantly and convincingly proves His friend-ly and gracious favor by His daily and everlasting goodness, as the psalmist writes: "His steadfast love endures forever"; that is, He unceasingly showers the best upon us. He is the Creator of our bodies and souls, our Protector by day and by night, and the Preserver of our lives. He causes the sun and the moon to shine on us, fire, air, water, and the heavens to serve us. He causes the earth to give food, fodder, wine, grain, clothes, wood, and all necessities. He provides us with gold and silver, house and home, wife and child, cattle, birds, and fish. In short, who can count it all? And all this is bountifully showered upon us every year, every day, every hour, and every minute. Who could measure even this one goodness of God, that He gives and preserves a healthy eye or hand? When we are sick or must get along without one of these, then we begin to realize what a blessing it is to have a healthy hand, foot, leg, nose, or finger; then we begin to realize what a blessing bread, clothing, water, fire, and home are. . . . Therefore this verse should be in the heart and mouth of every man every day and every moment.

From *Commentary on Psalm 118* (Luther's Works 14:47, 49)

November 24

May the God of hope fill you with all joy and peace
in believing, so that by the power of the Holy Spirit
you may abound in hope.

ROMANS 15:13

Joy and Peace through Faith

his is the apostle's meaning: May God produce hope through the Gospel, may He give you grace, so that you work with and believe the Gospel, from which you come to know Christ the most deeply. From that may you then have all joy and a good conscience, as from a common blessing, and then also peace among one another. This joy and peace is not what the world gives through feeling and experience, but through believing, for you neither see nor feel the One who is your blessing, from whom you have joy and peace. In the world, however, you will feel strife and grief. But when you learn that Christ is common for everyone and equally for all, then you will have a good peace. There is nothing that one can begrudge another, for you are all equally rich. That is joy and peace through faith or in faith. . . . The Holy Spirit helps us and strengthens our hope, so that we do not flee or fear the misfortunes of the world, but rather stand firm even to death and overcome all evil . . . .

From the *Church Postil*, sermon for Advent 2 on Romans 15:4–13 (Luther's Works 75:90)

Our Help in Time of Need

he physician is helpful and welcome to the sick, but the healthy pay no attention to him. This woman perceived her need, and for that reason she ran after the sweet fragrance (Song of Solomon 1:3; 4:11). So also Moses must come first and teach us to perceive our sins so that grace may become sweet and welcome. Therefore, all is lost, no matter how kindly and delightfully Christ is portrayed, if one is not first humbled by knowledge of himself and is not eager for Christ, as the Magnificat says: "He fills the hungry with good things, and the rich He sends away empty" [Luke 1:53]. All of this is said and written for the comfort of the miserable, poor, needy, sinful, and despised people, so that in all of their need they know to whom they should flee for comfort and help. . . . How it hurts nature and reason when, in destitution, she takes off, and leaves behind everything that she senses, and clings to the bare Word alone, even when she senses the opposite. May God help us in time of need and of death to such courage and faith!

From the *Church Postil*, sermon for Lent 2 on Matthew 15:21–28 (Luther's Works 76:378–79)

I shall not die, but I shall live, and recount the deeds of the LORD. PSALM 118:17

The God of the Living

henever in the Psalter and Holy Scripture the saints deal with God concerning comfort and help in their need, eternal life and the resurrection of the dead are involved. All such texts belong to the doctrine of the resurrection and eternal life, in fact, to the whole Third Article of the Creed with the doctrines of the Holy Spirit, the Holy Christian Church, the forgiveness of sins, the resurrection, and everlasting life. And it all flows out of the First Commandment, where God says: "I am your God" (Exodus 20:2). This the Third Article of the Creed emphasizes insistently. While Christians deplore the fact that they suffer and die in this life, they comfort themselves with another life than this, namely, that of God Himself, who is above and beyond this life. It is not possible that they should totally die and not live again in eternity. For one thing, the God on whom they rely and in whom they find their consolation cannot die, and thus they must live in Him. Besides, as Christ says, He is a God of the living, not of the dead and of those who are no more (Matthew 22:32). Therefore Christians must live forever; otherwise He would not be their God, nor could they depend on Him unless they live. For this little group, therefore, death remains no more than a sleep.

From *Commentary on Psalm 118* (Luther's Works 14:87)

November 27

"If anyone keeps My word, he will never see death."

JOHN 8:51

We Will Rise with Him

Because we have the Word and are baptized in accordance with it, we also die gladly, relying upon it, and are certain that we have already risen with Christ according to the soul, and on the Last Day will also rise with Him according to the body. That is where St. Paul now takes his stand: If Christ rose only on His own behalf, our salvation is lost. Then the true and joyous Easter Day that we are keeping does not pertain to us, nor does the Last Day, which will be a day of redemption for all Christians. But if Christ has risen from the dead for our sakes and become the firstfruits of those who sleep [1 Corinthians 15:22–23], then our salvation stands firm and we, too, shall rise from the dead and keep the joyous Easter with Him on the Last Day. Thus he weaves Christ's resurrection and our own into one another and makes of them a single resurrection.

From *Eastertide Sermons on 1 Corinthians 15* (Luther's Works 58:149–50)

"The girl is not dead but sleeping." MATTHEW 9:24

Death Is Not Death

h, she is sleeping! Death, where are you? Among Christians, death is not death, but a sleep. Indeed, the burial place of Christians is called a . . . "dormitory." The heathen cannot give their graves that name. Only Christians say: "My grave is my bed, my dormitory. I am not dying, but I am falling asleep." John 11:25 [says]: "Whoever believes in Me, even if he dies, yet he shall live," and [11:11]"Lazarus has fallen asleep." But here you also see how many hindrances there are to this faith concerning eternal life. . . . There is despair, as if we were not going to live eternally. . . . The Law and the wisdom of the flesh assert repeatedly that death is death and that, conversely, the promises of eternal life are nothing and wholly in vain. For the Law knows how to kill and nothing else; this is what the conscience feels. Therefore, here we must direct our attention zealously to this word of Christ: *"She is sleeping."* though it is drowned out by so many crowds and scandals. . . . Oh, if only (as the text says) this report of the power of Christ the Restorer of life would go out into all the land [Matthew 9:26]—or, rather, into the hearts of all—so that all would believe that He is such a one as considers us dead men to be living ones who shall be awakened from sleep. Thus we may joyfully scorn death, certain that He does not lie but shall awaken us, for though to ourselves we seem dead, to Him we are sleeping.

From *Annotations on Matthew* (Luther's Works 67:76–78)

The one who conquers, I will grant him to sit with Me
on My throne.

REVELATION 3:21

Where Is our Kingdom?

ccording to faith we are foreigners; that is, our kingdom is according to faith. I am a king in eternal life; I am a prince and am mighty over devil, death, [and] sin. Secular authority is under the devil, death, [and] sin. . . . [But] there [in eternal life] I am a squire. Therefore, my kingdom is indeed a glorious dominion compared to the one on earth, which is only a place to lie down for a night as an alien. But when it is time, we must leave the inn. . . . Christians travel on to blessedness; here they are aliens. Thus through God's Son you are a lord over sin [and] death. The [emperor is only a lord] over money. Even if I die, [what difference does it make]? I am lying down in the inn. . . . They all pass away, leave the world here and depart. Therefore, since that is the case even with the lords, remember this so that you do not become angry, because [you are] kings and priests.

From *Sermon for Easter 3 on 1 Peter 2:11–20* (Luther's Works 58:229–30)

November 30

The night is far gone; the day is at hand. So then let us cast off the works of darkness and put on the armor of light. ROMANS 13:12

The Light of the World

The doctrine of the Law, or the first light, is the moon. It teaches our obligation to bear fruits, as a good tree should. The other light is the sun. It speaks of the new man, of a different tree, telling us that we receive the Gospel from Christ. There we hear whence and how a man becomes good, namely, through faith. Thus the Gospel deals, not with our works but with grace and gifts, with the good that God does for us and presents to us through Christ. The Ten Commandments tell us about our duties toward God. Now, to be sure, the moon shines at night, but still it does not turn night into day. Christ, however, is the true Sun. He ushers in the morning and the day. He teaches us how to be saved and how to be delivered from death and sin. Therefore He says: "I am the Light which illumines the whole world"; for He alone liberates from sin, death, the devil, and hell. . . . Now again the proclamation is issued that sin is condemned solely in Christ, and that we are delivered from sin without our works, boasts, or deeds but only through the death of Christ. This is the message of the Gospel. This is the light and the true brilliance of the sun, which radiates through the entire world. So Christ's claim is just. The doctrine in itself is true; He is the Light of the world.

From *Sermons on the Gospel of John*, Chapters 6–8 (Luther's Works 23:324–25)

December 1

Commit your work to the LORD, *and your plans will
be established.* PROVERBS 16:3

Commit Your Work to the Lord

 omeone who is a magistrate, a householder, a servant, a teacher, a pupil, etc., should remain in his
calling and do his duty there, properly and faithfully, without concerning himself about what lies outside his
own vocation. If he does this, he will have his boast within
himself, so that he can say: "With my utmost faithfulness and
diligence I have carried out the work of my calling as God
has commanded me to; and therefore I know that this work,
performed in faith and obedience to God, is pleasing to Him.
If others slander it, that does not matter much." There are
always those who despise and slander faithful teaching and
living. But God has given a dire warning that He will destroy
such slanderers. And so while such men search for vainglory,
anxiously and long, and try to blacken the reputation of the
true believers by their slanders, what Paul said will happen
to them (Philippians 3:19): "They glory in their shame"; and
elsewhere (2 Timothy 3:9): "Their folly will be known to all."
Through whom? Through God, the righteous Judge, who
will both expose their slanders and bring forth the right of
the believers as the noonday (Psalm 37:6).

From *Lectures on Galatians* (1535) (Luther's Works 27:119–20)

December 2

I bear on my body the marks of Jesus. GALATIANS 6:17

A Life of Trials and Sufferings

he wrath of God is necessary because of "the body of sin" spoken of in Rom. 6:6 and because of "the law of my members" (Romans 7:23). For it is necessary that "the body of sin" and the law of the flesh or the members "be destroyed" (Romans 6:6), since it is impossible for "anything unclean to enter the kingdom of heaven" (Revelation 21:27). But such destruction comes about through crosses, sufferings, deaths, and disgraces. Therefore God kills in order to make alive; He humiliates in order to exalt, etc. And this is what the apostle glories in when he says that he knows nothing except Jesus Christ, and Him not glorified but crucified (see 1 Corinthians 2:2). He bears on his body the marks of his Lord (see Galatians 6:17). For to bear Christ crucified in oneself is to live a life full of trials and sufferings, and for this reason He becomes for carnal men "a sign that is spoken against" (Luke 2:34). Therefore one should resolve to receive with open arms every trial, even death itself, with praise and joy, just as one should receive Christ Himself. For it is true that Christ always comes in the form He assumed when He "emptied Himself" of the form of God (see Philippians 2:7). Thus James 1:2 says: "Count it all joy, my brethren, when you meet various trials." And in Isaiah 48:9 we read: "For the sake of My praise I restrain it for you, that I may not cut you off." And in Psalm 18:3: "I will call upon the Lord, and I will be saved from my enemies."

From *Lectures on Hebrews* (Luther's Works 29:130)

December 3

In this the love of God was made manifest among us,
that God sent His only Son into the world, so that we
might live through Him.

1 JOHN 4:9

Our Divine Treasure

ecause He says, "Whoever believes in God's Son will not be lost, but have eternal life" [John 3:16], death, the devil, and the fright of the Law must be gone, and our merit and worthiness must add nothing. So the very great, eternal, divine treasure that we shall have is set before us: that we will be without fear and fright before the frightful judgment and damnation which came over human nature through Adam's fall, and instead have redemption, victory over it, and every good. However, this is also offered, given, and presented to us out of pure grace, so that it can be received in no other way than through faith. He paints this grace and gift in Christ with brief and yet very excellent and rich words in order to magnify it and make it comforting in every circumstance. Everything at every point—the Giver, the recipient, the gift, the fruit, and its benefits—is so unspeakably great that it is only hard to believe because of its greatness. However, before we look at that, we want first to hear the reason why Christ says this. It is given by the words He speaks: "So that whoever believes in Him will not perish" [John 3:16], etc. In this way, He wants to show the world the misery and need in which it is stuck, namely, that this is how it is: it is altogether lost, and would have to remain eternally lost, if Christ had not come with this preaching.

From the *Church Postil*, sermon for Pentecost Monday on John 3:16–21 (Luther's Works 77:365)

This took place to fulfill what was spoken by the
prophet . . . . MATTHEW 21:4

The Promise Fulfilled

he evangelist cites [this prophecy] so that we may see how Christ has come not for the sake of our merit, but for the sake of divine truth. For He was promised long ago before we, to whom He comes, existed. Therefore, just as God promised the Gospel out of pure grace, so He has also fulfilled it to demonstrate His truth—that He keeps what He promises—in order to stir us to build confidently on His promise, for He will fulfill it. And this is one of the Scriptures in which the Gospel was promised, of which Paul says, "God promised the Gospel beforehand through His prophets in the Holy Scripture, concerning His Son, Jesus Christ," etc. (Romans 1:2). We have now heard how, in this verse, the Gospel, Christ, and faith are pointed out with the utmost excellence and consolation.

From the *Church Postil*, sermon for Advent 1 on Matthew 21:1–9 (Luther's Works 75:57)

"Say to the daughter of Zion, 'Behold, your king is coming to you.' "

MATTHEW 21:5

All Wrath Is Laid Aside

o not flee, and do not be afraid, for He does not now come as He came to Adam, to Cain, to the flood, to Babylon, to Sodom and Gomorrah, nor as He came to the people of Israel on Mount Sinai. He does not come in wrath; He does not want to call you to account nor to affix blame. All wrath is laid aside; nothing but gentleness and kindness remain. He indeed wants to deal with you in such a way that your heart will have pleasure, love, and full confidence in Him, that from now on you will cling to Him and find refuge in Him much more than you before were terrified and fled from Him. See, He is nothing but gentleness toward you. He is a different man completely. He acts as if He were sorry ever to have terrified you and to have caused you to flee by His punishment and wrath. For that reason He wants to make you bold again and to comfort you and kindly bring you to Himself.

From the *Church Postil*, sermon for Advent 1 on Matthew 21:1–9 (Luther's Works 75:36–37)

Rejoice in the Lord always; again I will say, rejoice.

PHILIPPIANS 4:4

Joy Is a Result of Faith

 his joy is a fruit and result of faith . . . . It is impossible for a heart to rejoice in God which does not first believe in Him. Where there is no faith, there is only fear, flight, timidity, and sorrow as soon as God is even thought of or named; indeed, there is hatred and enmity toward God in such hearts. The reason for this is that the heart finds itself guilty in its conscience and has no confidence that God is gracious and favorable, since it knows that God is the enemy of sin and horribly punishes it. . . . Therefore, this Epistle was not written for sinners, but for saints. The sinners must first be told how to be freed from their sins and receive a gracious God; then the joy will follow of itself when they are freed from their evil conscience. . . . St. Paul is here speaking about that kind of joy. There is no sin there, no fear of death or hell, but rather a glad and all-powerful confidence in God and His kindness.

From the *Church Postil*, sermon for Advent 4 on Philippians 4:4–7 (Luther's Works 75:157–58)

Then they will see the Son of Man coming in a cloud
with power and great glory.

LUKE 21:27

Christ's Coming

 ere "power" may again signify the hosts of angels, saints, and all creatures that will come with Christ to judgment. (I believe this is the correct interpretation.) Or it may mean the power and strength that make this coming of Christ so much more powerful than the first, which was weaker and inferior. He says not only that He will come but also that they shall see Him come. At His birth He came also, but was seen by no one. He comes now daily through the Gospel, spiritually, into believing hearts; no one sees that either. But this coming will be public, so that all must see Him, as Revelation 1:7 says, "And every eye will see Him." And they shall see that He is none other than the bodily man Christ, in bodily form, as He was born from Mary and walked on earth. But when He says, "They will see the Son of Man," He clearly indicates that it will be a bodily coming, a bodily seeing in bodily form yet in great power, with the great host of angels and all glory. He will sit on a bright cloud, and all the saints with Him. The Scriptures speak much of that day, and everything is pointed to it.

From the *Church Postil*, sermon for Advent 2 on Luke 21:25–33 (Luther's Works 75:102–3)

*"Then the King will say to those on His right, 'Come,
you who are blessed by My Father, inherit the kingdom prepared for you from the foundation of the
world. For I was hungry and you gave Me food, I was
thirsty and you gave Me drink, I was a stranger and
you welcomed Me, I was naked and you clothed Me,
I was sick and you visited Me, I was in prison and
you came to Me.' "*

MATTHEW 25:34–36

Come, Lord Jesus

 herefore see to it that you are among those who are
kind and merciful here upon earth for Christ's sake,
or who even suffer for His sake, then you may joyfully await the Last Day, and need not be afraid of the judgment; for He has already selected you and placed you among
those who will stand at His right hand. For we, who are
Christians, should hope for the coming of this judgment and
desire it with our whole heart; as we pray for it in the words:
Thy kingdom come, Thy will be done, deliver us from evil; so
that we may also hear the glad and welcome words: Come,
ye blessed, into the kingdom of My Father. This is the verdict
we await; for this reason we are Christians, and just for the
sake of this hope we are so severely oppressed, first by Satan
and by our own flesh, which would not have us believe this

December 9

and rejoice over it; then by the tyranny and enmity of the world. For we must constantly see and hear the maliciousness which Satan and the world practice against the Gospel. There is so much misery on earth that we ought to be tired of this life and cry aloud: Come, dear Lord, and deliver us.

From the *Church Postil*, sermon for Trinity 26 on Matthew 25:31–46 (Luther's Works 79 (Lenker) 5:389–90)

To [Jesus] all the prophets bear witness that every-
one who believes in Him receives forgiveness of sins
through His name. Acts 10:43

Proper Reading of the Scriptures

herefore, whoever wants to read the Scriptures correctly and with profit, let him make sure that he finds Christ in them. Then he will certainly find eternal life. On the other hand, if I do not study and learn in the writings of Moses and the Prophets that for the sake of my salvation Christ descended from heaven, became man, suffered, died, was buried, rose again, and ascended to heaven, in order that through Him I might have reconciliation with God, forgiveness of all my sins, grace, righteousness, and eternal life, then my reading of Scripture will not help me for salvation one bit. From reading and studying Scripture I can, to be sure, become a learned fellow, able to preach about it. But all that will not help me at all, for if I do not know or find Christ, then I will not find salvation and eternal life either. Instead, I will find bitter death, for our dear God has decreed that there is no other name given to human beings by which they can be saved, except in the name of Jesus (Acts 4:12).

From *Sermon on the Glorious Passage from John 5* (Luther's Works 58:249–50)

December 10

"I will put enmity between you and the woman, and between your offspring and her offspring; He shall bruise your head, and you shall bruise His heel."

GENESIS 3:15

It All Points to Christ

dam and Eve and their children believed in [Christ] because they possessed the promise of the woman's Seed, who would bruise the serpent's head (Genesis 3:15). That is what Adam preached; he also received numerous signs which impelled and encouraged him to look to Christ. Moses' Law, Baptism, sacrifice, kingdom, and priesthood were to endure but a short time, not permanently. For how long? Until the woman's Seed should appear. And all who understood this were saved, as, for example, the patriarchs. Similarly, we today also preach, teach, baptize, and have our government. None of this has any permanency; but it all points us to Christ who became incarnate and for whom we must wait and hope. These are only mementos and monitors. Thus Christ remains our Savior in the future and in the present. The little children who marched in Christ's van sang their hosannas, just as the patriarchs had done; we, who with the whole world follow in His train, sing the same song. The only difference is that they preceded Christ and we follow Him. Whatever was ordained was all focused on Christ. Therefore Christ was this Rock, for He was to come from this nation. They and we share the same faith . . . .

From *Sermon on the Gospel of John*, Chapters 1–4 (Luther's Works 22:448–49)

December 11

The law was given through Moses;
grace and truth came through Jesus Christ.

JOHN 1:17

Christ Justifies

o observe the whole Law is tantamount to pointing out in fact that the Christ has not yet come. If this is true, then all the Jewish ceremonies and laws about foods, places, and seasons must be observed; and we must still look for the Christ, who is to make the kingdom and priesthood of the Jews obsolete and is to establish a new kingdom throughout the world. But all Scripture testifies, and the facts themselves show, that Christ has already come, has redeemed the human race by His death, has abrogated the Law and has fulfilled what all the prophets predicted about Him. Therefore He abolished the Law and granted grace and truth (John 1:17). Accordingly, the Law does not justify; neither do its works. It is faith in the Christ who has already come that justifies.

From *Lectures on Galatians* (1535) (Luther's Works 27:15)

December 12

From their race [the Israelites], according to the flesh,
is the Christ, who is God over all, blessed forever.

Romans 9:5

Divine Conquerer

o conquer the sin of the world, death, the curse, and the wrath of God in Himself—this is the work, not of any creature but of the divine power. Therefore, it was necessary that He who was to conquer these in Himself should be true God by nature. For in opposition to this mighty power—sin, death, and the curse—which of itself reigns in the whole world and in the entire creation, it is necessary to set an even higher power, which cannot be found and does not exist apart from the divine power. Therefore to abolish sin, to destroy death, to remove the curse in Himself, to grant righteousness, to bring life to light (2 Timothy 1:10), and to bring the blessing in Himself, that is, to annihilate these things and to create those—all these are works solely of the divine power. Since Scripture attributes all these to Christ, therefore He Himself is Life, Righteousness, and Blessing, that is, God by nature and in essence.

From *Lectures on Galatians* (1535) (Luther's Works 26:282)

And His name shall be called Wonderful Counselor,
Mighty God, Everlasting Father, Prince of Peace.

ISAIAH 9:6

Name above All Names

 he kingdom of Christ is beyond grasp, reason, and experience. Here the flesh must be put to death with all its wisdom and judgment, and it must be grasped only by faith. We must believe that Christ's righteousness is ours. . . . Lest we come short in the matter of faith He gives us counsel, that is, the Word, so that we may abide in so wonderful a government of His kingdom. . . . ["God,"] that is, strong, Power. Here it is not the person or nature of this king that is depicted but only His wonderful government of the kingdom. Therefore, He has counsel, He has full power, He can come to the aid of the weary and those spent by trials. . . . He gives the strength to triumph through the Word and the Holy Spirit. . . . This ["Everlasting Father"], then, indicates the work and business of this King, not His person. This name fits no one else. He always increases His reign, He always begets children and rules over them, He always remains the Father, He does not assume the role of tyrant, His children are always His beloved. This is beyond question the most delightful kingdom.

From *Lectures on Isaiah* (Luther's Works 16:100–101)

"For as the lightning comes from the east and shines as far as the west, so will be the coming of the Son of Man."

MATTHEW 24:27

False Teachers Remain

 e says now: "Take heed, I am warning you. . . . When they say, 'Look, here is Christ! There He is!' do not believe it. I am telling you beforehand: false prophets and false christs will arise and perform great signs and wonders, so as to lead astray, if it were possible, even the elect" [Matthew 24:23–25], who nevertheless are to be saved eternally. Further, He says, "If they say to you: 'He is in the wilderness' or 'He is in the inner rooms,' do not believe it" [Matthew 24:26]. For these false teachers will remain until the Last Day, which will come like lightning [Matthew 24:27]. So the false prophets will remain and deceive the people until that blessed day dawns, when we will be standing in the pulpit, or lying in bed, and in an instant we will be standing before Christ's judgment seat.

From *Sermons on the Gospel of Matthew*, Chapters 19–24 (Luther's Works 68:286)

December 15

A voice cries: "In the wilderness prepare the way
of the LORD; *make straight in the desert a highway*
for our God."

ISAIAH 40:3

Prepare the Way of the Lord

 his, then, is the preparation of Christ's way and John's proper office. He is to humble all the world and proclaim that they are all sinners—lost, damned, poor, needy, miserable people; that there is no life, work, or estate (however holy, beautiful, and good it may appear) that is not damnable unless Christ our Lord dwells therein, unless he works, walks, lives, is, and does everything through faith in Him; that they all need Christ and should desire to share His grace. See, where it is preached that all people's work and life is nothing, that is the true voice of John in the wilderness and the pure and clear truth of Christian doctrine, as Paul says, "They are all sinners and lack the glory that they should have had toward God" (Romans 3:23). This is truly humbling and cutting out and destroying over-confidence. That is truly to prepare the way of the Lord, to give room, and to make way.

From the *Church Postil*, sermon for Advent 4 on John 1:19–28
(Luther's Works 75:179)

December 16

"The poor have good news preached to them."

MATTHEW 11:5

Fix Your Eyes on Jesus

o you not hear what Christ says? "I give you My peace, God's grace, and the forgiveness of sin. You must not look at yourself; you must fix your eyes on what I give you. As you know, you have My Baptism, Sacrament, and Gospel, which are nothing but tokens of grace and peace." Let those tremble before wrath and displeasure who live smugly and brazenly, are impenitent and wicked, and do not know Christ. For you are a person who desires God's grace and the forgiveness of sins, who wants to be comforted by Him, who is frightened, and who is conscious of his misery. Therefore these words are addressed to you. . . . Why, then, are you so foolish as to refuse to accept and take to heart these beautiful and comforting words and tokens, in which He tells you and all fainthearted souls: "I do not want My Christians to be frightened. . . ." Therefore whenever you feel any fear or sorrow, you may rest assured that this certainly does not come from Christ. Nor must you give way to this; but you must take courage from these words, in which He exhorts you and bids you be unafraid.

From *Sermons on the Gospel of John*, Chapters 14–16 (Luther's Works 24:185)

This is the name by which He will be called:
"The LORD is our righteousness."

JEREMIAH 23:6

Two Kinds of Righteousness

here are two kinds of righteousness: mine and Christ's. The Gospel proclaims that we must be put into the righteousness of Christ and must be translated from our righteousness into the righteousness of Christ. Thus Paul says in Romans 3:24 that we "are justified by His grace as a gift"; and in 1 Corinthians 1:30 he says that Christ was made by God "our Wisdom, our Righteousness and Sanctification and Redemption." . . . . When Moses lifted up the bronze serpent (Numbers 21:9), no one could be healed by his own effort until he looked at that serpent. Thus if sin bites us, we cannot be freed either until we look at Christ crucified. Therefore you must cling to the wounds and the blood of Jesus Christ if you do not want to be lost forever.

From *Lectures on 1 John* (Luther's Works 30:252–53)

December 18

Return to your stronghold, O prisoners of hope;
today I declare that I will restore to you double.

ZECHARIAH 9:12

We Live in Hope

ne could take this doubling to mean the people or the Spirit multiplied because of hearing the Gospel. . . . However, I am much more pleased with another statement which we find in Isaiah (Isaiah 40:2): "She has received from the Lord's hand double for all her sins." And here we have, "Today I declare that I will restore to you double." . . . This is pure grace when He restores double grace in the place of sins which have been taken away, that is, He removes from us both the Law and sin. . . . It was not enough that we be freed from sin unless the author of sin also be taken away. That, of course, is the Law, which causes sin to abound, and it makes demands on us and accuses us so that no conscience can ever be joyful. But that redemption is brought about by the blood of the King. In sum, the prophet is doing the following: he describes the way in which that King has arrived at this kingdom of salvation and righteousness. Through the Word we are justified and freed. We are moved from the kingdom of darkness into the kingdom of light by the power of Christ's blood. Then we live in hope.

From *Lectures on Zechariah* (Latin text) (Luther's Works 20:98–99)

December 19

"For God so loved the world, that He gave His only Son, that whoever believes in Him should not perish but have eternal life." John 3:16

God's Intention for the World

n these words you hear even more forcibly and clearly what God's will and intention is toward the world, that is, toward those who have sin and because of it are already under the judgment and verdict of damnation. He takes out of the way everything that wants to frighten us because of sins. He says simply and clearly that Christ was sent and His kingdom was established not so that He would condemn and damn. This judgment and verdict were already there over all people through the Law, because they are all born in sin, are already sentenced to death and the hangman with his rope, and the only thing lacking is for the sword to be drawn. Then Christ steps into the middle at God's command, orders judge and jailer to leave off, and rescues and makes alive those who were condemned. The reason He comes is to help the world, which He finds already damned. This is shown also by the words He speaks—"in order to save the world"—for that is enough for us to understand that the world must have been damned. Why else does it need to be saved?

From the *Church Postil*, sermon for Pentecost Monday on John 3:16–21 (Luther's Works 77:376)

*For the grace of God has appeared, bringing
salvation for all people, training us to renounce
ungodliness and worldly passions, and to live self-
controlled, upright, and godly lives in the present age.*

TITUS 2:11–12

In the Present World

e says "in the present world" [Titus 2:12] much more to point out the power of the saving grace of God, since the world is so wicked that the godly person must live all alone, without any example, like a rose among thorns, and suffer all kinds of misfortune, disdain, shame, and sin. It is as if he would say: "Whoever wants to live a sober, righteous, and godly life must renounce all enmity, must take up the cross, must not allow himself to be misled, even if he lives all alone, like Lot in Sodom and Abraham in Canaan [Genesis 13:12], among none but dead drunk, lewd, unrighteous, false, and ungodly people." It is the world and remains the world, of which he must deprive himself and live contrary to it, rebuking its worldly desires. That means living soberly in a tavern, chastely in a brothel, godly in a theater, righteously in a den of murderers. Such a world makes life confined and unpleasant, so that we wish, cry out, and call for death and the Last Day, and await them with great longing, as the next words show. Grace must lead in such a difficult life, since nature and reason are lost here.

From the *Church Postil*, sermon for Christmas Day on Titus 2:11–15
(Luther's Works 75:198)

December 21

We preach . . . Christ the power of God
and the wisdom of God.
1 CORINTHIANS 1:23–24

True Christian Theology

rue Christian theology, as I often warn you, does not present God to us in His majesty, as Moses and other teachings do, but Christ born of the Virgin as our Mediator and High Priest. Therefore when we are embattled against the Law, sin, and death in the presence of God, nothing is more dangerous than to stray into heaven with our idle speculations, there to investigate God in His incomprehensible power, wisdom, and majesty, to ask how He created the world and how He governs it. . . . Therefore if you want to be safe and out of danger to your conscience and your salvation, put a check on this speculative spirit. . . . Begin where Christ began—in the Virgin's womb, in the manger, and at His mother's breasts. For this purpose He came down, was born, lived among men, suffered, was crucified, and died, so that in every possible way He might present Himself to our sight. He wanted us to fix the gaze of our hearts upon Himself and thus to prevent us from clambering into heaven and speculating about the Divine Majesty.

From *Lectures on Galatians* (1535) (Luther's Works 26:28–29)

"Blessed is the one who is not offended by Me."

MATTHEW 11:6

Guard Yourself

uard yourself here diligently against offense. Who are those who offend you? All who teach you to do works instead of to believe; those who make Christ into a lawmaker and a judge and won't let Him be a helper and a comforter; who frighten you into acting with works before God and toward God in order to atone for your sins and to merit grace. . . . For if you want to believe correctly and truly obtain Christ, then you must put aside all works with which you would act toward God and before God. They are only an offense which leads you away from Christ and away from God. No works are valuable before God except Christ's own work. You must let His work act for you toward God, and do no other work before Him than to believe that Christ is doing His work for you and places it toward God. In this way your faith remains pure, does nothing other than keep quiet, lets Him do good and accepts Christ's work, and lets Christ practice His love on you. You must be blind, lame, deaf, dead, leprous, and poor, or you will take offense at Christ. The Gospel does not lie to you which shows Christ doing good only among the needy.

From the *Church Postil*, sermon for Advent 3 on Matthew 11:2–10 (Luther's Works 75:154)

December 23

And she gave birth to her firstborn son and wrapped
Him in swaddling cloths and laid Him in a manger.

LUKE 2:7

The Nativity of Our Lord—
Christmas Eve

"To you this night is born a child
Of Mary, chosen virgin mild;
This little child of lowly birth
Shall be the joy of all the earth.

"This is the Christ, our God Most High,
Who hears your sad and bitter cry;
He will Himself your Savior be
From all your sins to set you free."

My heart for very joy must leap;
My lips no more can silence keep.
I, too, must sing with joyful tongue
That sweetest ancient cradlesong:

Glory to God in highest heav'n,
Who unto us His Son has giv'n!
While angels sing with pious mirth
A glad new year to all the earth.

From *From Heaven above to Earth I Come* (*LSB* 358:2–3, 14–15)

December 24

*And the angel said to them, "Fear not, for behold, I
bring you good news of great joy that will be for all
the people. For unto you is born this day in the city of
David a Savior, who is Christ the Lord."* LUKE 2:10–11

The Nativity of Our Lord—
Christmas Day

 hrist takes our birth away from us and absorbs it
into His birth, and gives us His, that in it we might
become pure and new, as if it were our own, so that
every Christian may rejoice and glory in Christ's birth as if
he also, like Christ, had been born bodily of Mary. Whoever
does not believe this, or doubts it, is no Christian. That is the
great joy of which the angel speaks. This is the comfort and
exceeding goodness of God that, if a man believes this, he
can boast of the treasure that Mary is his true mother, Christ
his Brother, and God his Father. For all these things are true
and happen when we believe. This is the principal thing and
the principal treasure in every Gospel, before any doctrine
of good works can be taken out of it. Christ must above all
things become our own, and we become His, before we can
take hold of works. But this cannot occur except through the
faith that teaches us rightly to understand the Gospel and
properly to lay hold of it. This is knowing Christ correctly,
so that the conscience is happy, free, and satisfied. Out of
this grow love and praise to God, who in Christ has given

us such superabundant gifts free of charge. This gives courage to do, avoid, and suffer everything as is well pleasing to God, whether in life or in death, as I have often said. This is what Isaiah means: "To us a Child is born, and to us a Son is given" (Isaiah 9:6)—to us, to us, to us is born, and to us is given. Therefore, see to it that you do not find pleasure in the Gospel only as a history, for that does not last long; also not only as an example, for that does not stick without faith. But see to it that you make this birth your own and trade places, so that you are freed from your birth and receive His. This happens when you believe.

From the *Church Postil*, sermon for Christmas Day on Luke 2:1–14 (Luther's Works 75:216)

When they saw it, they made known the saying that
had been told them concerning this child.

LUKE 2:17

The Christian's Highest Work

he shepherds freely confess and publicly preach the word that was spoken to them about the child, which is the highest work in the Christian life. In this we are to risk our body and life, our wealth and honor. For the evil spirit does not attack so harshly those who believe correctly but live secretly and by themselves. He will not put up with it when we go forth and spread, confess, preach, and praise this for the good of others. Therefore, Luke says here that the shepherds did not only come and see, but they also preached what they heard in the field about this child, not only before Mary and Joseph but also before everybody. Do you not think there were many who thought [the shepherds] were fools and insane in that they attempted, as coarse and unschooled laymen, to speak of the angels' song and sermon? . . . But the shepherds, full of faith and joy, cheerfully were fools before men for God's sake. A Christian also does the same. For God's Word must be considered as foolishness and falsehood in this world.

From the *Church Postil*, sermon for the Second Day of Christmas on Luke 2:15–20 (Luther's Works 75:252)

But when the goodness and loving kindness of God
our Savior appeared, He saved us.

TITUS 3:4–5

Build Your Faith on These Words

 he divine nature is nothing other than pure beneficence and, as Paul says here, "kindness and love of people" [Titus 3:4], which daily pour out their good things in abundance on all creatures, as we see. See that these words are spoken to you, since God's kindness and love of people are revealed and offered to everyone. Build your faith on these words; daily train and strengthen yourself in them. If you hold without any doubt that it is true and that God is and wants to be kind and people-loving toward you, then He certainly is. Then you can with all confidence ask and desire whatever you want, whatever presses on you, whatever is necessary for you and for others. But if you do not believe it, then it would be much better if you had never heard it. By your unbelief you make these precious, comforting, gracious words into lies. You take the position that you do not regard them to be true, which is a very high and great dishonor and slandering of God; you could commit no greater sin. But if you believe, then it is impossible that your heart will not laugh for joy in God, and become free, sure, and courageous.

From the *Church Postil*, sermon for the Second Day of Christmas on Titus 3:4–8 (Luther's Works 75:233)

December 27

The Word became flesh and dwelt among us,
and we have seen His glory, glory as of the only Son
from the Father, full of grace and truth.

JOHN 1:14

Jesus' True Deity

ere [John] expresses who the Word is, of whom he and Moses have spoken—namely, the only Son of God, who has all the glory that the Father has. Therefore, he calls Him the only, the only-begotten, so as to distinguish Him from all the children of God, who are not natural children as this one is. His true deity is shown in this way; for if He were not God, He could not be called the only-begotten Son compared to the others. This is as much as saying that He and no other is God's Son. This cannot be said of angels and saints, for none of them is God's Son but are all brothers and created creatures, children [of God] adopted by grace, not born by nature.

From the *Church Postil*, sermon for the Third Day of Christmas on John 1:1–14 (Luther's Works 75:315)

December 28

Great indeed, we confess, is the mystery of godliness:
He was manifested in the flesh. 1 TIMOTHY 3:16

The Promised Savior

He paints His person in this way: He is the promised Savior come from heaven—that is, the true Son of God from eternity, for if He comes from heaven, then He must have been with God eternally. However, He descended or came down from heaven not as an angel descends and appears, and then again vanishes and goes away. Rather, He has taken human nature onto Himself and (as John 1:14) says) "has dwelt among us" on earth, etc. That is why He calls Himself here "the Son of Man" [John 3:13], that is, true man who has flesh and blood just like us. However, this descent of the Son of God properly means that He has subjected Himself to our misery and distress; that is, He has taken on Himself God's eternal wrath merited by our sins and become a sacrifice for them, as He here says that "He must be lifted up" (John 3:14). However, because this man comes down from heaven, for His own person He must be without any sin, innocent, and of divine purity. Thus He is not said to be born of flesh, as we are, but of the Holy Spirit, and His flesh is not sinful, but a purely holy flesh and blood. This was so that He could make our sinful flesh and blood pure and holy through His purity and holy, unblemished sacrifice.

From the *Church Postil*, sermon for Trinity on John 3:1–15 (Luther's Works 78:49)

December 29

To all who did receive Him, who believed in His name,
He gave the right to become children of God, who were
born, not of blood nor of the will of the flesh nor of the
will of man, but of God. JOHN 1:12–13

The True Son of God

 hrough God's creation and blessing we were born of the blood of our parents; some poor, pitiable, and deserted children are adopted and reared as heirs by pious people; our students are pupils and disciples of their preceptors, whom they honor—some more, some less—according to the command and will of God, as their fathers. But the fatherhood by blood, by law, or by honor justifies and saves neither the fathers nor the children. The high honor and glory of the sonship of God is attained solely through the birth of or from God, through believing in the name of the man called Jesus Christ, true and natural son of Mary, born of her in time and begotten eternally of the Father. . . . This Jesus Christ, our Lord, alone imparts this birth, granting believers in Him the privilege, the right, and the power to become God's children. He alone bestows sonship. Therefore they and only they are children of God who are born of God, that is, who believe in Jesus Christ, the Son of God and of Mary. And these believers are not "born of blood nor of the will of the flesh nor of the will of man, but of God." . . . Whoever remains faithful to the

Word and accepts the testimony of John—also impressively emphasized by Isaiah's testimony to Christ in chapter forty—and believes in Christ's name falls heir to this inexpressible glory of sonship with God, whether he be emperor or king, burgher, peasant, servant, shepherd, or beggar. Thus all, without exception, whether male or female, who hear the Word of Christ and believe in Him are privileged and able to say in truth: "Through Christ I am God's child and heir of all His heavenly goods, and God is my Father."

From *Sermons on the Gospel of John*, Chapters 1–4 (Luther's Works 22:100–101)

Surely goodness and mercy shall follow me
all the days of my life, and I shall dwell in the house
of the LORD *forever.*

PSALM 23:6

Lord God, Keep Us to the End

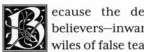ecause the devil never stops tormenting the believers—inwardly with terror, outwardly with the wiles of false teachers and the power of the tyrants— the prophet here at the end earnestly asks that God, who has given him this treasure, would also keep him in it to the end. He says: "Oh, may the dear God grant His grace that goodness and mercy might follow me all the days of my life and that He might soon make manifest what He calls goodness and mercy," that is, that he might dwell in the house of the Lord forever. It is as though he would say: "Lord, Thou hast begun the matter. Thou hast given me Thy holy Word and received me among those who are Thy people, who know Thee, praise and magnify Thee. Continue to give Thy grace, that I may remain with the Word and nevermore be separated from Thy holy Christendom." Thus he also prays in the Twenty-seventh Psalm (Psalm 27:4): "One thing," he says, "I ask of the Lord, that will I seek after; that I may dwell in the house of the Lord all the days of my life, to behold the beautiful worship of the Lord, and to visit His temple."

From *Commentary on Psalm 23* (Luther's Works 12:178–79)

December 31